Otto Hietsch

Wörterbuch [Dictionary] Bairisch – English

Otto Hietsch

Wörterbuch [Dictionary] Bairisch → English

Von Apfelbutzen bis Zwickerbusserl

SüdOst Verlag

Gewidmet Frau Ingrid Hietsch

Bibliografische Information der Deutschen Nationalbibliothek

Die Deutsche Nationalbibliothek verzeichnet diese Publikation in der Deutschen Nationalbibliografie; detaillierte bibliografische Daten sind im Internet über http://dnb.dnb.de abrufbar.
ISBN 978-3-86646-307-3

1. Auflage 2015
ISBN 978-3-86646-307-3

Illustrationen: Nina Schneider, http://nina-schneider.com

Titelbild: vg-design-fotolia.com, magann-fotolia.com, Jeanette Dietl-fotolia.com, Gregory Johnston-fotolia.com, oleksaey–fotolia.com

Inhalt

Vorwort

Als Bearbeiter dieser komplett neu gestalteten Ausgabe des Wörterbuchs *Bairisch-English* erfülle ich einen lang gehegten Wunsch des 2010 im Alter von 86 Jahren verstorbenen Professors Dr. Otto Hietsch: sein ehemals in 3 Bänden erschienenes Werk als kompaktes einbändiges Wörterbuch zu veröffentlichen. Dabei wurden die gängigsten bairischen Begriffe und Redensarten ausgewählt, und jede Seite strotzt nur so vor Wissensgut und feinem Humor. Darüber hinaus lernt der Benutzer für Bayern typische kulinarische Köstlichkeiten kennen und erhält Einblicke in die bunte und lange Tradition Bayerns.

Geboren wurde Professor Dr. Otto Hietsch am 14.01.1924 in Wien. 1942 legte er das Abitur ab und studierte zunächst in seiner Geburtsstadt Anglistik, Germanistik und Philosophie, ehe er 1948 nach Durham (Newcastle upon Tyne) übersiedelte und dort den englischen akademischen Grad *Magister Litterarum* erwarb. Von 1951-1954 verbrachte er in Padua, wo er sein Studium mit Romanistik und Pädagogik erweiterte. Bereits im Alter von 40 Jahren wurde er 1964 zum ordentlichen Universitätsprofessor für Anglistik in Braunschweig ernannt. 1967 erging an ihn der Ruf, an der neu gegründeten Universität von Regensburg an der Anglistik-Fakultät den Bereich Linguistik aufzubauen. Seine Hauptforschungsgebiete waren die Erfassung der englischen Gegenwartssprache, Kulturbeziehungen zwischen den englisch- und deutschsprachigen Ländern, Lyrik und Lieder in Übersetzung, Dialektologie, historische Linguistik u.v.m. Alsbald entdeckte er seine große Leidenschaft, nämlich das Bairische dem Englischen im zweisprachigen Kulturvergleich an die Seite zu stellen. Immer mit Papier und Bleistift ausgerüstet, schaute er „dem Volk aufs Maul“ und sammelte reichlich bairisches Sprach- und Kulturgut, das sich nun in dem Werk *Bairisch-English* wiederfindet.

Ich hoffe, dass es mir gelungen ist, ein zweisprachiges Lexikon zu gestalten, das Ihnen, liebe Leserinnen und Leser, stets ein munterer, origineller und informativer Begleiter durch das Land und das Leben der Bayern sein wird.

Mein herzlicher Dank gilt den Verlegern Heiner Gietl und Josef Roidl von den Gietl Verlagen, die mir dieses aufwändige Unterfangen ermöglicht haben und mir immer unterstützend zur Seite standen. Zuletzt aber möchte ich Frau Nina Schneider nicht vergessen, die mit ihren lebendigen und ausdrucksstarken Illustrationen dafür gesorgt hat, dass das Lexikon auch optisch zu einem echten Buchschmankerl geworden ist.

So wünsche ich viele vergnügliche und interessante Momente beim Schmökern – in Erinnerung an Professor Dr. Otto Hietsch!

Andreas Dick (Bearbeiter)

Foreword

As the Editor of this completely revised edition of the *Bairisch-English* dictionary, I am fulfilling one of the most fervent wishes long cherished by Professor Dr. Otto Hietsch, who died in 2010 at the age of 86: namely, to publish his dictionary, a work which had hitherto appeared in 3 volumes, as a compact, single volume. In so doing, the most common Bavarian terms and sayings were selected, and every page is jam-packed with a wealth of wisdom and subtle humor. Furthermore, those using the book can learn about Bavarian culinary dishes and gain an insight into Bavaria's long and colorful tradition.

Professor Dr. Otto Hietsch was born in Vienna on 14.01.1924. He graduated from grammar school in 1942 and started studying English, German and Philosophy in his native city, before moving to Durham (near Newcastle upon Tyne) in 1948, where he was awarded the English academic title *Magister Litterarum* (Master of Literature). He spent the years 1951-1954 in Padua, where he broadened his studies, adding to them French and Educational Science. At the age of only 40, he was appointed Professor for English Philology in Brunswick. In 1967 he was asked to build up the Chair for Linguistics in the Faculty for English Studies at the newly founded University of Regensburg. The main areas of his work were to analyze present-day English, cultural relations between English-speaking and German-speaking countries, poetry and song in translation, dialectology and historical linguistics to name but a few. Before long, he discovered his enormous passion, namely putting Bavarian side by side with English, in a bilingual comparison of the two cultures. Always equipped with a pencil and paper, he listened very carefully to the language of the common people and collected a wealth of Bavarian lexical and cultural information, which is now to be found in his work *Bairisch-English*.

I hope that I have succeeded in creating a bilingual dictionary which, for you, dear readers, will always be a cheerful, original and informative companion throughout Bavaria and Bavarian life.

My sincere thanks go to the publishers Heiner Gietl and Josef Roidl from the publishing house Gietl Verlagen, who enabled me to carry out this elaborate venture and who were always on hand with their assistance and support. Last but not least, nor do I wish to omit to mention Ms. Nina Schneider, whose vibrant and expressive illustrations ensure that this book has become a real gem in visual terms, too.

I wish you many an amusing and interesting moment browsing through the book – in memory of Professor Dr. Otto Hietsch!

Andreas Dick (Editor)

The Bavarian Anthem

Music by Max Kunz (1812-1875)   Words by Michael Öchsner (1816-1893)

2. *Gott mit dir, dem Bayernvolke, dass wir, uns're Väter wert, fest in Eintracht und in Frieden bauen uns'res Glückes Herd! Dass mit Deutschlands Bruderstämmen einig uns ein jeder schau und den alten Ruhm bewähre unser Banner, weiß und blau!*

2. May the Lord save you, Bavarians, make us walk our forebears' path; fortified through peace and union, steadfast build our fortune's hearth! May He will that German nations are like brothers for the view, keep the ancient glory going of our banner white and blue.

Gerd Maier

Wos i mog

Auf d' Nacht in am oidn Wirtshaus hocka
und d' Wirm vom Kachlofa spürn.
De Bauern zuaschaugn beim Tarocka,
a weng dablecka, wenn s' valiern.

A frische Hoibe ab und zua
und zuaschaugn, wia da Foam zammasitzt.
Sunst mog i nix ois wia mei Ruah,
denn d' Unruah hod no nia nix gnützt.

Dazwischn nei a Liadl singa,
ned plärrat, na, schee staad und fei.
Grod a so mog i 's, so muaß klinga,
schee boarisch, griawig muaß 's hoid sei.

Und drunta nei a Pfeifal raucha,
de blaua Ringl nocheschaugn.
Na, mehra daat i gor ned braucha,
des san de Sachan, de mia taugn.

Things I Like

At night, an old inn feels snug and pleasant,
When mildly wafts the tiled stove's heat.
I kibitz on the farm folks present
And tease a bit those in defeat.

At times, I order a fresh stein,
Watch frothiness give up its lease.
Else, none but rest and calm be mine –
Unrest 's no good, right mars the peace.

Still, in between I feel like singing
(Not blaring, mind) a quiet tune;
A tune to set deep chords a-ringing,
And my Bavarian soul will croon.

A dreamy pipe, too, smoked at leisure,
Its bluey wisps trail out of sight.
Aye, brimful's then my cup of pleasure –
Such are the things that spell delight.

A

A-a [a-ˈa:] *interj* & *n* - *baby talk* **1.** (the presence of some) excretion *(Kot)*: plop-plop; *schau, Hundi ~* look, doggie plop-plop. - **2.** excretion *(Stuhlgang)* - (1) *interj* a child's warning shout of a pressing personal need: *Mami, ~!* Mummy (*AmE* Mommy, *or* Momma), plop-plop! - (2) *n* an adult's reference to the act - *~ machen* to have motion *(Stuhlgang haben)*: to do a big job, to do number two; *hast du jetzt scho ~ gmacht?* have you done your (big) business yet?

abblatteln *v/i colloq. (abbröckeln)* of the plaster on old houses, of wall paint, etc.: to peel, to come off; *die Farbe blattelt von den Wänden ab* the paint is peeling off the walls.

abbrocken *v/t* to pull off or break off a flower or fruit from a plant or tree *(abpflücken)*: to pick, to pluck.

abbusseln *vt/refl* [an intensive of *busseln*↓] *colloq.* **1.** *v/t* to kiss effusively: to cover with kisses, to shower (*or* smother) with kisses; *unsere kleine Juliane ist so ein goldiges Buzerl, dass wir sie am liebsten den ganzen Tag knuddeln und ~ könnten* our baby Juliana is such a sweet little darling we could cuddle and cover her with kisses all day. - **2.** *v/refl* (1) to kiss each other lovingly: to kissy-kissy, *AmE hum. also* to play post office, to play smacky lips. - (2) slightly *contp.*, if the act of osculation is performed with sovereign disregard for other people around: to smooch; *sich in der hintersten Kinoreihe ~* to be necking in the back row of the cinema.

abfieseln *v/t dial. (abnagen)* to pick (a bone, etc.) clean; *er hat die Boandl vom Hendl gründlich abgefieselt* he did a thorough job of picking the bones of his chicken.

abfretten *v/refl colloq. (sich abmühen)* to take a lot of trouble (but with little success), to wear oneself out, *colloq.* to knock oneself out (doing s.th.), *BrE colloq. also* to toil and moil; *sie muss sich beim Heizen immer mit diesem alten Ofen ~* she has quite a job (*or*, she has a terrible time) keeping that old stove going.

abbusseln

Abrahams Wurstkessel [-ʃt-] *m* - -s [for absurd effect, the venerable name of Abraham (according to John viii. 37, the progenitor of the Jewish people) here collates with something almost ludicrously mundane] *hum.* a crudely medieval picture, possibly lifted from a Biblia Pauperum, helps to describe man's estate when yet unborn - "sausage" embryos are afloat in a huge "cauldron" before being transmuted into human shape later on; the phrase is used to deflate a potential or real braggart, putting him in his place in one of two ways, **1.** he is made to look a callow youth, at least by comparison: *damals warst du noch in ~ ~* you were then still living in a cabbage patch, *or* under the gooseberry bush, *or, AustralE,* under a gum-tree, you were then still coated with fuller's earth || with a triumphantly sensual leer: *du bist ja noch in ~ ~ gelegen, wie ich schon fleißig Kinder gemacht hab* you weren't even a gleam in your father's eye while I was already busy fixing up kids; and **2.** he is given to understand that he may claim no privileges: *du bist ja auch nur in ~ ~ herumgeschwommen!* *you aren't a bit better than the rest of us coming out of Abraham's cauldron, you aren't any different from the common run of us, *NorBrE also* we're all Jack Thompson's bairns, *AmE also* you aren't number one on the hit parade, you aren't the only fish in the sea.

abwatschen *v/t* [emphatically for *watschen* 'to cuff', 'to slap'] *colloq.*, rudely descriptive **j-n** ~ **1.** to beat s.o. again and again with the open hand: to cuff s.o. left and right. → **2.** to beat s.o. severely in an election, a match, etc.: to beat the pants off s.o., to take s.o. to the cleaner's; *der Vorsitzende wurde am Aschermittwoch weit gründlicher abgewatscht als seine drei Stellvertreter; er war vor zwei Jahren noch mit 93 Prozent gewählt worden* on Ash Wednesday the chairman was much more thoroughly trounced than his three deputies; two years ago, he had been voted in by 93 per cent.

Allerwelts...: ~kirtag *m* -(e)s/pl. rare: -e, **~kirchweih** *f* -/pl. rare: -en *folklore* "All-Bavarian Sunday Fair", a festive occasion, on the third Sunday in October, to engage in various merrymakings and to have roast goose as a traditional meal; established in 1869, it is also known as *großer Kirtag*, distinguishing it from the more specific, and more religious, *kleiner Kirtag.*

Alm *f* -/-en, *dial.* **Alma** *f* -/-; in SW Bavaria, **Alp** *f* -/-en, **Alpe** *f* -/-n **1.** *agr., econ.,* & *folklore* a summer branch of the home farm in the valley, situated well above the line of grain fields *(Bergweide [mit niedrigem, kleinem Wohn- und Wirtschaftsgebäude])*: alpine pasture, mountain dairy (farm), alp; *auf die ~ gehen* to go up the alp; *eine sonnige, blumenübersäte ~, und in der Ferne träumerisches Geläut von Kuhglocken* a sunny, flower-strewn mountain meadow, and in the distance the dreamy sounds of cowbells; *bis zum Zweiten Weltkrieg gab es auf den Almen um Sennerinnen und Senner ein ur-*

wüchsiges Leben und Treiben; es ist heute leider oft verblasst oder gar erloschen, und einsam liegt das Galtvieh auf enger Weide vor der offenen Stalltür until the Second World War, dairymaids and lads led a simple and wholesome life, watching over their herds; sadly, this has dwindled or even disappeared, and the young calves lie penned in, alone, before the open stable door || the punch line of a famous yodelling song, one that is often laughingly quoted with an erotic leer: *auf der Alm, da gibt's k[o]a Sünd* there's no sin on pastures high - its sequel is sometimes ad-libbed by scoffing townsfolk into ..., *weil die Männer müde sind*, the whole couplet best to be rendered as

Alm

Dairymaids commit no sins
'cos their lads are Tired Tims.

2. *tourist trade* often as part of a proper name, chosen to conjure up a cowbell-cum-dairyhut rusticity whereas the place actually embodies citified comfort and luxury: (fashionable) mountain lodge.

Ạlm...: **~abfahrt** *f* -/-en, more often **~abtrieb** *m* -(e)s/-e; in SW Bavaria, **Viehscheid** *m* -(e)s/-e, *dial.* **Viechschoad** *m* -s/- in late September or early October: descent, *or* bringing (*or* driving) down the cattle from the mountain pastures - this, provided that no animal has come to grief, is a festive procession with yodelling, jangling of bells, and cows decorated with ribbons, paper bows, and a tower of wildflowers on their horns. - **~auffahrt** *f* -/-en, more often **~auftrieb** *m* -(e)s/-e in early May: ascent, *or* taking (*or* driving) up to the mountain pastures. - **~hütte** *f* -/-n alpine hut, dairyhut. - **~ruf** *m* -(e)s/-e, **~schrei** *m* -(e)s/-e, *dial.* **~schroa** *m* -s/- *mus.* a primitive, yet by no means inartistic or unmelodious, type of short song used as an identifying "signature tune" from one dairyhut to another: (dairyfolk's) mountain cry. - **~wirtschaft** *f* - *econ.* mountain-dairy farming.

Ạndachtsjodler *m* -s/- *mus.*, usu. *eccles.* a slow and stately yodel sung in harmony as a centrepiece of any ceremonious gathering: devotional yodelling song.

ạnlangen *v/t colloq.* to handle *(anfassen)*: to touch - (1) *concr. lang mir fei das Reindl ja* (or, *ja das Reindl) nicht an, du* *könntst dir sonst die Händ verbrennen!* don't you touch that saucepan, you might burn your hands!; (2) *fig.*, in a brusque refusal to be involved in the slightest way: *den [die; das] würd' ich nicht mit der Kneifzangen* (or *einem Stecken,* or *einem Steckerl) ~! BrE* I wouldn't touch him [her; it] with a barge pole, *AmE* ... with a ten-foot pole.

Ạntn *f -/- dial.* [< the awkwardly slow rolling gait of a duck *(Ente)*] *school sl.* dull girl: dopey duck, daffy duck.

ạntrenzen *v/refl colloq.* to dirty one's clothes by drinking hastily or carelessly, or by being unexpectedly interfered with in the act: to spill things on one's clothes; *trink langsamer, sonst trenzt du dich noch an!* drink slower, or you'll spill it all over yourself!; *der Kleine hat sich mit dem Apfelsaft von oben bis unten angetrenzt* the baby has spilled apple juice all over himself.

ạnwanzig *adj colloq. (aufdringlich)* clinging; *der ist aber ~* he sticks like glue, *or* like a tick, he's a leech *or* limpet; *die ist aber ~* she's a clinging vine.

ạper *adj* [< L *aperire* 'to open, to make visible (the ground')] of fields, roads, etc.: *(schneefrei)* free from snow, thawed-out; **~n** *v/i* of snow *(tauen)*: to melt, to thaw; *es apert* the snow is melting, it is thawing; *die Sonne wird den Schnee in ein paar Tagen zum ~̽bringen* the sun will melt (*or* strip) the snow in a matter of days.

Ạpfel...: ~butzen *m -s/- dial. (Kerngehäuse e-s Apfels; → Butzen)* apple core. - **~kücherl** *n* -s/often pl.: - [second el., a dim. variant of *Kuchen* 'cake'] *cul.* a slice of apple dipped into batter, cooked in hot fat, and sprinkled with sugar and cinnamon: apple fritter. - **~strudel** *m* -s/- *bak.* a pastry consisting of sliced apples rolled in a blanket of paper-thin dough, and baked in the oven: apple strudel.

Apfelbutzen

Appọrtl *n* -s/-(n) *colloq. (Gegenstand, der geworfen wird, damit ihn der Hund wieder zurückbringt)* object thrown for a dog to retrieve; command to a dog: *such's ~!* seek!, find!, go fetch!, fetch it!, (go) get it!

Aprịl...: ~aff *m* -en/-en, **~ochs** *m* -en/pl. rare: -en [the ancient heathens (and, following them, modern Christians have) looked upon the beginning of a new year as a great occasion to celebrate; and as March 25th, which was supposed to be the Incarnation of our Lord, used to be New Year's Day, April 1st was its octave, when its festivities culminated and ended] *folklore,* low *colloq.* the person sent on stupid errands, or imposed upon in some ridiculous way, on April 1st: April Fool, *ScotE also* gowk ([gaʊk] 'cuckoo'); „~!", *schreien die Kinder, wenn es ihnen gelungen ist, jemanden hereinzulegen* "April Fool!", the children shout when they succeeded in playing a prank on someone; or, in gloating elaboration,

Am ersten April
schickt man den Narren,
wohin man will!

On the first of April
You may send a fool (*or*, a gowk)
wherever you will.

Ạrmdrücken *n* -s *folklore* wrist-wrestling, arm-wrestling **1.** a popular entertainment and test of strength, practised in Upper Bavarian inns, etc. between two men seated opposite one another across a table; with their left hands joined on the surface between them, the opponents clasp right hands firmly and brace their right elbows on the table; at the 'go' signal, both try to force the other's hand down to achieve a victory. - **2.** *sports* an official international sport with the above rules, requiring a table of specific size and padded elbow cups.

Armdrücken

Ạrsch *m* -(e)s/Ärsche, *colloq. Ärscher*; *dial.* **Ọrsch**, **Oasch** [ɔaʃ], **Oosch** [o:ʃ] *m* -(s)/-(a) **A. I.** *concr.* in low colloq. & rustic speech - the human or animal buttocks *(Gesäß)*: *BrE* arse [a:s], *AmE* ass [æs]; *sich [j-m] den ~ auswischen* to wipe [some]one's arse; *auf den ~ fallen* to fall on one's arse; *j-m einen Tritt in den ~ geben* to give s.o. a kick up the arse; *den ~ in die Höh hebm [rausstrecken]* to lift [to stick out] one's arse. **II.** *fig.* **1.** low colloq. phrases, each marked by vigorous diction, though not necessarily obscene - simply based on the fact that the buttocks, anatomically, are positioned "down and behind" on the human body: (1) said of an inactive person, also of a visitor giving no sign of rising to leave when, in the opinion of the host, he should: *der hat Blei im ~* he has (*or*, he's got) lead in his pants. - (2) said *contp.* of a person's, usu. a woman's, large bottom: *die [der] hat einen ~ wie ein Biergaul* (or, *wie ein Brauereipferd)* she [he] 's got an arse like the back of a bus. - (3) *iron.*, said of a person who often forgets or loses things: *du taatst dein ~ aa vagessn, wenn er net angwachsn waar!* you'd surely lose your arse if it was loose. - (4) a warning not to get carried away by emotions, and thus possibly make rash decisions: *wir wollen doch die Kirche im Dorf oder, wie man so zartfühlend sagt, den ~ in der Hosn lassn* by all means let the church stand in its own churchyard or, as the dainty saying goes, let the arse sit and fill the back of its pants. - (5) a warning to a person not to become too proud of his or her own abilities, position of authority, etc.: *mach den ~ nicht größer, als wia die Hosn is!* don't chuck (*or* throw) your arse around (*or* about), and let it fit the seat of your pants! - (6) a verbal threat: *wenn der mein Haus noch einmal betritt, werf ich ihn mit dem ~ voraus* (or, *~ über Kopf) die Stiegn runter!* if the dares (to) enter my house again, I'll throw him out arse over elbow (*or*, arse over tip [*or* tit], *or* arse first). - (7) a telltale snort of contempt indicative of the speaker's utter lack of interest in or concern about a matter: *das geht mir am ~ vorbei!* I couldn't care less, *BrE also* I don't give a tinker's curse (*or* cuss), *AmE also* ... a tinker's damn. - (8) a humbly *joc.* acknowledgement of one's own lowly position, which rules out all hopes of ever attaining any appreciably higher rung on the social or professional ladder: *ja mei, dafür hab ich meinen ~ zu tief unten!* oh my, I'm much sooner made out to be the arse-end Charlie of the ladder. - (9) said of a person who is naturally kind and helpful: *die is so gutmütig, die würd'* (or *taat) sogar ihrn ~ hergebm* she's so good-natured she'd even give away her last pair of knickers. - (10) an *iron.* couplet glibly fastening the blame for a noiseless but evil-smelling anal wind on the complainant; indeed, often used by the crafty 'culprit' to clear himself:

Wer es hat zuerst gerochen,
dem ist's aus dem Arsch gekrochen.

*The arse from which the stench dispersed
Belongs to him who smelt it first.

(11) *hum.*, a quick excuse for an audible escape of air from one's bowels: *wenn der ~ net brummt, is der Mensch net gsund!*, or, on the authority of Dr. Martin Luther, *aus einem verzagten ~ kommt kein fröhlicher Furz!* wherever thou be, let the winds go free!, a healthy gas from a merry ass! - (12) *iron.*, with specific reference to a remote, backwoods part of the country where life is said to be so primordial as to show features that are diametrically opposed to what modern man is used to: *dort bellen die Hunde mit dem ~* *in that area, dogs do their barking with their backsides. - **2.** vulgar phrases based on the, above all, physiological fact that the human buttocks are felt to be good for voiding waste matter only (cp. the phrase under *Feierabend 2, [2] b*): (1) a blunt suggestion that a person's action just performed is, or his intended action would be, utterly foolish: *du hast wohl* (or, *du hast, mir scheint) den ~ offen!* your arse is showing!, you're just plain full of shit!, *AmE also* you're out of your fucking mind!, stop thinking with your arse! - (2) a fierce refusal to have any truck with a person: *mit dir red't mein ~!* you're on my shit-list!, you can kiss my arse!, *AmE also* talk to my ass, man [woman]! - (3) a threat of vicious verbal (and possibly also physical) attack: *dem fahr'* (or *hupf') ich mi'm nackerten ~ ins Gsicht!* I'll bawl the livin' hell outa him!, *AmE also* I'll chew his ass out! - (4) a crude rejection of an offer, or in angry reply to the question what should be done with something:

schiab dir's in 'n ~!, damit kannst d' dir 'n ~ auswischn! you (can) keep it to wipe your dirty arse on! - **B.** *contp.* a pars-pro-toto vulgarism angrily shouted out about [or, often, hurled at] a person: *[du] blöder ~!, [du] ~ mit Ohren!* [you] shitarse!, [you] dumb arse!

Ạrsch..., *dial.* **Ọrsch...**, **O̲asch...**, **O̲osch...** *vulg.*: **~backn** *f -/- dial. vulg.* either of the two fleshy parts of the body on which a person sits *(Gesäßhälfte)*: (one of the) arse- [*AmE* ass-] end(s) - in a crudely facetious tease offered in response to a time enquiry: *es ist drei Viertel auf ~* (with the rhymed addition, ..., *kannst dir a Trumm rohackn [< herunterhacken]* '... you may cut yourself off a chunk') it's half-past shithouse time (, and time to shit again). -

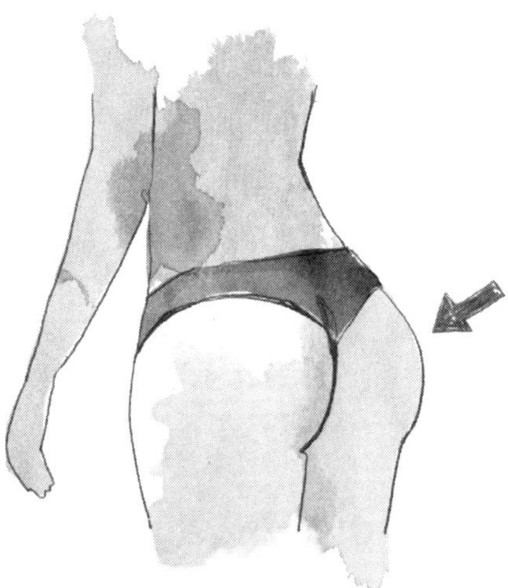

Arschbackn

~geige *f -/-n, dial.* **~geign** *f -/-* a term of gross abuse for a male: bugger, sod, turd; *das ist vielleicht eine ~!* what a turd!, he's a bugger, isn't he?; *was willst du denn mit dieser ~?* you don't want to have anything to do with that bugger (*or* sod)! - **~gesicht**, *dial.* **~gsicht** [-ks-] *n -s/-er* **1.** a fat, puffy face *(feistes, ausdrucksloses Gesicht)*: arse face, bum face; *der mit dem ~* the one with the arse face. → **2.** as a pars-pro-toto - (1) a person with a fat, puffy face: arse face, bum face; *das junge ~ dort drüben* that arse-faced (*or* bum-faced) youth over there. - (2) a worthless or annoying person: shit face, *BrE also* pillock, *AmE also* fart face, horse's ass. - **~kriechen** *n -s* sycophancy *(würdelose Liebedienerei)*: arse-kissing, arse-licking, bum-sucking, brown-nosing. - **~kriecher** *m -s/-* a sycophant: arse-kisser, arse-licker, bum-sucker, brown-nose(r), *AmE also* brownie.

ạ̈rschlings, *dial.* **ạrschlings** *adv, vulg.* in reverse order; wrong(ly), confused(ly) *(rückwärts; verkehrt)*: *BrE* arse first, *AmE* ass-backwards, backasswards.

aso̲; less often, **asọ** *adv, dial.* for the sake of emphasis, monosyllabic *so* is prefixed by unaccented *a-*, which adds body and weight to the slim monosyllable, and gives added status to the preceding word - **1.** in imperative or doctrinaire utterances: *mach's ~!* do (*or* make it, *or* go) like that!; *i geh ~* I'll go the way I am (*i.e.*, I'll wear the [casual] outfit you happen to see me in just now); *das kann man ~ und ~ sehn* this can be looked at from one angle or from another. - **2.** in a statement acknowledging a new fact (yet with less surprise than is conveyed by, say, *aha!*

and *ah so!*): ~! I see. - **3.** when stating a high opinion: *mir schmeckt's scho ~, i sag dir's!* I like this food no end, I tell ye.

auf geht's! *interj* a cheerful invitation, sometimes to oneself, but more often for others to join the speaker in starting work, or in having fun, with zest and vigour: here we go!, off like blazes!, let's get cracking!, let's whoop it up!, let's get the show on the road!; to others also: let's go, boys [girls]! || as a spirited elaboration of that phrase ("Papa" Schichtl, 1851-1911, having been a well-known showman at the Munich *Oktoberfest*↓, who for years performed "real" decapitations with his guillotine): ~ ~ *beim Schichtl!* as one earwig said to another, "'ere we go!" || a rallying call to join the crowd of merrymakers at the Munich *Oktoberfest*↓: ~ ~ *zur Wies'n!* to the Meadow off we hie!

aufkoppen *v/i* [→ *koppen*] *colloq.* said of certain vegetables that one has eaten - to cause eructation *([aus dem Magen] aufstoßen)*: to repeat; *mir koppen Zwiefel immer auf* I find that onions repeat.

aufmandln *colloq.* **1.** *vt/i agr.* [second el., *Mandl 3*↓] *Getreide ~* to put sheaves together in the harvest field for drying *(Garben zur Nachreife aufstellen)*: to stook [-u:-], *NorBrE also* to set (the) sheaves up in a hattock, to set up, to hattock, to stack, to stowk [-(a)ɔ:-], [-əʊ-]. - **2.** *v/refl* [second el., *Mandl 1* & *2*↓] often *iron.* or *contp.* whenever said with reference to a person, usu. male, whose slight frame is at odds with his, at the moment, aggressive and overbearing manner — to become impatient and angry: to work oneself into a lather, to get one's dander (*or*, quills) up, *AmE also* to rear up on one's hind legs.

auf Wiederschauen *interj* a slightly less frequent variant than *auf Wiedersehen*: goodbye, *colloq.* see you, be seeing you || a good-natured warning that the object about to be given away on a loan basis should be duly returned: *du weißt [Sie wissen] ja, da steht „ ~ ~ " drauf!* mind you, it's got a back to it!, *or* ... it's on an elastic band - it comes back!

Auf Wiederschauen

ausfratscheln *v/t colloq. (aushorchen)* to elicit information from s.o.: to pump s.o., to put the screws on s.o., *AmE also* to give s.o. the third degree.

ausgeschamt, often **ausgschamt** *adj* [for *ausgeschämt*, the p.p. of an unauthenticated *ausschämen* 'to have lost, or to be void of, all feeling of shame'] *dial.* insolent *(unverschämt)*: brazen-faced, (damn) cheeky; *so ein ~s Weibsbild!* the shameless hussy!; *die Bande, die ~e, die hätt' wohl all's von der Erbschaft eingsacklt!* that brazen-faced gang, what a cheek! they'd (just) as soon have grabbed all the inheritance; *obwohl über die ~n Bierpreise jedes Jahr ausgiebig gegrantelt wird, kommt zur nächsten Wies'n aber doch alles wieder gern nach München* although widespread grumbling about the steep prices of beer is an annual feature, folks nevertheless all gladly flock back to Munich for their "Meadow brew" the year after.

Ausgezogene, *dial.* **Auszongne** *f* -n/usu. pl.: -n, short for **ausgezogene Nudel** *f* -n -/usu. pl.: -n -n, also known as **Kirtanudel**, **Schmalznudel** *f* -/usu. pl.: -n, or **Knieküchel** *n* -s/usu. pl.: -(n) [→ *Küchel*] *bak.* tiny slabs of sweetened yeast pastry, (at one time, and sometimes still) gently pulled out over the housewife's knees to leave the centre very thin but the rim a bulgy ring, then fried in lard and dipped in sugar *(schmalzgebackene, durch Rundumziehen des Teiges außen wulstige Nudel)*: brown doughnut with a thin yellow-white "hub cap".

auspapierln *v/t* [second el., < *Papierl*, here: 'tissue paper (to wrap flowers), or kraft paper (to wrap items of food, such as a snack meat loaf) in'] *colloq.* to unwrap: to undo, e.g. a bouquet of flowers before presenting it to the hostess; *er geht fürstlich ins Wirtshaus essen, und ich bleib da und kann mein Wurstbrot ~!* he lords it at the inn with knife and fork, and I am left behind to dig my teeth into a slice of bread and sausage!

aussackeln, *dial.* **aussackln** *v/t colloq.* [cp. *einsackeln*] **1.** *rare* to remove from a bag *or* sack [... from bags *or* sacks] *(aus einem Sack [aus Säcken] leeren)*: to unbag, to unsack. → **2.** [lit., 'to turn a dupe's pockets inside out (and thus to empty them of all their contents)'], also **ausziehen**, *dial.* **ausziang** *v/t colloq.* (1) to charge someone too much money for something *(schröpfen)*: to fleece. - (2) to cheat someone out of all his money or possessions, e.g. at a game of chance *([völlig] ausnehmen)*: to clean out, to take to the cleaner's; *ees Hundling, ees habts mi schö ausgsacklt!* you bastards, you've cleaned me out good and proper!

Austrag *m* -(e)s *husb.* **1.** ([old farmer's] state of) retirement; *in den ~ gehen* to go into retirement, *colloq.* to have been put out to pasture; *im ~ leben (den Hof übergeben haben)* to be retired; *den Bauern zum Gehen in den ~ verlocken* to entice the farmer to retire. - **2.** *(Altenteil)* quarters for the retired farmer. - **~häusl** *n* -s/-(n) old farmer's cottage, a small cottage adjacent to a farmhouse set aside as old-age residence for parents or grandparents. - **Austrägler**, *dial.* **Austragler** *m* -s/- = *Austragsbauer*;

Austräglerin, *dial.* **Austraglerin** *f* -/-nen = *Austragsbäuerin.*

Austrags...: ~**bauer** *m* -n/-n (~**bäuerin** *f* -/-nen), ~**landwirt** *m* -(e)s/-e (~**landwirtin** *f* -/-nen) retired farmer (retired farmer's wife *or* woman farmer) living on the premises of the farm in a small cottage *(Austragshäusl)* or room *(Austragsstüberl)* set aside as an old-age residence.

Austragstüberl *n* -s/-(n) old farmer's room, *i.e.* a small room in which the retired farmer lives.

Auswärts *m* -/no pl. [literally, '(season of leaves sprouting) outward', the time when the days are 'getting longer'] *dial.* & *poet. (Frühling*; opp. *Einwärts*↓*)*: spring; *im ~* in spring; *für den naturverbundenen Menschen liegt der Schnee nicht wie ein Leichentuch auf der Landschaft, sondern als Zudecke, unter der Blumen, Gräser und Saaten schon dem ~ entgegenträumen* for nature-loving folks, the snow is not so much a deathly pall covering the landscape but rather a protective blanket, under which flowers, grasses, and seeds dreamily await the coming of spring || a piece of old weather lore: *wenn's um Lichtmess stürmt und schneibt, / ist der ~ nimmer weit!* *storms and snows at Candlemas / herald springtime flowers and grass.

auswatten *v/t colloq.* **1.** to decide by a game of *Watten*↓; *eine Mass (Bier), eine Runde (Bier) ~* among card-players, usu. in a pub: to stake one litre (of beer), one round, on a game of *Watten* (with all the cronies drinking the prize together, as a rule, from one earthenware mug). - **2.** *fig. colloq. ([ein Problem] aushandeln)* to come to an agreement on, to settle (an issue); *wir müssen das noch ~* we've to speak about that and decide matters, we've to argue that question out; *das watten wir dann schon aus* we'll get square on that all right, *AmE* we'll get that squared away, we'll ante for it. - **3.** *fig.* to make an arbitrary and, by implication, unfair decision; *ich habe das Gefühl, die Lehrer haben unsere Noten ausgewattet* it seems to me the teachers tossed (*AmE* flipped) coins to decide our marks (*AmE* grades), ... the teachers decided our marks (*AmE* grades) by drawing (*or* picking) cards.

auwehzwịck *interj* [in a rendering faithful to the sense and the elements used, 'ooh, a pinch can hurt, too'] sometimes *hum.* - a none too deeply felt shout of surprise or mild annoyance when something unusual, and often slightly unpleasant, happened: hi-yi ouch!, (oh,) my aching back!, (oh,) my shattered nerves!, (oh,) my battered curves!, *AmE also* of all the nutty snozzlewobbles!

auswatten

B

Baaz *m* -es [< sound symbolism] *colloq.*, sometimes with a playfully pleasant undertone **1.** mud, or any other slushy mass: goo, *AmE also* gumbo, glob; *Kinder und Wildschweine spielen für ihr Leben gern im ~* children and wild boars just love to wallow in the mud. - **2.** any other sticky substance the speaker has, often inadvertently, come upon: goo, *BrE also* gunge, *AmE also* gunk; *was ist denn das für ein ~ da unten in der Tasche? ... da muss die Schokolade zergangen sein!* what's all that goo at the bottom of this bag? ... the chocolate must have melted. - **baazig** *adj colloq.* said of, or resembling, a sticky substance: gooey, *BrE also* gungy.

bạcherlwarm *adj* & *adv* [first el., an endearing dim., with the suffix *-erl* added to the stem form of *bạchen*, the dial. variant of *bạcken* 'to bake'] *colloq.*, always *apprec.* pleasantly warm (and fresh, crisp, etc.): nice and warm [hot]; *wenn's an einem eiskalten Winterabend ~ vom Ofen herweht, dann ist es in der Bauernstubm gwiß am gemütlichsten* on an icy-cold winter evening, with the stove oozing cosy warmth, the farm-house room's most snug and safe, I'm sure.

Baiern 1. *m pl., hist. (Baiwaren, Bajuwaren)* (ancient tribe of the) Bavarians. → **2.** *n* -s *hist. geog. (Altbayern)* Old Bavaria, i.e. the tribal heartlands around Munich, Landshut and Regensburg (extending at one time south to include a large part of what is today Austria and South Tyrol); cp. *Bayern.*

Bạmbs or **Bạms** [bɔmps] *m* -/-en *dial.* any young child whom a negative personal quality or stigma is attached to by the speaker or writer, e.g. (1) that of being spoiled or ill-mannered: brat, holy terror; *de ~en bringa mi no um!* those brats 'll be the death of me; or (2) that of illegitimate birth: love child, *AmE also* come-by-chance; *Simon ist der ~, den er von der Veronika hat, die jetzt auf seiner Besitzung Berchtoldszell im Gebirg den Haushalt führt* Simon is the love child he'd got Veronica pregnant with who is now keeping house at his place at Berchtoldszell, down in the mountains.

Bạmpf *m* -(e)s *colloq.*, often *contp.* food that tastes soft and thick and heavy *(dicker Brei, Kleister)*: mush, goo, sticky mess, *BrE also* gunge; *ich mag keinen Erdäpfelschmarrn, das ist mir zu viel ~* I don't care for mashed potatoes, they're too mushy.

Bärendreck *m* -s *comest., colloq. (Lakritze[nstange* or *-schnur])* "bear's dung," a confectionery made from liquorice, *AmE also* licorice, a black substance produced from the sweet-tasting dried root of Glycyrrhiza glabra, a leguminous plant.

Bärwurz "bear root" **1.** *f* -/-en, *also* **Bärenwurzel** *f* -/-n, **Bärendill** *m* -s/-e *bot.* an umbelliferous plant *(Meum athamanticum)* whose natural habitat are the high-lying meadows (all above 3000 ft. in altitude) of the Rachel and Lusen mountains, in the Bavarian Forest; its root, shaggy in appearance, and similar in taste to celery, is dug in autumn: (true) spicknel, baldmoney, bear fennel. → **2.** *m* -(es)/-(e) *bev.* a pungent brandy distilled from this root (commonly known as *Waldlerschnaps*), sometimes diversified by the addition of various woodland berries.

Bärendreck

Bạtzl *n* -s/-(n) *colloq.* **1.** a small lump *(Klümpchen)*: twiddly-bit (of earth, mud, etc.); → *Hirnbatzl.* - **2.** *emot.*, hence also **Bạtzerl** *n* -s/-(n) a very small amount *(ganz kleine Menge)*: smidgin (*or* smidgen); *könnt ich bittschön noch ein ~ Kartoffelbrei haben?* could I have another smidgin of mash, please? - **3.** *med.* a pimple or other minor skin blemish *(Pickel)*: hickey; *soll ich dir das ~ ausdrucken?* do you want me to squeeze out your hickey for you? - **4.** *agr.* a white, often globular root crop, the size of a fist or a baby's skull: turnip.

Bạtzl... *colloq.*: **~augen** *n pl.* **1.** *med.* protuberant eyes *(hervortretende Augen)*: bug-eyes, goggle-eyes, pop-eyes; *der hat fei ~* his eyes stick out like organ stops (*BrE also* ... like chapel hat-pegs). - **2.** often *contp.* momentarily bulbous eyes, due to intense curiosity or greed: beady eyes, goo-goo eyes, pop-eyes; *gib Obacht, du kriegst am End vor lauter Schauen noch ~!* mind, if you don't stop staring your eyes will pop out; *er hat vor lauter Gier solche ~ gekriegt, dass man sie mit der Knopfgabel hätte putzen können* he became all agog and gawping with greed, making his eyes shine like shoe buttons || in stark irony, also: *hast du deine ~ vielleicht auf einen gewissen jungen Mann geworfen?* have you by any manner of means set your beady blue eyes on a certain young man?

Bauch... *colloq.*: **~butzen** *m* -s/-, **~knöpfl** *n* -s/-(n) [second el., dim. of Knopf 'button'] *anat., hum.* navel *(Nabel)*: belly button. - **~platscher**, **~pflatscher** *m* -s/- [second el., echoic for the thud caused by the impact of a heavy object on a hard surface] *sports*, esp. in swimming and ice-skating — the awkward pancake landing of a diver or skater, whose front of the body falls flat against the water, or ice, respectively: flop(per),

BrE also belly flapper, *AmE also* belly whop(per), belly buster. - **~weh** *n* -s **1.** *med.* abdominal pains: bellyache. - **2.** *fig.* an ironic way of expressing one's feeling of dislike: *die Hausarbeit ist mir so lieb wie ~* housework is my pet hate (*or*, pet aversion). - **~zwicken** *n* -s *med.* *(Bauchgrimmen)* sudden and severe stomach cramps: gripes; *er hat ~* he's got the gripes; *gegen ~ ist ein Stamperl gut, bei ~ ist ein Stamperl fällig* a little pick-me-up is good for (*or*, comes in handy with) the gripes.

Bauern...: **~bub** *m* -en/-en *(Bauernjunge)* country lad, farmer's boy, *AmE* farmboy. - **~fünfer** *m* -s/- **1.** *hist., contp.* Roman numeral V which, along with other simple Roman numerals, continued to be used by the rural population long after Arabic numerals had found widespread acceptance in the seventeenth century. - **2.** *hist. jur. (ländlicher Hilfsschöffe)* peasant juryman, one of a group of five called by the judge in doubtful cases from the market assembly to assist at a trial. - **3.** *contp.* an invective hurled in anger at any male person thought to have acted foolishly or clumsily: clodhopper, country yokel, *AmE also* country clod, alfalfa grower, pea picker, rube. - **~hammel** *m* -s/-(n) *contp.* country boor, peasant lout. - **~lackel** *m* -s/-(n) *contp.* = *Bauernhammel.* - **~trampel** *m* -s/-(n) *contp.* a derisive term for a woman of unrefined manners, often quickly ostracized by city dwellers because she is of rural descent: country bumpkin, *AmE also* hayseed, hick, hillbilly.

Baumschule, *dial.* **Ba(a)mschui** *f* -/-n [basically, a StandG technical term in forestry and horticulture, 'nursery of young trees'] *colloq., hum.* or *sarc.* a playful re-interpretation of the compound merging the arborial and the human aspect of the element *-schule*; it now raises serious doubts about a young (or not so young) student's formal education: backwoods school (in which natural ignorance is bliss); *er ist, mir scheint, in die ~ 'gangen* seems to me he was dragged up rather than brought up; *du hast ja nicht einmal einen Abschluss von der ~* gee-whizz, did you ever get a nursery-leaving certificate ... or was it that from a tree nursery?

Bayer *m* -n/-n a native of Bavaria: Bavarian; *woher* (or *wieso*) *weißt du, dass er (ein) ~ ist?* how do you know (that) he's (a) Bavarian?; *Herzog Ludwig der ~* Duke Lewis of Bavaria || a brief sampling of familiar quotations on a Bavarian's reputedly simple and easy-going nature: (1) *Gott ist kein ~, er lässt sich nicht spotten* God is no Bavarian, He does not allow Himself to be made fun of (*or*, you can't make fun of Him). - (2) *Alles kann man dem ~n abkaufen, nur nicht seine Dummheit* you can get a Bavarian to part with anything except his credulous good nature. - (3) *Für den* (or, *dem*) *~n ist das Leben ein sich täglich erneuerndes Fest* a Bavarian looks upon life as a perpetual feast (*hum. also*, as a pageant of highdays, holidays and bonfire nights).

Bayerin *f* -/-nen woman from Bavaria, Bavarian (woman).

Bayern *n* -s, *polit. geog.* Bavaria; *sie stammt aus* ~ she's a native of Bavaria; *bei uns in* ~ in Bavaria, where I come from; *der Freistaat* ~ the Free State of Bavaria; cp. *Baiern.*

Baze or **Bazi** *m* -/Bazen *or* Bazi *colloq.*, often in dial. context - either an angry or an indulgently, sometimes even fully, appreciative epithet for a male: **1.** said with bitterness about a dishonest person *(Gauner)*: crook, rogue, scoundrel; *das war der größte ~, der je auf Gottes Erdboden herumgelaufen ist!* he was the biggest crook that ever was graced to walk on God's earth, *NorBrE also* ... the biggest rogue unhung. - **2.** *hum.* or in slight annoyance - a person, esp. a child, who plays tricks but is regarded with fondness *(Schelm)*: rascal, *BrE* scallywag, *AmE* scalawag; *wo hat denn der ~ meine Schlüssel versteckt?* where has that rascal hidden my keys? - **3.** *hum.* or *euphem.* in mock abuse, often from the buyer to the seller, after a business has been concluded among longtime partners, and a formal act of hospitality is then asked for to wind up the deal *(Schlawiner)*: old rogue *or* villain, (blasted) so-and-so; *jetzt fahrst aber a Trumm Gselchtes her, du ~, du (ganz) schlechter!* well, it's high time now you dish out a big chunk of smoked meat, you old rogue! - **4.** *apprec.* one who achieved something against heavy odds, or one who did so barely "on the brink of legality" *(Tausendsas[s]a)*: cunning devil, sly customer; *mei, des is' dir ein ~!* my, there's a cunning devil for you!

begriffsstutzig *adj colloq.* slow in understanding *(schwer von Begriffen)*: slow off the mark, slow on the uptake, dense; *er ist derart ~, dass man ihm das Einfachste zweimal sagen muss* he's so slow off the mark that you have to repeat the simplest things.

beinand [a short form of StandG *beieinander* 'together', brought about by haplography and end-clipping] *adv, colloq.* in (jovial) company, happily well met || *phr.* **1.** hearty greetings by one joining the circle of family or friends, entering a cosy inn which is pleasantly filled, etc.: *grüß Gott ~!* (God) bless you all (in here)!; *guten Abend ~!* good evening, everybody! - **2.** a cheerful or mocking comment on seeing, or hearing of, a clique gathered together: *da ist ja eine saubere Blasn ~!* there's a fine get-together of good fellers (*AmE also* a swell bunch [*if ironical*: a happy family]) for you!

Belle or **Belli** *m* -/- **1.** *colloq.* a person's head *(Schädel)*: noddle, (coco)nut, *BrE also* crust (of bread), *BrE dial. also* top-knot, top-piece, *AmE also* dome, noodle || *phr.* (1) *hau dir bei der Tür da nicht* (dial. *net) den ~ an!* mind your nut on that door! - (2) *mir brummt der ~* my head's going round and round. - (3) *mei, hat der einen (*dial. *an) [Trumm] ~!* my (*AmE also* gee), what a pumpkin (*AmE dial.* punkin) he's got (for a head)! - **2.** also **Schellensiebner** or **Schellsiebener** *m* -s/- *cards* the second highest of the permanent trump cards *(Kritische)* in the game of *Watten*↓: seven of bells.

Bẹtthupferl *n* -s/- [second el., the verbal stem of *hupfen*, the dial. variant of *hüpfen*, + dim. suffix *-erl*, 's.th. or s.o. that hops, skips, or jumps'] **1.** *colloq.*, often *dial.* something in the eat-drink-or-read line that gives pleasure, or at least satisfaction, before feeling ready to fall asleep for the night: pick-me-up-and-lay-me-down titbit (*AmE only* tidbit); such go-to-bed-with treat varies, of course, in content and name according to age and education - (1) if demanded by and given to children who incline towards things that are sweet and sugary: beddy-bye goody (*BrE also* sweetie, *AmE also* candy); *magst (no') a ~?* would you like a goody for bye-byes?; (2) if an adult has the lurking suspicion that going without supper, or even without a prenocturnal snack, might increase the risks of infarction and apoplexy: pre-beddy bite; (3) if a good many adults presume "liquor is quicker" to bring about sound sleep: nightcap; and (4) if an entertaining or, conversely, a dull book is believed to have the same effect: beddy-bye read. - **2.** blatantly *erot.* a sexually desirable female: dainty dish; *waar des net a pfundigs ~?* wouldn't she be a delicious goody to jump into bed with?

Bi̱er *n* -(e)s/-e beer, an alcoholic beverage for which, in the states of Bavaria and Baden-Württemberg, under a law dating from 1516, only malt, hops, culture yeast, and water may be used as ingredients; naturally, the merry devotee gives the drink many names, such as *Gerstensaft* 'barley juice' and *Hopfensaft* 'hop juice', and indeed generally looks upon it as *flüssige Nahrung* 'liquid food'; what is more, beer is *das fünfte Element in Bayern* 'the fifth element in Bavaria' which, in addition to the four classical elements (viz., earth, water, air and fire) is thought to be basically indispensable to the Bavarian's minimal world of existence, while humanity of large, inside our blue-and-white pales, can lustily enjoy *die fünfte Jahreszeit* 'the fifth season', between the end of winter and the beginning of spring when strong brown stout *(Starkbier)* is sold during a fortnight early in Lent. || a *prov. phr.* warning against superfluous or absurd action; specifically, not to supply a commodity to a place where there is already plenty of it: *~ nach München bringen* to carry *or* take coals to Newcastle, *AmE* to sell refrigerators to Eskimos; *Speiseeis an die Italiener (zu) verkaufen, das hieße doch ~ nach München bringen - oder?* selling ice cream to the Italians - that's carrying coals to Newcastle, isn't it?

Bi̱er...: **~bauch** *m* -(e)s/...bäuche usu. *contp.* a greatly protruding abdomen assumed to be caused by a surfeit of beer; any man with such an unsightly excrescence: potbelly, *AmE also* beer belly. - **~deckel** *m* -s/-, *dial.* **~filzl** *n* -s/-(n) [dim. of *Filz* 'felt'] = *Deckel*. - **~dimpfl** or, in its original, rounded form, **~dümpfl** *m* -s/-(n) [second el., *Dümpfel* 'stout person' (cp. E *dump* 'short thick object')] **1.** *colloq.* one very fond of drinking beer: beer quaffer, beer slinger, beer tippler, *contp.* guzzler;

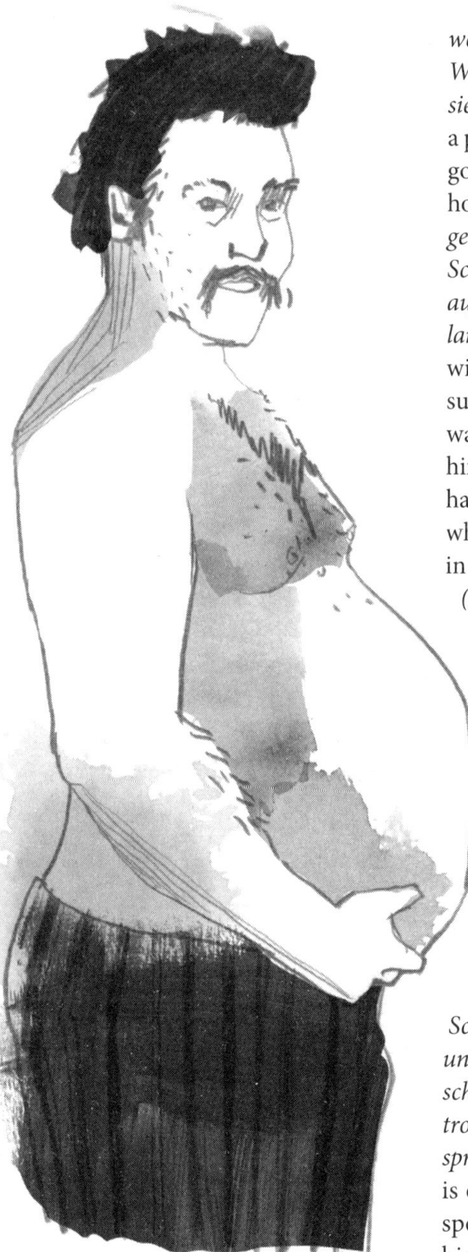

Bierbauch

wenn du am Freitag auf d' Nacht ins Wirtshaus neinschaust, dann siehst du sie alle drin hocken, die ~ looking in at a pub on Friday night you'll catch them going into a huddle, the whole lot of honourable froth-blowers; *die ~n schlagen sich vor lauter Freud auf den Schenkel und der Sepp der Bedienerin auf den Hintern, die ihm dafür eine langt* the beer quaffers slap their thighs with merry laughter, and Joe follows suit taking aim at the bottom of the waitress, who duly clouts (*or*, pastes) him one in return. - **2.** *hum.* or *contp.* a habitual drinker, usu. old and destitute, who makes the round of public houses in search of leftovers in beer mugs *(Noagerl↓)*: *BrE* scrounger of heel-taps, *AmE* backwash scavenger. - **~garten** *m* -s/...gärten *folk customs* an outdoor tavern, usu. resembling a garden, where beer and other drinks are served among congenial surroundings: beer garden; *für unsern Bayer ist der ~ bei schönem Sommerwetter eines seiner Lieblingsplatzerln - da ratscht er gern mit alten Freunden, träumt solo halbwach selige Stunden dahin, nimmt gern dabei die vielen Schatten spendenden Kastanien wahr, und munter wird dann der Blick auf die schäumend-volle Mass Bier, die der trockenen Kehle köstliche Labung verspricht* to our Bavarian, the beer garden is one of his favourite balmy-weather spots - just look at him chatting with his old cronies, yet dreaming also through solitary hours of bliss, drowsily taking in the comforts of the many shady chestnut trees, but thrilling to the sight of his frothy mugful of beer that offers such delightful promises for his parched throat. - **~krug** *m* -(e)s/...krüge tankard, beer mug (often provided with a pewter lid); *if made of stoneware*: (beer) stein. - **~noagerl** *n* -s/-(n) [see *Noagerl*] *dial.* dregs of beer: backwash, tail-end || *hum.* said of a disappointingly stale joke: *abgestanden wie ein ~ am Aschermittwoch* as moth-eaten as Joe Miller's old working jacket. - **~stüberl** *n* -s/-(n) *archit.* a cosy, usu. wood-panelled annex to a restaurant or inn, where men meet over beer and cards: snug (room), snuggery.

bieseln

bieseln, *dial.* **bịsln** [both: -z-] *v/i* [echoic] *colloq.* to urinate: to piddle, to pee, to weedle, *NorBrE* to scoot; *ich muss ~ (gehen), ich muss zum* $\overset{x}{\sim}$ I must go for (*or* do, *or* have) a pee; *ins Bett ~* to wet the bed, to pee in bed (cp. *zündeln 1*); *der schau(g)t aus, wie wenn er in die Hosn bislt hätt* he's looking as if he'd wet his britches. - **Bieselwasser** *n* -s *colloq.* urine: piddle; *Mami, wo soll ich das Potschamberl mit dem ~ hinschütten?* Mummy (*AmE* Mommy, *or* Momma), where do you want me to pour my piddle potty on to? || *fig.* in an ungracious comparison (cp. also *Pfeiferlwasser*): *die Limo schmeckt wie ein ~* the lemo tastes like pee-water. - **Bieserl** *n* -s/pl. rare: -(n) low or domestic *colloq.* a girl's pudend: wee-wee. - **biesi-biesi**, **bịsi-bịsi**: only in **~machen** used esp. to and by children — to make water: to tinkle, to wee, to wee-wee, to widdle; *sie muss ~ (machen)* she wants to have (*or* do) a wee-wee, *AmE* she wants to make weewee.

Bịffe *m* -/-; rarely in its StandG form, **Bụffel** *m* -s/- 'buffalo' *dial.*, usu. the centrepiece of a blunt way of verbal criticism or reproach - a rough rude (young) man *(Flegel)*: bumpkin, lout, yokel, *AmE also* dumb ox, yahoo; *geh, flack di' net so hi', du gscherter ~, mir san' doch da net dahoam!* don't you plant that carcass of yours like that, you country bumpkin (*or, AmE,* you big yahoo), we aren't at 'ome 'ere!

Bịssgur(r)n *f* -/- by folk etymology also, **Bịssgurkn** *f* -/- *contp.* a woman with a fierce temper *(zänkisches Weib)*: old nag, (hell)cat, spitfire.

Blasius *m* - *pr. n.* [this is the Latinized form of Gr *Blasiós*, the name of one of the Fourteen Holy Helpers (in his lifetime an Armenian prelate and physician said to have perished for his religion about A.D. 316)] *R.C.* St Blaise; ~ *ist der Schutzpatron für Halsleiden; an seinem Tag, dem 3. Februar, entzündet der Priester zwei geweihte Kerzen, hält sie jedem Gläubigen kreuzweise unter das Kinn und betet, „Auf die Fürsprache des heiligen Bischofs und Blutzeugen Blasius bewahre dich der Herr vor jeder Halskrankheit und jedem anderen Übel"* St Blaise is the patron saint asked to intercede against the danger of throat afflictions; on his day, February 3rd, the priest blesses and lights two candles, holds them in the form of a St Andrew's Cross below the chin of each faithful, and prays, "At the intercession of St Blaise, Bishop and Martyr, may the Lord protect you from every evil of the throat, and from every other evil."

Blasius...: **~segen** *m* -s *R.C.* Blessing of St Blaise; *den ~ erhalten* (or *bekommen*) to receive the Blessing of St Blaise, to take part in the ceremony of Blessing the Throat. - **~tag** *m* -(e)s *R.C.* St Blaise's Day, Blaise Day, Feast of St Blaise; *auch in vielen Kirchen Englands findet heute noch an jedem ~ zu Ehren des Heiligen ein Gottesdienst mit „Besegnung gegen Halskrankheiten" statt* also in many churches of England, on Blaise Day, the saint is still honoured to this day by an annual service of "Blessing the Throat."

Blaukraut *n* -(e)s *bot.* *(Rotkohl)* red cabbage.

Blụnze *f* -/-n *gastr.*, rare, since stilted for next. - **Blụnzen** *f* -/- **1.** *gastr.* a sausage made from pig's blood, often containing small cubes of bacon: *BrE* black pudding, *AmE* blood sausage, blutwurst || placing an order at an inn: *zwei ~n mit Sauerkraut BrE* one plate of black pudding and pickled cabbage, *AmE* two blood sausages with sauerkraut. - **2.** *contp.* a fat, unshapely person, often an elderly female: *BrE* jelly-belly, jelly-wobble, lump of lard, rubber-guts, fat slag, *AmE* blubberpot, five by five; *das ist (dir) eine ~! BrE* (look,) she [he] 's a right pudding, *AmE* ... a tub of lard.

Boandlkramer, Boanlkramer *m* -s/- [first el., with intrusive <d>], dim. of *Boan*, dial. for *Bein n* 'bone'; second el., dial. for *Krämer* 'small shopkeeper'] *colloq.* **1.** *lit., euphem.* an almost everyday-life impersonation of Death who, contrary to medieval concepts, is not pictured as a skeletal Grim Reaper but as an altogether jovial fellow, dressed in a cloak and a broad-brimmed hat, a friend rather than a foe to mankind: *Bonny Bone Grocer. - **2.** *obs.*, often *contp.* an emaciated person: bag of (skin and) bones, human skeleton, skinnymalink. - **3.** *obs., hum.* or *iron.* an undertaker *(Leichenbestatter)*: corpse polisher, shroud tailor.

Bọck *m* -(e)s [by popular etymology, < *Einbeck*, a village in southern Lower Saxony, S of Hildesheim, whence Bavarian dukes in the sixteenth century imported large quantities of beer; on Corpus Christi Day, 1614, however, thanks to the services of a Hanoverian master brewer duly invited to practise his art down south, "Ainpöckisch Bier" was tapped for the first time in Munich] *bev.* a dark strong beer, the first that is drawn from the vats in springtime: bock (beer).

Bọckerl *n* -s/- [dim. of *Bock* 'billy goat,' due to its butting and jerking] *railway colloq.* "Puffing Billy," choo-choo (train), lokey, *i.e.* a small steam locomotive used on branch lines, now largely replaced by diesel engines. - **~bahn** *f* -/-en *colloq. (Lokalbahn)* local line, *AmE colloq.* milk run, milk train.

Bọcksbeutel *m* [< *Bock* 'he-goat,' and *Beutel* 'bag,' 'purse,' 'scrotum': due to the similarity of its shape to the testes of a goat] *vinic.* Franconian wine bottle: a flattened globular bottle with a short neck, for white table wine produced along the river Main in Germany *(Steinwein)* or for similar wine produced elsewhere; the flagon resembles the one used for Australian Burgundy; **~straße** *f* - "Bocksbeutel Road," Franconian Wine Road, taking its name from the many wine-producing villages on the river Main in the Würzburg area.

Bocksbeutel

B<u>o</u>snickel, *dial.* **B<u>o</u>snigl** *m* -s/-(n) [see *Nickel*] *colloq.* an irascible and spiteful person *(boshafter Mensch)*: irritable old cuss, nasty thing, *AmE also* (old) meanie.

Bṛackl, with hardening of the initial consonant also **Pṛackl** *m* -s/-(n) [the stem form of *Brocken m* 'lump' (with vowel variation) + dim. *-l*] *dial.*, often *hum.* **1.** a solidly built human, usu. male - (1) if an adult: big bundle, hulk of a man, *AmE also* man mountain, big hunk of beef; *a ~ Mannsbild is er scho!* he ain't half a whale of a feller; (2) if a child: regular little dumpling. - **2.** a robust or uncommonly large specimen of an animal e.g. a fish or hare: great big thing; *a (Trumm) ~ Fisch* a whopping (big) (*or*, a [great big] whopper of a) fish.

brạndeln *v/i colloq.* **1.** *(brandig riechen)* to smell of burning, or of something burnt (e.g., food); *es brandelt* there is a smell of burning (in the air); *für mich brandelt's da wo* I can smell burning. - **2.** *(brandig schmecken)* when sampling some food that was (overly) exposed to fire: *das brandelt (ja) noch* it still has (*or*, there still is) a burnt taste.

Brät, Brat *n* -s *comest.* meat finely ground and seasoned, to be used for meat loaves, frying sausages, etc. *(feingehacktes [Bratwurst-] Fleisch)*: sausage meat; cp. *Leberkäs.*

Braterei *f* -/-en grill *or* barbecue stand, a temporary (fairground) restaurant serving barbecued meat or fish *(Hühner~, Ochsen~, Steckerlfisch~, Wurst~).*

Brat...: **~hendl** *n* -s/-n *(Brathuhn)* roast chicken. - **~kartoffeln** *f pl. cul.* fried *or* sauté potatoes. - **~wurst** [-ʃt] *f* -/-würste [-ʃtə], *dial.* -würscht [first el., < *Brät n* 'finely ground and seasoned sausage meat'] *cul.* a Franconian speciality: fried sausage of smoked pork and beef || a *hum.* observation by a native speaker when people of lusty appetites are consuming prodigious portions of sausages and sauerkraut, washed down by seas of foaming beer (say, at Nuremberg's centuries-old *Bratwurstglöcklein*↓): *Da Hunga treibt d' Brodwürscht nei'* 'Hunger makes folks wolf 'em down on a string'. - **~würstl**, *dial.* **~würschtl** *n* -s/-(n) *comest.* (small) sausage for frying.

Bratwurstglöcklein *n* -s *hist.* ever since 1313 (excepting the few years after its destruction in 1945), a Nuremberg scene set for convivial gatherings both of the highest civic grandees and of visiting strangers: "Fried Sausage Inn," a snug eating place crowded with all sorts of antiques, and a smoky kitchen where crisp titbits are frizzling on the gridiron.

Bräu -(e)s/-e or -s **1.** *n* (1) *(Bier[sorte])* (brand of) beer, *colloq.* brew; *Thomas~ ist meine Marke* Thomasbräu is my brand (of beer). - (2) *(Brauerei)* brewery [Note: The use of the word in that sense as a *neuter* noun is frowned upon by real Bavarians, who think it to be an abomination typically committed by "Prussians" only - cp. *Bräu 2 (1).*] - (3) *(Bierlokal)* beer tavern *or* restaurant (often serving only beer of a certain brand), *BrE also* pub. - **2.** *m* (1) *(Brauerei)*; often to be found in proper-name compounds, e.g. *(der [!]) Hof~* || *Bayern ist bekannt wegen seiner guten ~e* Bavaria is known for its good breweries. - (2) *(Brauereibesitzer)* brewer.

Brauerei *f* -/-en brewery || a Bavarian's ingenuous way of describing his gargantuan thirst (and duly hearing the same metaphorical hyperbole echoed from across the Channel): *ich könnt' eine ganze ~ austrinken* (or, more coarsely, *aussaufen*)! I've got a thirst that would swallow a brewery, I could drink a brewery dry.

Brennsuppe, *dial.* **Brennsuppm** *f* -/- [first el., *(ein)brennen* 'to fry in fat', 'to make a brown roux [ru:]'] **1.** *cul.* a simple type of soup, once a common morning dish among the poor country population, usu. made from two finely chopped onions, two or three tablespoonfuls of flour allowed to brown in butter, one quart of water poured on and allowed to simmer, at last caraway seeds, chopped chives, parsley, and one teaspoonful of vinegar added: (1) cream soup (made of a base of flour, butter, and stock), thickened soup. - (2) when dark: brown roux soup, brown vegetable soup. - **2.** *dial. phr.* heard in protest when one has been told an obvious falsehood or a tall tale, the message conveyed being, "I am nobody's fool!": *ich bin fei nicht auf der ~ dahergeschwommen!* I wasn't born yesterday, you know; I didn't come down with the last shower (*or,* ... fall off a Christmas tree), you know; *AmE also* I didn't just roll into town on the hay wagon.

Brẹtt *n* -(e)s/-er board, = *Totenbrett*↓ || the following usages reflect some unrefined folk parlance of today, although the custom (leading to such utterances) of resting the deceased on a board, carrying the body to its burial, and tipping it into the grave may well hark back to pagan times and has, of course, long since been discontinued: **1.** said of someone who is about to die: *der kommt bald aufs ~* *he will soon be on the board, he is aching *or* begging (*or,* is a [prime] candidate) for the board. - **2.** said of a dead person: (1) *er liegt schon auf dem ~* he's already (lying) on the board, they've already got him on the board. - (2) *er ist schon längst hinuntergerutscht* he slid into the grave ages ago.

Note: Although the concept and the fact of "death boards" do not exist in Anglo-Saxon countries, English folk speech is similarly outspoken on the occasion of death and burial; note such phrases as "to buy the farm" and "to be pushing up (*BrE* the) daisies" - the latter idiom neatly corresponding to BavG *die Radieserl [↓] von unten wachsen sehen.*

Bre̲ze *f* -/-n [a rare pseudo-standard form of *Brezel*↓ and *Brezen*↓]; **Bre̲zel** *f* -/-n *bak.* pretzel, a crisp knot-shaped biscuit flavoured with salt, a favourite relish with beer: **1.** the earlier form made with water and salt, and grey in colour. - **2.** = *Laugenbrezel*; *~architekt m* -en/-en *hum. (Bäcker)* baker, *AmE sl.* dough roller, dough slinger; **Bre̲zen** *f* -/- = *Brezel*; *~wochen f pl.* pretzel season, i.e. carnival time, in which pretzels are much in vogue.

Bro̲tzeit *f* -/-en **1.** *(Zeit für einen Imbiss)* snack-time; *~ machen* to have a snack, usu. bread and sausage or cheese, with beer or another drink || a semi-proverbial saying: *die ~ ist die schönste Zeit!* snack-time is the best time!; → **2.** *cul. (Imbiss)* mid-morning *or* afternoon snack, as a break during working-hours || in the Old Sausage Inn of the City of Regensburg: *historische ~* "historical snack", i.e. small

Brotzeit

sausages roasted on an open charcoal grill, served with plenty of sauerkraut and beer; *klassische* ~ "classical snack", i.e. a small Regensburg sausage and a piece of brown bread, to be eaten cold.

brụnzen *v/i vulg.* to urinate: to (take *or* to have a) piss.

Bschoad [pʃoɑt] *m* -s/-e [< StandG *Bescheid (geben)* '(to spread) the glad tidings (of a wedding or christening [dinner], or of some other positive event on the farm')] *dial.* a parcel of food items from the festive dinner, meant to be delivered to absent friends and relatives, so that they may have the vicarious opportunity to share in the fun: choice titbits (*AmE* tidbits) from the wedding [christening, or other celebration].

Bschoad...: **~binkerl**, **~packerl**, **~tüachl** *n* -s/-(n) *colloq.* **1.** piece of (ornamental) cloth or linen, often simply a large handkerchief or napkin, tied at four corners, which holds food to take home from a festive meal: take-home bag (*or* sack), *colloq.* goodie bag, *AmE esp.* doggie-bag; *für jeden Erntehelfer richtete die Bäuerin, wenn er nach dem „Erntebier" den Hof verließ, ein ~ „für die Leut dahoam"* after the "harvest beer", as the hired hands prepared to leave, the farmer's wife fixed each of them a goodie bag "for all the folks back home". → **2.** *fig.* angry message for others to take notice of what one thinks of them: bundle of complaints (*or* grievances); *nach seinem Vortrag gaben die Bürger der Stadt dem Finanzminister ein ~ nach München mit: bei ihnen werden nämlich bei Steuerzahlungen für jeden Tag Terminverlust neun Prozent Verzugszinsen berechnet* after his address, the townspeople gave the Minister of Finance a hefty bundle of complaints to take with him back to Munich: as it was, the citizens were required to pay a default interest of nine per cent for every day they had missed paying their taxes.

Bụ̈chsenmacher ['byksn-] *m* -s/pl. rare: - [in StandG, the compound refers to the ancient and honourable craft practised by a 'gunsmith'; but with *Büchse f* dragged into the aura of sex anatomy, a rude and lewd double entendre is quite likely "to rear its ugly head"] *vulg. hum.* a family man whose children are all female: *snatchmaker.

Bụ̈rscherl *n* -s/-(n) *colloq.*, often *emot.* little fellow, laddie. - **1.** with positive connotations: *ein aufgewecktes* ~ a clever (little) lad, a bright one; *ein sauberes* ~ a nifty lad, a boy beautiful, *AmE also* one easy to look at. - **2.** with negative connotations; often *iron.*: *ein abgebrühtes* ~ a dyed-in-the-wool young crook; *ein sauberes* ~ a bad egg, a sight for sore eyes || a verbal threat: *wart' nur, du staubigs ~ du, bis ich dich (d)erwisch'!* you just wait, you young limb of the devil, till I get my hands on you!

Bụssel, also **Bụssl** *n* -s/-(n) *colloq. (Küsschen > Kuss)* kiss; *dem Kind ein ~ geben* to give the child a kiss; *dafür kriegst [verdienst] du ein* ~ you get [deserve] a kiss for that || *ein flüchtiges* ~ a peck; *ein lautes* ~ a smack.

bụsseln *vt/i colloq.* to kiss (heartily); *die haben (sich) gebusselt wie nicht gscheit*

busseln

they beslobbered each other as if kissing was going out of fashion.

Bụsserl *n* -s/-(n) [an often warmly affective variant of *Bussel*↑] *colloq.* **1.** *([süßes] Küsschen)* (sweet) little kiss; *ein ~ auf die Wange* a playful kiss on the cheek || *phr.* (1) *hum.* asking, in a cheerfully relaxed atmosphere, for permission to give a lady a chaste little kiss (and taking this request to be implicitly granted): *ein ~ in Ehren kann niemand verwehren!* (a) in prose: there's nothing wrong with a harmless kiss; a friendly kiss can do no harm; who could object to a friendly little kiss? (b) in rhyme: there's nothing amiss in an honest kiss. - (2) *ich möchte mir ein ~ holen, wenn's gestattet ist* and I'll steal a small kiss, if you don't mind. - (3) *jetzt möcht' ich aber ein richtiges ~, Schatzi, das erste war ja nix!* but now, darling, let's have a real sweet kiss - the first one was just an excuse (*or*, an apology) for one. - **2.** *bak.* a small hard conical biscuit (*AmE* cookie) made of egg-white, honey or sugar, and finely ground nuts: almond (hazelnut, coconut, etc.) kiss, *BrE also* rock cake.

Bussi *n* -s/-(s) [the nursery dim. variant of *Busserl*↑] *colloq.* **1.** nursery, lovers', and bird- or dog-fanciers' talk — sweet little kiss: kissie, kissie-wissie; *schau, das Hunderl will dir ein ~ geben!* look, the doggie wants to give you a kissie(-wissie). - **2.** *hum.* or *iron.* a light-hearted expression of thanks, in mock imitation of a doting parent or lover, for a minor service rendered or to be rendered: ~ *aufs Bauchi!* you are a precious darling!

Butz- and *dim.* **Butzl**- [< *Butz m* 'little person *or* thing', ? < the base of *putzig* 'amusing', 'cute']: ~**kuh**, more often *dial.* ~**kuah** *f* -/usu. pl. -kühe, or more often *dial.* -küah *for. (Tannen-, Fichtenzapfen)* fir *or* pine cone; *~küah klaubm* to (go and) pick up fir *or* pine cones; *~klauber(in f) m, ~sammler(in f) m* (1) someone collecting fir *or* pine cones. → (2) *contp.* a stingy, niggardly person *(Geizhals)*: skinflint, *BrE also* penny pincher; *AmE also* nickel nurser.

Butzen *m* -s/- *dial.* **1.** *bot.* also **Butz** *m* -en(s)/-en *(Gehäuse)* the heart of an apple, pear, etc.: core; *wirf den ~ vom Apfel grad beim Fenster raus!* why, just throw the apple core out (*BrE* out of) the window. - **2.** *art (Verdickung)* lump, clump, irregularity (in glass, metal, etc.).

Buzerl *n* -s/-n [? < the base of *putzig* 'amusing', 'cute' + dim. suffix *-erl*] - **Buziwackerl** *n* -s/-n, **Buziwacki** *n* -s/-(s) [second el., a twin diminutive tacked onto the base of *wackeln* 'to waggle one's head' and/or 'to walk with short unsteady steps'] *hum.* a parent's or an auntie's affectionate form of endearment for a small child (though some mothers tend to protract the word's use into, or even beyond, the child's adolescence): toddlekins, toddles, tumble boy [lady], fiddlede-flumps, polliwog, *NorBrE* & *ScotE* weeny little bairn.

C

Charivari *m* -s/-(s) [< F *charivari* [ˌʃɑrɪvəˈriː] 'mock serenade of discordant noises made with pans, horns, etc. after a wedding'] *folklore* a distinctive feature of a male Bavarian's regional costume: ornamental fob chain; *an der Trachtenweste darf der mit Silbertalern, Sauzähnen, Hirschgrandeln usw. behängte ~ nicht fehlen* the ornamental fob chain is a must with a Bavarian's festive waistcoat, and from it dangle sundry trinkets like silver thalers and the eye-teeth of a boar and a stag.

Christkind *n* -(e)s [< Jesus Christ, as a new born child] **1.** *relig.* & *art* the representation of the Infant Jesus, a happy, smiling baby with plump cheeks and blond curls: Christ Child, Holy Child; *das liebe ~* (the) Baby Jesus || said on or after December 25: *gehen wir (in die Kirche) das ~ anschauen in der Krippe* let's go (to the church) and have a look at (*AmE* the) Baby Jesus in the manger. - **2.** *colloq.* & *folklore* also in the dim. form, **Christkindl** — the legendary bearer of gifts on Christmas Eve, usu. depicted as a curly-haired child (in the Bavarian tradition, often a girl) in shining robes: Santa Claus, Santa, *BrE also* Father Christmas, *AmE also* St Nicholas (a fat and jolly, white-bearded old man in a red coat, who comes in a sleigh drawn by reindeer).

Christkindlmarkt, in Franconia **Christkindlesmarkt** *m* -(e)s/ ...märkte *com.* & *folklore* Christmas Market, a traditional feature of the Advent Season dating back to medieval times: there are rows of stalls offering a colourful variety of small things for sale, Christmas-tree tinsel, of course, being the most abundant commodity.

Christmette *f* -/pl. rare: -n *R.C.* a joyful fixture at Noel many of the faithful religiously adhere to, in spite of heavy snowfalls or other inclemencies of the weather: Midnight Mass (at the local parish church, on Christmas Eve); *in die ~ gehen* to go to *or* to attend Midnight Mass *or* Christmas Mass.

Christkind

CSU [ˌtse:-es-ˈu:] *f* - *polit. abbr.* short for *Christlich-Soziale Union* 'Christian Social Union,' the Bavarian sister-party of the *CDU (= Christlich-Demokratische Union* 'Christian Democratic Union'*)* in the rest of Germany.

D

Dạm *m* - (rare)/- [< StandG *Daumen m*] *dial.* thumb - in *phr.* **1.** *alle ~ lang* repeatedly, at very short intervals: again and again, time and (time) again, over and over again. - **2.** said of a clumsy person, e.g. one who hardly manages to hit the nail on the head: *der hat lauta ~* he's all fingers and thumbs, his fingers are all thumbs.

da̱misch *dial.* **1.** *adj* (1) dizzy *(taumelig)*: woozy; *hamma den Föhn oder is sonst was los, mir is* (or, *i bi') ganz ~ im Schädel* is the foehn blowin', or is somepm else the matter, I feel all woozy in me 'ead. - (2) foolish *(dämlich, verrückt)*: daft, crazy; *in München ist der Faschingsball der ~en Ritter eine Urgaudi, da kannst du dich noch ganz narrisch verkleiden* in Munich's carnival season the Ball of the Crazy Knights (*or*, the Dimwitted Knights Errant) is huge fun, you can dress up for it in the zaniest guise; *so ein ~er Ritter, der fahrt wie ein Verrückter!* what a crazy fool, he drives like one possessed! - (3) much: terrific; *ich hab' ~es Glück gehabt* I had terrific good luck, I was mighty lucky; *er könnt' fei ~e Scherereien haben* he could have (*or*, land [himself] in) no end of trouble, mind. - **2.** *adv* very *(sehr)*: awfully; *das hat sie ~ durcheinander gebracht* this upset her no end; *es ist draußt ~ kalt* it's beastly cold outside.

Dạmpf...: **~nudel** *f* -/-n *cul.* a sweet yeast dumpling cooked in milk and sugar *(in Milch gedämpfter Hefeteigwürfel)*: stewed dumpling; such sticky sweet rolls are usu. served on Fridays as a main dish with hot vanilla sauce || *fig.* said on an appropriate occasion of a short-tempered person: *er ist aufgegangen wie eine ~* he blew his top, he had steam coming out of his ears. - **~plauderer** *m* -s/- *contp.* or *hum.* *(Schwätzer)* a person who talks too much, esp. about uninteresting things: chatterbox, windbag; *er ist ein alter ~*

Dampfplauderer

BrE he's a proper Peter Waggie, he has been inoculated with a gramophone needle, *AmE* he talks a blue streak; *das waren (dir) ~ (, ich sag dir's)!* they were chatting away nineteen to the dozen (, I can tell you).

dasig *adj*, chiefly *pred.* [related to E *dazed* 'having all sense of feeling taken away', 'benumbed'] *colloq.* **1.** confused *(verwirrt)*: muddled; *ganz ~* all in a muddle. - **2.** intimidated *(verschüchtert)*: crestfallen, subdued; *sie ist ganz ~ dagestanden* she stood there (looking) quite crestfallen. - **3.** depressed *(niedergeschlagen)*: downhearted, (down) in the dumps; *warum so ~ heute?* why so very downcast today?

Daube *f* -/-n *curl. (Zielklotz)* target, mark, i.e. a ten-centimetre square piece of wood sticking up from the ice at the end of a curling lane; *auf die ~ schieben* or *schießen* to shoot for the mark.

Deckel *m* -s/- [short for *Bierdeckel*] *colloq. BrE* beer mat, *AmE* coaster || a man standing his friends a round of drinks tells the waitress to mark his beer mat with a pencil stroke: *mach das auf meinen ~!* put it on my mat (*AmE* coaster)!

deftig *adj colloq.* **1.** of food: simple and substantial, plain and filling; *ich mag halt einen Eintopf, wie's der Pichelsteiner ist - das ist was ~es, da kannst du richtig reinhauen* give me a hot pot like the Büchelstein stew any time - that's something hefty to really sink one's teeth into. || → *Obatzte*. - **2.** of behaviour, jokes, etc. *(grob)*: coarse || → *krachledern* 2.

Depp *m* -en (less often: -s)/-en (less often: -e) *colloq.* **1.** a person who has done or said something silly or stupid *(Dummkopf)*: chump, *BrE also* clot || in a good-natured and friendly rebuke: *so soll's ja auch ausschaun, du ~!* that's what it's supposed to look like, you chump. - **2.** a downright stupid or irritating person, an idiot *(Trottel)*: dolt, blockhead, *BrE also* berk, burk, *AmE also* lunkhead || if such name-giving is to carry even greater acerbity: **Knall~** raving lunatic, blithering (*AmE also* first-class) idiot. - **Depperl** *n* -s/-n [dim. of *Depp 1*] *colloq.* a mild and friendly rebuke: little silly.

derblecken *v/t* [*blecken* is the causative of *blicken*, hence 'to make s.o. see (*scil.*, one's teeth or tongue as an act of jest or mockery)'] *dial. (hänseln)* to tease, *colloq.* to rag, to pull s.o.'s leg; *([j-n] verulken, [j-m] einen Streich spielen)* to play a prank on; *die Eingeborenen ~ gern einen Nichtbayern, indem sie ihn um Mitternacht zum Wolpertingerfangen in den Wald schicken* natives love to play a practical joke on a non-Bavarian by setting him to catch a mysterious forest animal (in *AmE*, a cryptically elusive snipe) around midnight.

Dezimal *n* -s/-(e) *husb.* "decimal", an old area measure *(Feldmaß)* of 33.3 square metres, still used when buying a plot of ground (for building, etc.); cp. *Tagwerk 2.*

Diezl *m* -s/-, as a nursery word also **Diddi** and **Dizzi** *m* -/- [cognate with StandG *Zitze* and StandE *teat*] *dial.* = *Luller*↓.

Diridari *m* - *hum.* money: the wherewithal, what it takes (to get along), *AmE also* bees and honey, mint sauce, do-re-mi [this one from a pun on dough 'money', plus the second and third notes of the diatonic scale].

Dirn *f* -/rarely -en *husb. (Bauernmagd)* female farm-hand, farmer's maid; *Stall*~ milk-maid, dairymaid. - **Dirnderl** *n* -s/-(n) *emot.* very young girl: (sweet) little lassie *or* chippie. - **Dirndl** *n* -s/-(n) **1.** chiefly in rural use: (teenage) girl, lass; → **2.** a peasant dress traditionally worn by girls and women, usu. a dress and apron whose form and colour vary from region to region: Bavarian costume, dirndl (costume).

Distelscheißer *m* -s/- *vulg. hum.* "thistle crapper", a border patrolman on his beat (maliciously described here as stopping in his tracks to answer a call of Nature amid the sylvan solitude of the Bavarian-Bohemian frontier).

Docke *f* -/-n *art* & *folklore* also known as *Wickelkind* and *Fatschenkind*↓ a simple, crudely painted wooden toy, rather like a skittle or chessman, representing a child in swaddling clothes: wooden dolly; *von den armen Bauern einst für ihre Kinder gedrechselt, sind die Berchtesgadener ~n heute als Ausfuhrware und Christbaumschmuck sehr begehrt* once made on wood-turning lathes by the poor peasants for their children, Berchtesgaden baby dolls are now much in demand as an article of export and a Christmas-tree decoration.

Domspatz *m* -en/-en in Regensburg: "Cathedral Sparrow" *mus.* more fully, usu. pl. *Regensburger ~en* (a member of the) Regensburg Boy Choir, one of the most famous cathedral choirs in Germany, dating from a Carolingian singing-academy.

Donau *f* - *river-name* Danube [ˈdænju:b], the principal river of Central Europe, second only to the Volga in volume and to the Rhine in importance, extending 2,888 kilometres, or 1,775 miles, from the Black Forest to the Black Sea.

dorert, **dorat**, with its dial. sp.s **doarat** & **dourat** *adj dial.* **1.** unable to hear at all *(taub)*: deaf ([-e-]; in dial. speech [-i:-]). - **2.** unable to hear well *(schwerhörig)*: hard of hearing || *phr.* (1) used with, sometimes acid, humour by or of one who does not like, and is therefore unwilling to take any notice of another person's requests or proposals; often accompanied by an appropriate gesture: *auf dem Ohr bin i* [*is er,* etc.] ~ I [he, *etc.*] cannot (*dial.* canna) hear on that ear (*or*, on that side [of my (his, *etc.*) head]), I'm [he's, *etc.*] deaf on that ear. - (2) a *sarc.* or sympathetic note that those afflicted with hardness of hearing are also often emotionally handicapped in fully sharing a lively conversation, and therefore tend to be more prone than others to agree to what has been said: *wer ~ is, reimt guat* *a nod is as good a rhyme as any to come from one who can't hear.

Dorf...: **~depp** *m* -en/pl. rare: -en, **~trottel** *m* -s/pl. rare: -n *contp.* in former times, a physically or mentally handicapped person who was often held responsible for any misfortune that had befallen the community: village idiot.

Drachenstich

Drạchenstich *m* -(e)s *folklore* a festive play and pageant, with some 1,200 costumed people and 200 horses, staged at Furth im Wald, on the Czech border, between the second and the third Sunday in August: "Killing the Dragon," the oldest German folk drama, featuring a knight who struggles against a most realistic dragon *(Drack↓)* spitting fire and fury; historically, the show developed from a simple lindworm float in a former Corpus Christi procession.

Drạck *m* -s *dial.* **1.** *(Drache)* ugly dragon, monster of a dragon. → **2.** *emot.* for a human being - (1) *contp.* a fierce, hot-tempered girl or woman: hellcat, spitfire. - (2) *apprec.* a clever, crafty person, often a male: wizard, (old) fox, *AmE also* clevershins.

Drạller, less often **Trạller** *m* -s/- [< *Drall m* 'spin, *i.e.* a fast turning movement' + agentive *-er*] *colloq.* a child's toy that is made to spin and balance on its point by twisting it sharply *(Kreisel)*: (spinning) top.

Drẹckbatzen *m* -s/- [second el., 'something, initially moist, "baked" together into a roundish lump'] *colloq.* lump *or* clod of dirt || *phr.* **1.** *concr. auf j-n ~ werfen* to pelt s.o. with lumps of dirt. - **2.** *fig.* (1) *j-m (z.B. einem Gesinnungsgegner) ~ hinterherwerfen* to say unfair and damaging things about s.o. (e.g., a political opponent) in his absence: to sling dirt *or* mud at s.o., to feed *or* spill the dirt behind s.o.'s back. - (2) *j-n wie einen ~ behandeln* to refuse to recognize s.o. one knows in order to be rude: to treat one like dirt; *wenn er ihnen auf der Straße begegnete, dann hat er sie übersehen, grad als ob sie ein ~ wären* when passing in the street he took no

Dult

notice of them, just as though they were lumps of dirt.

Dụlt *f* -/-en *folklore (Jahrmarkt und Volksfest)* (market) fair; *auf der ~* at the fair || *Auer ~ (Münchner Trödel- und Jahrmarkt)* "Au Fair," the largest fair-cum-flea-market in Germany, held three times a year in Munich, near the Isar, and comparable to Maiden Lane in London or the Flea Market in Paris. -~**platz** *m* -es/...plätze fairground.

durchwạchsen *p.p.* [literally, 'marbled,' 'streaky' (meat)] *meteor., colloq.* of changeable weather: spotty, fair to middling; *der Wetterbericht sagt für morgen schwüles, gewitter~es Wetter voraus* the forecast for tomorrow is hot and humid weather, with intermittent storms.

Dụtt *m* -(e)s/-s or -e *hairdressing* a woman's long hair fastened in a small round shape at the back of her head *([hochstehender] Haarknoten)*: knot of hair, bun.

E

E̲delweiß *n* -(es)/-(e) *bot.* edelweiss ['eɪdlvais], *scient.* Leontopodium alpinum, a small composite herb with woolly leaves and flowers, growing in the high altitudes of the Alps (of which it has long been regarded as their symbol); the continued existence of the plant is now in danger, one of the few remaining areas of retreat being the Allgäu mountains.

E̲i̲erpecken *n* -s *folklore* a children's Easter game originating from an ancient religious rite, in which an egg is firmly held in the fist and knocked against another person's egg (first by the slender end, then by the other) to see whose is stronger, and which egg eventually can score the most victories: conkers, *AmE also* bumping, *Cumb.* dumping, *Northumb.* jarping.

eingeschlafen *p.p.* & *adj* [literally, 'fallen asleep'] numb - in a *colloq.* phrase stigmatizing a drink that has little or no flavour: *das schmeckt wie ~e Füße* that tastes like dishwater.

einkasteln *v/t colloq.* **1.** *jur.* to put s.o. in a prison or in a mental hospital *(einsperren)*: to lock up, to put away. - **2.** *mot.* to park so near to another car that it cannot move *(einklemmen)*: to box in. - **3.** to surround s.th. with a border so that it looks pleasant or can be clearly seen *([mit einem Stift] eckig umranden)*: to box, to frame.

Einmerkerl *n* -s/-(n) [< a nominal nonce formation blending elements of verbal *einlegen* 'to insert' and *merken* 'to notice' + dim. *-erl*] *colloq.* **1.** an object, sign, etc. that shows the position of something *(Einmerkzeichen)*: marker. → **2.** a piece of paper, leather, etc. that shows you the last page, or some interesting word or passage, you have read in a book *(Lesezeichen)*: bookmark. → **3.** a knot made into a person's handkerchief, serving as a reminder not to forget doing a particular thing in the near future *(Erinnerungszeichen)*: visual memento.

einsackeln, *dial.* **ei(n)sackln** *v/t colloq.* [cp. *aussackeln*] **1.** to put into a bag *or* sack [... into bags *or* sacks] *(in einen Sack [in Säcke] füllen)*: to bag (up). → **2.** to manage to get money, prizes, etc., often by mere good luck, perhaps also through some shady deals *(einheimsen)*: to bag, to grab, to pocket, to rake in; *er hat mordsviel eing(e)sackelt* he raked in a tidy lot || → *ausgeschamt*. - **3.** to defeat someone in a fight, competition, or argument *(besiegen)*: to put in a bag *or* sack, *AmE also* to put in the soup.

einsagen *vt/i* often *educ.* to help a pupil, or sometimes also to brusquely interfere with an adult speaker who falters, by suggesting how to continue *([etwas] vorsagen)* **1.** *v/t j-m etwas ~* to whisper s.th. to s.o.; *der Hans hat sich vorgelehnt, um dem Freund die richtige Antwort einzusagen* Jack leaned over to whisper the right answer to his friend. - **2.** *v/i j-m ~* to prompt s.o.; *nicht ~!* no prompting!

einsagen

Einwärts *m* -/no pl. *dial.* & *poet.* the time of year when the days are getting shorter (*Herbst*; opp. *Auswärts*↑): autumn, *NorE* the back-end (of the year), *AmE also* fall (of the leaves); *so geschätzt die Schlüsselblume im Auswärts, so verachtet ist die giftige Herbstzeitlose im ~* the cowslip is highly prized in spring, and the poisonous meadow saffron is as sincerely despised in autumn.

Eis...: **~bahn** *f* -/-en *curl.* curling lane. - **~heiligen**, **~männer** *m pl. meteor.* & *folklore* Ice Saints, Icemen, *i.e.* St Pancras, St Servatus and St Boniface, whose feast-days are the 12th, 13th and 14th of May: this period is often particularly cold, but it is also said to mark the end of ice and snow for that year. - **~schießen** *n* -s *curl.* = *Eisstockschießen*. - **~schütze** *m* -n/-n (**~schützin** *f* -/-nen) *curl.* (lady) curler. - **~stock** *m* (e)s/...stöcke *curl.* "ice stick," a large, heavy, saucer-shaped piece of wood or plastic with curved handle used in Bavarian curling; *~schießen n -s curl.* Alpine curling, a popular game similar to Scottish curling but with no concentric circles around the goal *(Daube*↑*)*, no sweeping along the way, and no stone; instead, the "ice-stick" is thrown along the lane as near to the goal as possible while knocking the sticks of the enemy team further away; the best throw wins one point, and 21 points win the game; *~weitschießen n -s curl.* long-distance Bavarian curling, whereby the longest shot wins the game and not the one placed nearest the goal.

Eiweckerl, sometimes also **Eierweckerl** *n* -s/-(n) [so called after its shape which, to the fanciful mind, resembles two eggs joined as if by melting] *bak.* a small oval cake whose dough contains butter, sugar, and milk (but no egg!): twin bun.

Eiweiß *n* -s/- *cul. (Eiklar)* the white or colourless part of an egg: white of egg, egg white; *drei ~ steif schlagen* beat three egg whites until stiff.

entzwịrlen, **entzwịrln** *v/t* [< *Zwirl m* ↓] *dial.* with reference to something that is knotted or twisted (*concr.* and *fig.*) - to unravel *(entwirren)*: to undo; *zwischen ein paar Eishockeyspielern ist es zu einer handfesten Rauferei gekommen, und die Schiedsrichter haben damit ihre liebe Not gehabt, das Knäuel von Heißspornen wieder zu ~* some of the ice-hockey players were in a violent punch-up, and the umpires had their work cut out for them trying to undo the knot of hotspurs.

Ẹnzian *m* -s/-e [< MHG *encian*, *entian*, a borrowing from LateL *jentsiana* < L *gentiana*; said to be named after *Gentius*, an Illyrian king] **1.** *bot.* a usu. blue mountain plant: gentian. → **2.** *bev.* a spirit distilled from the roots of that plant: gentian brandy.

Ẹrdapfel *m* -s/...äpfel **1.** *(Kartoffel)* potato, *poet.* earth apple, *colloq.* tater, *dial.* spud, *IrE* murphy, Irish apple *or* apricot - various names on various levels of usage for one and the same food item which, in past centuries, is said to have "graced" the Upper Palatinate farmhouse dinner table with cloying regularity; here is a dialect quatrain which mourns such eternal recurrence:

Erdäpfl in der Fröih;
Mittags in der Bröih,
Af d' Nacht in die Häut;
Erdäpfl in Ewigkeit!

*Taters when crows the cock;
Noons, soaking in the stock;
Nights, unpeeled they're a sore -
Taters for evermore!

2. *hum. phr.* the confessions of one who can well dispense with potatoes: (1) *die Erdäpfel sind mir lieber, wenn sie zuerst die Sau gefressen hat* (or, *wenn sie zuerst durch die Sau getrieben werden)* *potatoes taste better to me (*or*, taste best) after they've been eaten by the pig, and the pig has become pork. - (2) *die Erdäpfel sind eh im Schweinernen drin* *taters are part of pig-turned-pork, anyway.

F

Fạngamandl *n* -s [actually, a substantivized imperative phrase, 'catch a man', *„fang a Mandl (↓)!“*, a type of construction that has been common in our two languages since the Middle Ages], also **Fạngsterl** *n* -s [similarly, the remnant of an inviting question, *„fangst du mich [uns]?“ + -erl*] a children's game in which one player chases the others *(Fangen)*: tag, tick, tig; *spielen wir ~!* let's play tag!

Fasching

Fạsching *m* -s/-e and, at times, -s *folklore* **1.** the period of public enjoyment and merrymaking, with eating, dancing, drinking, and often processions and shows, held in the weeks before Lent, at the latest from January 7 to Shrove Tuesday *(Karnevalszeit)*: carnival; *im ~* in the carnival (season); *auf den ~ gehen* to go to a carnival ball; *in München und in anderen größeren Städten geht es mit dem ~ schon früh los, und zwar am 11.11. um 11 Uhr 11, denn dann besteigt das dortige Faschingsprinzenpaar den Thron* in Munich and in other major cities, the carnival season starts quite early, indeed at 11.11 a.m. on the eleventh day of the eleventh month of the year, when the local royal carnival couple ascend the throne to begin their rule.

Fạsten *n* -s *R.C. relig.* fast, fasting, an abstinence, esp. as a religious observance, from all solid food; liquid food is exempt, as tipplers are quick to spread the semi-proverbial message: *Flüssigkeit bricht ~ nicht* "drink won't break your fast". - **~bier** *n* -(e)s/-e *brew.* a strong beer with an original wort *(Stammwürze)* of at least 16 per cent, brewed as a special treat for habitual froth-blowers in the period between Ash Wednesday and Easter: fasting-season beer, Lenten beer.

Fạtsche *f* -/-n [< It *fascia* 'bandage'] *med.* *(lange Binde)* (roller) bandage, elastic *or* gauze bandage. - **fạtschen** *v/t* **1.** *med.* *([mit einer Fatsche] fest umwickeln)* to bandage, to swathe with bandages. - **2.** *hist. folklore* with reference to a baby: to wrap tightly in many coverings, to swaddle.

Fạtschenkind *n* -(e)s/-er, warmly also **Fạtschenkinderl** *n* -s/-(n) **1.** *med. hist.* & *folklore* baby (wrapped) in swaddling clothes. - **2.** *art* & *folklore* wooden dolly, painted in a way as to represent a baby in swaddling clothes; = *Docke*↑. - **3.** *R.C. art* to be seen at Christmas, since baroque and rococo times, in churches, and now also in folklore museums: Christ Child as a manger figure, dressed in elaborate knitwear adorned with thin gold wire.

fei *adv* an unassuming element in colloquial speech (hence invariably unstressed), but conveniently ready to lend weight or emotive colour to the utterance immediately following; it may connote **1.** sheer emphasis, or at least inviting attention: *das gibt's ~ oft!* that's quite often the case (*or*, this happens quite often), you know; *die Suppe war ~ heiß* the soup was good and hot; *auf den Bergen ist 's ~ sonnig* it's nice and sunny on the hills; *es ist ~ windig heut! BrE* it isn't half windy today; *die Kathi find't die neue Arbeit ~ bärig* Cathy's new job suits her down to the ground, *AmE also* ... suits her to a T (*or* tee); *der glaubt ~ alles* he'll believe any mortal thing. - **2.** pleased surprise, praise or self-praise: *weißt (du) was, das Grablichtl brennt ~ immer noch!* well, what do you know! the grave-light's still burning; *du bist ~ ein tüchtiges Bürscherl! ScotE* you're a brave good laddie, I say!; *das hab ich ~ selber gemacht!* I did this all by myself, mind. - **3.** a plea: *gib ~ Obacht!* do be careful!; *lass das ~ bleiben!* leave that well enough alone!; *sag ~ nix, von wem du das (gehört) hast!* don't let on please who told you!; *komm mir ~ nicht zu spät!* don't you be late, I'm asking you. - **4.** a note of humorous or gentle warning to come up to the speaker's expectations: *dass du mir ~ was Gutes bringst!* be sure to get me something good!; *dass du mir ~ brav bist!* I want you to be a good boy [girl], d'you hear me?; *den Regenschirm borg ich dir ~, aber Wiedersehen macht Freude!* I'll be glad to lend you my umbrella, but it's on an elastic band - it comes back!; *so was Grobes mag ich aus deinem Mund ~ nimmer hören!* next time I hear such a thing I'll tell you to rinse your mouth out with soap-water! - **5.** disappointment or criticism: *das is ~ a Schlauch!* my, that's a very trying thing!; it takes it out of you, no kidding!; *erzähl mir ~ nicht, dass ...* don't you (dare) tell me that ...!; *eine gute Zigarrn is das ~ net, hast d' mi'?* that's an apology for a cigar, you get me? - **6.** grudge, past or present: *das hat sie ihm ~ lang nicht vergessen!* oh, she's held this against him for quite a while! - **7.** a negative value judgment (here, in broad dialect): *des is ~ nix!* that ain't any good! - **8.** a protest of one's innocence, or an apology for an oversight: *das hab ich ~ net gsehn* gee, I didn't see that.

Feierabend, *dial.* **Feieroomd**, **Feieromd**, **Feiramd** [ˈfaɪrɑbnd, ˈfaɪərɔmd] *m* -s *colloq.*, often *dial.* **1.** the end of (the day's) work *(Ende der Tagesarbeit)* - (1) *nach ~* after work, in the evening. - (2) *~ machen*, in Upper Bavaria also *~ lassen* to call it a day, to knock off (work); *der macht oiwai ehnda ~* he's always faster to knock off work than the rest (of us [*or* them]). - (3) *~ läuten R.C.* to ring the bell for evening prayer [prɛə], *or* ... for the evening Angelus [ˈændʒɪləs]. - **2.** the part of the day after work *(Tageszeit nach Arbeitsschluss)*: evening (hours) || (1) *phr.* as a greeting: *bald ~!, lass ~!, mach ~!* a pleasant evening to you!, have a nice evening! - (2) *prov.* [a] lifting restrictive measures is likely to have consequences: *wenn die Katzen fort sind, haben die Mäuse ~* when the cat's away the mice will play. - [b] death of the taskmaster spells freedom for the bond servant: *wenn der Kopf ab* (or *hin*, or *weg) ist, hat der Arsch ~* when the noodle's off the arse will be relieved of his dirty chore. - [c] incompetence makes for comfort in life: *ein Ungeschickter hat immer ~* a clumsy clot never runs the risk of being assigned a tricky job. - **3.** *fig.* the cessation of any activity, or indeed of any status in life, that has been in evidence for some length of time *(Schluss)*: (1) retirement, or dismissal, from work: *er hat ~ gemacht* he called it quits; *mit dem habe ich ~ gemacht* I gave him the sack (*or*, the boot, *BrE also*, the chop). - (2) closing time of a public house - here, the *hum.* warning of the landlord: *~, meine Herren, der Wirt ist müde!*, or *~, ~, liabe Kunden, mir müassnt schlaffa geh'!* time, gentlemen, time, it's a lovely night outside. - (3) said with resolute impatience: *jetzt is aber ~!* that's enough!, enough is enough!, now leave off!, now give over! - (4) a rather callous remark about a person's critical state of health: *der wird bald ~ haben* or *machen* [cp. above, 1 (2)], *für den wird man* (or, *werden s') bald ~ läuten* he's about to take the last cue from life's stage, they'll soon be ringing the final curtain for him. - **4.** the day before a Sunday or a holiday: (1) Saturday - *morgen ist schon wieder ~* weekend Saturday's coming round again tomorrow. - (2) the eve of a holiday - *heut (*dial. *heint) is ~* it's a holiday tomorrow. - (3) the day before a double holiday - *morgen ist doppelter ~* we're in for a two-red-letter-day stretch tomorrow || *R.C. ~ läuten* to ring the church bells in the afternoon of the day preceding a Sunday or holiday.

Fẹnster... *archit.* [three words ending in *-l*, a suffix here evoking merely an aura of colloquial ease, but not suggesting that the technical feature mentioned is small]: **~bankl**, **~brettl** *n*

-s/-(n) *(Fenstersims)* window-sill. - **~reiberl** *n* -s/-(n) *(Fensterriegel)* (rotary) window catch || *fig.* in allusion to the Alpine custom of "window courting", but taboo in polite use: *sie hat ein loderes* (or *lockeres)* ~ she is ready for promiscuous love-making: she plays around, she plays the field, she shakes a loose leg, *BrE also* she is an Essex girl.

fensterln *v/i* [this present-day form of affective morphology (< *Fensterl n* '[dear] little window') is as yet absent in its earliest documentation, sixteenth-century G *fenstern* (showing but the verbal suffix *-n* added to the noun form)] *folklore, colloq.* only possible in a rural setting, with the girl courted having her bed in an upstairs closet *(Menscherkammer)* of the farmhouse — to pay a secretive visit to one's lady love (by climbing a ladder, after nightfall); *darf ich bei dir heute Abend* ~ (or, *zum ~ kommen)?* may I go knock-knock (*or*, tappety-tap) at your window tonight?

fensterln

fieseln *vt/i colloq.* **1.** *v/t* often also **abfieseln**↑ *(sauber abnagen)* with reference to a bone of cooked meat: to gnaw bare; *ich tu(e) leidenschaftlich gern Knochen* ~ I really enjoy chewing on the bones, I love picking bones clean. - **2.** *v/i (mühsam hinarbeiten)* (to have) to work at an often uninteresting task, employing excessive time and effort over inconsequential details: to niggle.

Fieselarbeit, **Fieselei** *f* -/-en *colloq.* a piece of work demanding (but occasionally also catering to a person's penchant for) excessive care, attention, time, etc.: niggling chore; nitpicking grind (*or* drudgery).

Finger...: **~hakeln** *n* -s finger-wrestling, finger-tug **1.** a popular entertainment and test of strength, practised in Upper Bavarian inns, etc. involving a middle-finger tug-of-war between two male opponents across a table; - **2.** a traditional sport, formally organized since about 1950 with championship matches for the Alps, for Bavaria, and for the whole of Germany: both players sit on opposite sides of a table, one finger hooked into a leather ring *(Hakelriemen)*, and try to pull their opponent's hand past the 'out' mark near the edge of the table; any finger except the thumb may be used. - **~hakler** *m* -s/- finger-wrestler, finger-tugger, i.e. one who engages in the sport or contest of *Fingerhakeln*↑; in official games, classed by weight. - **~hut** *m* -(e)s/ pl. rare: ...hüte [actually, 'thimble'] *bot. (Wiesenglockenblume, Campanula patula)* spreading bell-flower.

fischeln *v/i* [< *Fisch* 'fish' + *-eln*] *colloq.*, often with an implied critical note on the sense impressions received. - **1.** olfactory: *es fischelt* there is a smell of fish (in the air). - **2.** gustatory: *die Suppe fischelt (aber) arg* (my [*AmE also* gee],) this soup tastes strongly of fish.

flacken, also **flaggen** *dial.* & *colloq.* **I** *v/i* **1.** to rest lazily *(faul daliegen)*: to laze (around); *dein Herr Sohn flackt no' im Bett* that son of yours is still lazin' in bed. - **2.** said of clothes, tools, etc. that have not been cleared away *(herumliegen)*: to be (left) lying around *or* about. - **II** *v/refl* to lean back, *or* to lie down *(sich [zum Ausruhen oder Schlafen] unbekümmert hinstrecken)*: to loll, to sprawl; *er hat sich in einen Sessel geflackt, alle viere von sich gestreckt* he was lolling in a chair, his arms and legs spread-eagled; *flacken wir uns da halt hin auf den Boden für die Nacht* let's flop down (*BrE also* kip down, *or* have a kip) on the floor here for the night.

Flascherl *n* -s/-(n) *colloq.*, nearly always used appreciatively — a little bottle of something delicious, usu. of the alcoholic persuasion: baby, bottle of goods; *machen wir noch ein ~ auf, grad weil's so grüabig is!* let's crack another wee bottle just 'cause things are so nice and cosy now || a fictitious commodity (one from a long list) an unsuspecting child or adult is sent for as a practical joke, preferably on April Fools' Day: *ein ~ Fischblut* a pint (*or, AmE,* can) of pigeon's milk.

Fletz, Flez, Flötz, Flöz *f* -/-, also *m* & *n* -es/-e *dial.* chiefly in farmhouses of the Bavarian Forest *(Hausflur)*: (paved) entrance-hall, *AmE also* hallway; *der Rinderstall lag im Haus und war durch die ~ zu erreichen* the cow stable, forming part of the main building, could be reached from the hall.

Fliegenschiss *m* -schisses/-schisse *low colloq.*; **Fliagnschiss** *m* -/- *dial.* **1.** *zo.* one of (usu.) many small specks on walls, tables, crockery, etc. that are the waste matter of flies *(Fliegenkot)*: fly-shit, fly droppings *pl.; kennst du denn nicht ~ von Bleistiftpunkten auseinander?* can't you tell fly droppings from pencil dots? - **2.** any minor or trivial matter, a small unimportant amount of money, etc. *(Geringfügigkeit)*: chicken-shit, peanuts *pl.; die Bank hat uns einen Tausender vorschießen wollen, aber das ist ja grad ein ~ zu dem, was wir brauchen* the bank offered to advance us a (*or* one) thousand but that's just chicken-shit (*or*, mere peanuts) compared to what we need.

Foam [foam] *m* -s [< MHG *veim* 'froth' - extinct in StandG except in *ausgefeimt* 'devoid of any frothy head forming in the glass once the beer has been freshly poured out', hence 'subject to suspicion', 'arrant'; the English cognate of G *Foam* is, of course, *foam* [fəʊm], but the word, one of the notorious "false friends", is inapplicable to beer] *dial. (Schaum [in e-m Glas Bier])* froth; *des Bier hat koan ~* there's no froth on this beer, this beer has no head, this beer is flat.

Föhn *m* -(e)s/-e *meteor.* chiefly in Upper Bavaria: *(warmer, trockener Fallwind)* foehn (wind), föhn (wind), a warm, dry wind blowing down a mountainside.

Fọtze *f* -/-n, usu. *dial.* **Fọtzn** *f* -/- low *colloq.* & *vulg.* **1.** a person's mouth: gob || phr. (1) usu. imperative: *halt dei' ~!* shut up!, shut your gob (*or* trap)!, *ScotE* steek yur gab! - (2) *j-m die ~ recht herhauen* to box s.o.'s ears left and right. - **2.** a person's eloquence: gift of (*BrE* the) gab || said in praise, but as often also in derision, of an orator's, politician's, or lawyer's verbal performance: *der hat dir eine ~!* there's a spieler (*or* spouter) for you! - **3.** *(Ohrfeige)* (1) slap (in the face), box on the ear; *j-m eine ~ geben* to slap s.o.'s face, to box s.o.'s ears. - (2) *fig.* a humiliating remark or action: slap in the face, facer, kick in the teeth. - **fọtzen** *v/t* low *colloq.* & *vulg. (ohrfeigen) j-n ~* to slap s.o. in (*or* on) the face, to box (*or* cuff) s.o.'s ears.

Fọtzenschmied *m* -(e)s/-e rare = **Fọtzenspangler** *m* -s/- [second el., < *Spange* 'metal clasp', one of the common articles produced in a tinsmith's workshop; the standard SouG occupational term is now *Spengler*, an umlaut variant preferred by seventeenth-century grammarians who were no longer aware of the word being derived from *Spange*] low *colloq., hum.* or *contp.* dentist: *BrE* fang-farrier, *AustralE* fang-carpenter, gum-digger, gum-puncher, *AmE* tooth plumber.

Fọtzhobel *m* -s/- [the musical instrument is held close to the mouth, and being moved from side to side resembles the to-and-fro of a cabinet-maker's plane] *mus., hum. (Mundharmonika)* harmonica: mouth-organ, *ScotE* moothie, *AmE also* corn-on-the-cob, French harp, mouth Steinway.

Frai̱s, *dial.* **Fro̱as** *f* -/often pl.: -(e)n **1.** *med.* (1) rare (a) any attack of excruciating pain. → (b) *fig.* in a phrase like the following, sympathetically addressed by a mother to her daughter, *heint schaugst wieda aus, wia wenn di d' Froas gmartert hätt'* you look like you 've been (dragged) through all the tortures of hell today. - (2) pl. only - a child disease due to brain injury at birth *([plötzlich auftretende] Kinderkrankheit mit Zuckungen und Krämpfen)*: infant spasms, infantile convulsions; *der Bua is in die ~n gfalln* the lad had his fits of (infant) spasms. - **2.** *fig. colloq.* a very strong and uncontrollable emotion *(Wutausbruch)*: fit of temper; *die Mutter wär' fast in die ~n gfalln, wia s' des schlechte Zeugnis vo ihrm Buam gsehn hat* mother was on the brink of throwing a fit when she first saw the bad report card of her son; *da könnte man die ~n kriegen* it's enough to send *or* drive you round the bend.

frẹtten *v/refl colloq.* **1.** to cause a sore by constant rubbing *(sich wund reiben)*: to chafe o.s.; *sich den Zeh ~* to get a sore toe from walking. - **2.** to eke out a primitive existence *(sich mühsam durchbringen)*: to scrape *or* scratch a living, to have a hard time making (both) ends meet. - **3.** to deal with a difficult problem or situation *(sich sehr mit etwas abmühen)*: to struggle to come (*or* get) to grips with s.th. - **Frẹtter** *m* -s/- *dial.*, often *contp.* **1.** someone who, though trying hard, ekes out but a scanty living *(Hungerleider)*: starving wretch, poor devil. → **2.** *agr.* the owner

fußeln

or tenant occupying a modest cottage and farming a small acreage of land with his family *([Klein-]Häusler)*: small-time farmer, *ScotE* crofter, cottar (*or* cotter). - **Frẹttn** *f -/- dial.*, often *contp.* **1.** a dilapidated small building, often an impoverished farm dwelling *(Keusche)*: hovel, shack; *a windige* or *windschiefe* ~ a crooked [-ɪd] old cottage. - **2.** *agr.* a small piece of land, comprising one or two tagwerks (i.e. 7,000 to 10,000 square metres), which is very much below the size of an ordinary farm *([armselig] kleines Anwesen)*: scanty smallholding, *ScotE* croft; *contp.* apology for a farm.

Frọsch... [typical of the anatomy of an amphibian of the family *Ranidae*, and by disparaging metaphor applied to a human being who is only sparsely endowed with facial beauty]: **~auge** *n* -s/usu. pl.: -n *colloq.*, mostly *contp.* protuberant eye *(hervorquellendes Auge)*: bug-eye, goggle-eye; *er hat ~n* he's pop-eyed, his eyes stick out like organ stops (*BrE also* ... like chapel hatpegs). - **~maul** *n* -s/pl. rare: ...mäuler *colloq.*, mostly *contp.* a broad, flattened mouth: frog's mouth.

frọtzeln *vt/i colloq.* **1.** *v/t* to tease *(necken)*: to pull s.o.'s leg, *BrE also* to take the mickey out of s.o., *AmE also* to josh, to razz. - **2.** *v/i* to joke *or* jest about s.o. *or* s.th. *(sich über j-n* or *etwas lustig machen)*: to make fun of s.o. *or* s.th. - **Frotzelei**, **Frotzlerei** *f -/-en colloq.* a playful, or at times malicious, attempt to make a fool of a person by calling him nicknames, copying him, telling him something that is not true, etc. *(Hänselei)*: leg-pull, *BrE also* mickey-taking, *AmE also* razzing, giving the needle.

fußeln, *dial.* **fuaßln** *v/i colloq.* **1.** said of a child, and some adult small in stature, invalid, or old - to walk with short quick steps *(trippeln)*: to toddle; *geh du nur zu, ich fußel (schon) langsam nach!* you lead the way, and I'll be toddling after at my speed (all right), if you don't mind. - **2.** to touch one's foot on s.o. else's, usu. under the table, in a sensually playful way, or in order to give a secret hint, say, about another person present or to the partner in a card game *(füßeln)*: to play footsie *or* footsy, *AmE also* to play footsies *or* toesies; *hast d' es gsehn, die beiden haben miteinander gefußelt, und wie!* did you see the two of them playing footsie with each other, and how!

Fuzerl *emot.*; with rather less warmth of feeling, also **Fuzl** *n* -s/-(n) *dial.* any very small remnant of material, food at table (encouragingly mentioned by the host), etc.: tiny (*or* wee, *or* weeny) bit; *hast d' ebba a ~ Papierl da? i müsst mir schnell amal was aufschreibm* I say, have you got some scrap of paper for me to make a quick note on?; *geh, nimm dir no' a ~ mehr!* take just a weeny (*or* a widdy) bit more.

G

gaach, **gach** *adj* & *adv dial.* **1.** *adj* (1) steep: *ein ~er Steig* a steep path; *Bergwanderungen müssen ja nicht zu ~en Klettertouren ausarten* mountain walking surely needn't be jazzed up into stiff rock climbing. - (2) quick, swift - *attrib.*: *ein ~er Bach* a swift stream || *pred.*: *net so ~!* a phrase used (a) to tell someone to wait or stop what he is doing: hold it!; or (b) to interrupt someone: hold it a minute! (with the possible addition, ... *mir fallt da grad was Gutes ein* I've just had a good idea); or (c) to tell someone to stop and think about something: hold your horses! - (3) unexpected: *ein ~es Glück* a stroke of luck; *ein ~er Schmerz* a sharp pain; *ein ~er Tod* a sudden death; *ein ~er Wechsel* an abrupt change. - **2.** *adv* steeply; quickly; unexpectedly - e.g. *es geht da ~ runter* the slope falls sharply (*or*, plunges down).

Gackerl *n* -s/-(n) [dim. of echoic *gack* 'cluck,' the low short sound a hen makes when sitting on her eggs or when calling her chickens] *colloq.*, esp. in baby talk — egg: eggie; *willst du ein weiches ~ oder ein hartes ~?* would you like your eggie boiled soft or hard? - **≗gelb** *adj* [the compound refers to the vivid yellow, the typical colour of the yolk of a hen's egg] *colloq.* intensely yellow: bright-yellow, *AmE also* punkin yellow; *die ~en Singerln, sind die nicht süß?* the chickabiddies, all brightly yellow, aren't they sweet?

Galt... [< *galt* 'barren,' 'sterile,' 'not (yet) able to produce offspring'; akin to E dial. *geld*]: **~alm** *f* -/-en, **~alpe** *f* -/-n = *Galtviehalm, -alpe.* - **~vieh** *n* -s *husb. (Jungvieh)* young cattle, in mountainous regions often taken to high-lying pastures for summer grazing and inspected only from time to time; *~alm f* -/-en unattended hill pasture, fenced in and with stabling; sometimes a disused mountain dairy (opp. *Sennalm, -alpe*↓).

Gambrinus *m* - or *pseudo-L* -ni [a playful derivation < *Gambrivii*, the name of a tribe mentioned by Tacitus] *hum.* Gambrinus [-ˈɑɪ-] **1.** a mythical Flemish king, the reputed inventor of beer; *zu den großen Festen Gambrini strömen alljährlich Menschen aus der ganzen Welt nach Bayern* for the great feasts of Gambrinus, every year a multitude of people flock to Bavaria from all over the world; *auf die beruhigenden Wirkstoffe des Hopfens führt man seit eh und je die Bierruhe zurück, die den Jüngern des ~ heilig ist* the sedative substances in hops have ever since been claimed to bring about the beery peace and quiet that is so sacred to the Honourable Guild of Frothblowers. → **2.** *railway* a fast name train plying between the beer cities of Munich and Dortmund.

Gams *f* -/-en; in hunters' jargon, with reference to the male animal, **Gams** *m* -/- *zo.* chamois ['ʃæmwɑː], Alpine goat; *flink wie eine* ~ nimble as a (mountain) goat.

Gams...: **~bart** *m* -(e)s/...bärte *folklore* the bristly black hair on a chamois buck's withers *(Widerrist)*, often worn as a decoration in the Alps by men in their hats of green or black felt as part of the regional costume: tuft of chamois' hairs, chamois tuft (*or* brush), gamsbart. - **~bock** *m* -s/...böcke chamois buck. - **~geiß** *f* -/-en chamois doe. - **~hüter** *m* -s/- *hunters' jargon* "chamois keeper", mountain fog shielding the stalked animals from view.

Gamsbart

gamsig *adj* **1.** *colloq.* *(sehr flink)* nimble as a (mountain) goat. - **2.** low *colloq.*, said of people — lecherous *(geil)*: randy, horny.

Gankerl ['gaŋkəl] *m* -s *colloq.* an imaginary evil spirit (sometimes described as a little devil) brought into play by adults to scare children *(Kinderschreck)*: bogey (man), child-bogey || a dialect speaker's baleful warning: *etz kimmt na glei da ~!* you (just) wait, the bogey man's on the prowl to get you!

Gansjung *n* -s *cul.* the traditional light hot meal at an annual fair, eaten late in the day *(Gänseklein)*: goose giblets *pl.*, a gravy dish of the heart, liver, neck, and wing parts of a goose, marked by dark thickening, and usu. served with a white-bread dumpling.

Gassi *n* -/- [dim. of *Gasse* '(narrow) lane'] *colloq.*, chiefly baby or dog talk **1.** rarely: narrow little lane. → **2.** *euphem.*, of or to a dog: business; *einen Hund ~*

führen to take a dog for a walk; *geh den Hund ~ führen, führ den Hund ~!* take the dog out to do his (*or* her) business!

Gatsch *m* -(e)s *colloq.* **1.** *meteor.* very wet earth in a sticky mass *(aufgeweichte Erde)*: mud; *durch den ~ soll ich da durch? da werd ich ja ganz dreckig und rutsch hundertmal aus!* me walk through all that muck?! I'll get totally muddy and slip and slide all over the place || a *hum.* or only slightly impatient suggestion to go away at once: *hupf in 'n ~ (und schlag Wellen)!* go jump in the lake!, take a long walk off a short pier!, go climb a rock!, *AmE juvenile sl. also* be like a bee and buzz off!, make like a tree and leave!, drum and beat it!, (put an egg in your shoe and) beat it!, take a rope and skip it! - **2.** *meteor.* partly melted snow: slush, sludge. - **3.** *cul. contp.* viscid food mixture whose ingredients are a blend of mystery, overboiled and hence disintegrated *(weiche, breiige Masse)*: goo, goop, mush, mixed mullish, *AmE also* goozalum, stickum, mung; *und diesen undefinierbaren ~ soll ich essen?* and I am supposed to eat this mystery mullish?; *räum den ~ da von meinem Teller!* get this mung off ma plate! - **gatschig** *adj colloq.* said of soft and wet ground, of boots covered with thick mud, etc.: muddy, slushy, *BrE also* squidgy.

Gaudi *f* - *colloq.* **1.** *(Spaß)* lark, (bit of) fun, sport; *aus* or *zur ~, zwecks der ~* for fun, for a lark; *nur so zur ~* just for fun, just as *or* for a joke, just for a giggle; *er hat es aus* (or *zur*) *~ gemacht* he did it for a lark; *aus* (or *zur*) *~ soll man beim Bergsteigen Geröll nie lostreten* when climbing, stones (*AmE* rocks) should never be set scattering (*or* kicked loose) for sport; *bei dem Fernsehratespiel geht es uns hauptsächlich um die ~, aber sollte wirklich ein Gewinn herausschauen, dann wollen wir ihn für einen guten Zweck spenden* we do the TV quiz mainly for the fun of it, but should a prize really come our way we'll give it to charity || *auf ~ aussein* to be out for kicks; *das* (or *es*) *war eine ~* it was (great) fun [cp. *Mordsgaudi*]; *Buben machen gern eine ~* boys are fond of having a lark. - **2.** *(Lärm)* a loud noise: racket, hullabaloo; *~ machen* to kick up a racket, to raise (merry) hell; *macht's net so eine ~!* stop making such a racket! - **3.** *(Schabernack)* prank; *das Maibaumstehlen ist eine landbekannte ~* in this neck of the woods, robbing the maypole is a well-known practical joke.

Gaudi

- **4.** *sarc. (Ärger)* trouble; *(Durcheinander)* mess || in annoyance, when noticing something unpleasant recurring: *jetzt geht die ~ (von vorn) wieder los* (or *an)!* (ah, well,) here we go again! - **5.** *([Ehe-* etc.*]Streit)* marital (*etc.*) quarrel: row, rumpus, fall-out; *bei denen hat's heute fei wieder eine richtige ~ gegeben* they had a royal fight (*or*, a regular set-to) again today.

Gaudi... *colloq.*: **~blech** *n* -s *colloq. (Faschingsorden)* carnival tin medal. - **~bursch** *m* -en/-en **1.** any innocently cheerful young man: glad lad, happy duck. - **2.** a young man who is the cause of enjoyment or activity in a group: party pepper-upper; *er ist unser ~* he's the life and soul of our party. - **3.** a young man out for a wild time of irresponsible fun: hell-raiser, *AmE also* whoop-it-upper; cp. *krachledern 2 (1).* - **4.** any male member of a carnival procession: carnival caroller, *AmE also* carni guy. - **5.** a fairground crier: barker, spieler, *AmE also* ballyhoo man.

Geldbeutel... [in medieval and early modern times, any ready cash the common man had about him was carried in a "money-bag" strung to his girdle (hence also the descriptive name of G *Beutelschneider* and E *cutpurse* for a money-seizing thief of stealthy violence)]: **~waschen** *n* -s, less often **~wäsche** *f* - *folklore* in Regensburg and elsewhere in the Upper Palatinate, in the morning of Ash Wednesday, by the side of a river, brook, or pond: "purse rinsing", a hilarious gathering of men who, as "rueful" Carnival bankrupts, now "clean" their purses to make room for "better" money.

Geldige *m* or *f* -n/-n [an adjective used as a noun, *geldig* 'moneyed', 'wealthy'] *colloq.* a person who is in a very comfortable financial situation: *er [sie] ist ein ~r [eine ~]* he [she] 's a rich one, ... is well-heeled, he [she] has no end of money, *BrE also* he [she] 's warm.

Geldsau *f* -/...säu *dial.*, often *contp.* wealthy person: moneybags *sg.*, pig in clover, *AmE also* bum on the plush; *scheinbar haftet dem Besitz eines Motorboots automatisch an, eine „~" sein zu müssen* owning a motorboat seems to carry the fixed notion of being one who has money to burn (*or*, who is filthy rich, *AmE also* who is wallowing in dough).

Geldscheißer; less often, since tinged with the patina of an age gone by, **Dukatenscheißer** *m* -s/pl. rare: - low *hum.*, or *vulg.* when used in angry rebuttals - a mythical somebody thought capable of producing valid and valuable currency, esp. (gold) coins, by the simple act of bowel evacuation: *Mr. Anal Moneymint || *phr.* (1) an unrealistic dream thought: *wär' das nicht was, einen ~ zu haben?* wouldn't that be something to have a private mint (*or*, a goldmine) working for one? - (2) an assurance that belief in the speaker's affluence, or mere solvency, is (very much) unfounded: *ich hab (fei gewiß) keinen ~* (1) I'm not made of money (, that's for sure), money doesn't grow on (any one of) the trees in my garden; (2) *on a rising scale of bitterness*: do you think I'm the goose that lays the golden egg (*or* eggs)?, don't you think I mint the bloody stuff!

gẹll (more *dial.*, **gọ̈i**) or **gẹlt**; when using the polite, or *Sie*, form of address, **gẹllns** (more *dial.*, **gọ̈ins**) [optative forms of StandG *gelten* 'to be valid', plus agglutinative *s* (< *Sie*) in the polite, formal way of addressing people - all in evidence throughout the South German dialects since the fourteenth century] *colloq. interj*, placed at the very beginning or the very end of an utterance, **1.** to elicit a positive response, often with a coaxing twinkle in the speaker's eyes: *gell, du borgst mir einen Fünfer?* you'll lend me a five (*or* a fiver), won't you?; *morgen kommen Sie (*or* kommen S') wieder, gellns?* you'll be back tomorrow, right (*or*, won't you)?; **2.** to make such a positive response an almost foregone conclusion by pitching a breezily emphatic *gell* in the interviewee's face: *Traditionalisten lehnen das Schuhplatteln (mit den gegenseitig ausgeteilten Fußtritten) als Effekthascherei ab, aber eine Mordsgaudi ist es trotzdem, ~!* traditionalists dismiss foot-and-thigh-slap dancing (with its give and take of kicks) as cheap showmanship, but the thing's great big fun all the same, you bet (*AmE also*, ..., yes siree)!; **3.** to add a touch of grimness to a warning: *hör mir fei auf mit dem Blödsinn, gelt!* you stop all this nonsense, got me?; *jetzt langt's (*or* reicht's) aber, ~!* now that's the limit, mind (*or*, ... I've had enough, really)!; **4.** to end an argument or discussion on a little triumphant note, say when someone is for once found short of a retort to a joke at his expense: *iatz hast d' dei Fett weg, göi!* now you've got yours, haven't you!; **5.** to refuse to listen to a person's plight, when the answering monosyllable *gell* (etc.), shot off indeed as a provocative echo, acts as the most cynical and uncompromising of cut-offs to any further discussion: *A - Kannst du was machen mit dem Wasserhahn? Der tropft! B - Gell!* A - Can't you do something about this tap? It's dripping! B - Isn't (*or* Ain't) it?

Gemü̱tlichkeit *f* - leisurely ease, friendly informality, cosy and jolly good-fellowship - for many Bavarians the very essence or life, and a recurring subject, therefore, of toasts and songs among well-wishers:

Ein Pro-sit, ein Pro-sit
der Ge-müt-lich-keit,
ein Pro-sit, ein Pro-sit
der Ge-müt-lich-keit!

Three cheers to us gath-ered
and to hap-py days,
three cheers to us gath-ered
and to hap-py days!

Gemütlichkeit

Gerọstete *f pl.* [< *geröstet* p.p. of *rösten* 'to roast', i.e. to cook by dry heat, either in front of an open fire or in an oven; 'to fry', i.e. to cook in hot fat or oil; 'to sauté', i.e. to cook quickly in a little hot oil or fat] *cul. (Röst-* or *Bratkartoffeln)* roast potatoes *pl.*; fried potatoes *pl.*; sauté potatoes *pl.*

geschẹrt, often pronounced and spelt **gschẹrt** *adj* [actually, the p.p. of the weakly conjugated verb *scheren* 'to shear': 'shorn', 'close-cropped'; historically, reference is to the bullet-shaped head of hair once compulsorily worn by bonded underlings and villeins as a conspicuous symbol of subservience to their land-owning overlords (note in the English Civil War the Puritan party of the "Roundheads", who wore their hair cut short)] *colloq. dial.* **1.** *adj* **a.** a rural attribute of more or less good-natured abuse, echoing the fact that once not only lowly farm labourers but also knackers, millers, gravediggers, hangmen, travelling journeymen, and even schoolmasters (who at inns all had to keep to segregated tables) were branded by the signal ignominy of crop-eared beardlessness; the word is often part of a greeting bandied among young peasant cronies, but also in other juvenile circles: *servus, ~e Nuss* (or *Ruam* [StandG *Rübe*])*!* hey, mucky Joe (*or* Farmer John)!, *IrE also* hey, bog-hopper!, *AmE also* hi, country hick! - **b.** boorish, coarse-mannered, uncouth; *dass sie dir nicht gratuliert haben, ist einfach ~* it's right bad manners that they failed to offer you their congratulations. - **2.** *adv* speaking broad (*or* plain) dialect; *wir reden hier oben fei arg ~* we don't half talk our broad dialect up here; *„Toilette" und „Nichteinheimischer" werden auf ~ bairisch zu „Scheißhaisl" und „Zuagroasta"* "Toilette" and "Nichteinheimischer" become "Scheißhaisl" and "Zuagroasta" in plain Bavarian.

geschnạppig *adj dial.* [kʃ -] *(schnippisch)* flippant: cocky, *AmE also* snippy; *ein ~es Ding* a cocky young thing.

Gesẹlchte *n*, with *adj decl.*: -n *cul. (geräuchertes Schweinefleisch)* smoked salt pork.

gesprịtzt *p.p.* & *adj colloq.* said of wine and cider: mixed with soda-water; *ein*

Achtel ~ ist gut gegen den Durst an eighth of a litre (of wine) mixed with soda-water is good for the thirst. - **Gesprịtzte** *m* -n/-n wine diluted with soda-water.

gestạnden *p.p. adj* mature(d); *ein ~er Mann*, colloq. also *ein ~es Mannsbild* a real man, *sl.* a he-man, *AmE sl.* a regular guy; *~e Milch* milk on the turn, *AmE* milk turning sour, milk on the verge of curdling; sour milk.

Gfrẹtt, less often **Gefrẹtt** *n* -s *colloq.* anything that is "chafing" *(→ fretten)* in this treadmill of everyday encounters *(Mühsal, Plage)*: toil, drudgery; *meist ist das Leben voller ~* life is mostly toil and trouble.

gịck *interj* [imitative of one of the noises made by barnyard fowl] only in the *colloq.* or *dial.* phrase *nicht ~ und nicht gack [net ~ und net gack] sagen* - **1.** to be irresolute: to hem and haw, to haw and gee, to shilly-shally, *AmE also* to teeter-totter. - **2.** to observe a stony silence: not to let out a peep, not to say boo.

Gịfthaferl *n* -s/-(n) *colloq.* an irascible person *(jähzorniger Mensch)*: venomous toad; *das ist dir ein ~!* there's one for you that's quick on the boil.

Gla̲ser, *colloq. also* **Gla̲serer** *m* -s/- glazier; glass-worker || *phr.* used in good-humoured or caustic annoyance to someone obstructing the view: *ist dein Vater ein ~?* your father wasn't a glazier, you make (*or* are) a better door than a window; *AmE* you know, it's hard to (*or* one can't) see through muddy water.

Gla̲sscherbenviertel, *dial.* **Gla̲sschermviertel** *n* -s/- *colloq.* slum area of a city: Poverty Row, Skid Row *or* Road, *AmE also* gas-house district, hell's (half) acre, East Side, *in N.Y. City also* hell's kitchen; *er ist im ~ groß geworden* he was born on Poverty Row, *AmE also* ... on the wrong side of the tracks; *auch in dieser idyllischen Altstadt gibt es ein ~, in dem so manche Familie von der Fürsorge lebt* even this idyllic part of the town has its Poverty Row, where many a family is on welfare.

Glụmp *n* -s; less often in its full form, **Gelụmpe** *n* -s *colloq. contp.* **1.** old, discarded things of little or no value *(Kram)*: junk, rubbish; *der Speicher ist voller ~* the attic is cluttered with junk. - **2.** any object or material either of poor quality *(Plunder)* or considered to be unsuitable for the purpose in hand: trash, rubbish; *wirf doch das ganze ~ weg!* throw out the whole lot! - **3.** said in annoyance at anything that disturbs the speaker's peace of mind *(Zeug)*: stuff, thing(s *pl.*); *überall flackt dein ~ da rum, weg damit!* your stuff's lying all over the place, away with it!; *ohne das richtige Werkzeug krieg ich das ~ nicht raus ... ~, verreckts!* I can't get this darn thing out without the proper tools ... to hell with it! - **4.** low *colloq.*, in typically female-to female talk - a woman's monthly menstrual period *(Regel)*: the curse, friend(s [to stay]); *sie hat wieder 's ~* the curse has struck again, her little friend has come to visit her again.

gma̲ht *p.p.* [the unumlauted participle form, with vowel elision in the prefix,

Goaßlschnalzen

of StandG *mähen* 'to mow'] *dial.* said of grass, grain, etc.: mown || *phr.* a pleased comment on an opportunity readily offering itself, or on a task that is easy to perform (conjuring up the picture of oneself strolling in comfort across a closely cut meadow, and not having to struggle through overgrown grass): *ein ~es Wiesl* (or *Wieserl), eine ~e Wiesn* a walkover, a pushover; *die Prüfung war ein ~es Wiesl* (also:) the exam was a cinch (*or*, was as easy as pie).

Gmoa... *dial.* [< 'rural *or* church community' (StandG *Gemeinde*) < MHG *gemeine* 'common (life of a rural or religious body of people)']: **~depp** *m* -en/pl. rare: -en **1.** *agr. (Dorfdepp↑)* village idiot. - **2.** *educ.* bottom boy (of the class), *AmE also* low man (*or*, bottom guy) on the totem pole. - **~fresser** *m* -s/- *hist.* "The Hungry Mouth of our Community", an opprobrious epithet for the local schoolmaster who, in past centuries, was only staying with the villagers on sufferance; grudgingly billeted on private houses during the week, he was often forced into cadging food from farmsteads where a pig happened to have been freshly slaughtered - as can be gathered from these lines,

Und was er nicht isst, das steckt er ein,
das arme Dorfschulmeisterlein ...

And what he won't eat, he pockets quick,
Our master of the chalk and stick ...

- **~stier** *m* -(e)s/pl. rare: -e **1.** *agr.* a potent breeding bull kept for service to the whole bovine community of the village or area: parish bull, town bull, village bull. - **2.** *hum.* or *contp.* a local man who has sex a lot and who thinks he is very good at it: parish bull, village stud, cock of the heap, *AmE also* stallion; *er moant, er is da der ~* he reckons he's the cock-o'-the-walk in this place.

Goaßlschnalzen *n* [< *Geißel f* 'lash'] *dial. folklore (Preisschnalzen)* whip-cracking: an Alpine custom performed with very long hempen whip-cords; the prize goes to the team *(Passe)*, usu. a group of nine, which is judged to achieve the greatest rhythmic precision.

Gockel *m* -s/- *zo.* **1.** *([Haus-]Hahn)* cock, *AmE* rooster; *er stolziert herum wie der ~ auf dem Mist* he struts about like a cock on his dung-heap; with erotic overtones: *ein guter ~ wird nicht fett* a good stud does not run to fat. - **2.** *hunt. (Fasanenhahn,* NorG *Hahn)* pheasant cock.

Gọckerl *n* -s/-(n) [dim. of prec.] *colloq.* **1.** *zo.* young *or* small cock, *AmE* rooster. - **2.** *cul.* chicken, *AmE* fryer, frier. - **~friedhof** *m* -(e)s/...höfe *hum.* paunch, *hum.* chicken gut; *er hat einen ~* he has a bay window, he's a portly poultry eater.

Gọsche *f* -/-n, much more often **Gọschn** *f* -/- *dial.* **A.** the mouth of an animal such as a dog or horse *(Maul)*: mouth, *less often* muzzle. → **B.** *vulg.* & *aggressive*, unless referring to oneself - the mouth of a human being *(Mund;* if aggressive, *Maul)*: gob, *AmE also* mug, kisser, (rattle)trap || *phr.* **1.** *eine große ~ haben* (1) *anat.*, rare - to have a large (*or*, big, *or* wide) mouth, *AmE also* ... a gatemouth *or* satchelmouth. - (2) *fig.*, also *die ~ weit aufreißen* to boast about what one can do, and say things which are not true in order to impress other people: to talk big. - (3) *fig.* to tell other people things that should have been kept secret: to have a big mouth, to be a bigmouth (*or* a blabbermouth). - **2.** *eine freche ~ haben* to speak rudely or disrespectfully to someone: to have the cheek of the devil. - **3.** *die ~ halten* to keep one's mouth (*or* trap) shut; *halt die ~* shut your face (*or* gob, *or* trap)!; *i halt scho die ~* I won't be shooting my mouth off any more. - **4.** *j-m über die ~ fahren* to fiercely interrupt someone's abusive or boastful flow of words: to choke s.o. off. - **5.** *sich die ~ zerreißen* to engage in malicious slander: to dish the dirt, to shovel dirt (*über j-n* about s.o.).

Grạffel, also **Grạffe**, **Grạffl** *n* -s *colloq.*, slightly *contp.* **1.** a heap of old and worthless objects *(Plunder)*: rubbish, junk; *allerhand ~* all sorts of rubbish. - **2.** disused and dust-covered articles, e.g. furniture, stored away somewhere, and conveniently forgotten *(Gerümpel)*: lumber; *was hebts denn das alte ~ auf?*, *was wollts denn mit dem alten ~?* what's the big idea of keeping all that lumber?; *mei, verkaufts doch das ganze ~ auf'm Flohmarkt!* why, go and sell all that junk on the flea market.

Grạmmel *f* -/usu. pl. -n [< *gram(m)eln* 'to make a crunching noise (as when biting crisp bits of food)'] *cul. (Griebe)* a small bit of fat bacon rendered down: scrap, crackling; *ich weiß, ich sollte auf die Linie achten, aber ~n mag ich halt für mein Leben gern* I know I should be watching my waistline, but I just love eating scraps.

Grạnd *m* -(e)s/-e, also **Wạssergrand** rural *archit.* an indestructible feature outside farmhouses as well as on pastures, to attract thirsty cattle: (stone) trough. - **Grạndl** *n* -s/-(n) [dim. of the above], also **Wạssergrandl** rural *archit.* a feature built into old farmhouse stoves of kitchen-ranges, to keep the inmates well supplied around the clock: hot-water tank.

Grạnt [-ʌ-] *m* -(e)s [< *greinen* 'to whine,' 'to whimper'; related to E *to groan*] *colloq.* **1.** ill humour *(üble Laune)*: grumpiness, grouchiness; *er schiebt heute einen* (or *seinen) ~* he's got the grumbles today. - **2.** (fit of) anger *(Wutanfall)*: tantrum; *einen ~ kriegen* to fly into *or* to throw a tantrum, to blow one's top *or* stack. - **grạnteln** *v/i colloq.* **1.** to mutter in a quiet but bad-tempered way *(murren)*: to grumble. - **2.** to find fault *(nörgeln)*: to bellyache, to beef. - **grạntig** *adj colloq.* bad-tempered and tending to complain *(mürrisch)*: grumpy, grouchy, cantankerous; *immer wenn sie Schädelweh hat, ist sie mords~* she's awfully grumpy whenever her head aches.

Grạntler [-ʌ-], **Grạntlhauer**, **Grạntlhu(a)ber** *m* -s/- *colloq.* **1.** bad-tempered person *(mürrischer Mensch)*: (old) grumbler, (old) grouch. - **2.** faultfinder *(Nörgler)*: bellyacher, *BrE also* (old) misery. - **Grantlerei** *f* -/-en *colloq.* continual *or* prolonged complaint: bellyache, beef, *AmE also* calamity howl, gripes; *ich kann deine ~en fei nimmer hören!* I'm sick and tired of listening to your bellyaches!

Gred *f* -/-n *dial.* [< L *gradus* 'step,' 'walk;' related to E *grade*] *archit.* always with reference to a rather small area outside a farmhouse that is covered with flagstones: paving, pavement; esp. **1.** *(Pflastervorplatz)* paved square in front of the house. - **2.** *(mit Steinplatten belegter Gang)* paved passage; *die ~ zwischen dem Wohnhaus und den Wirtschaftsgebäuden* the slabbed walk

Grantler

between the main house and its outbuildings (*or, BrE also,* outhouses).

greislich *adj* [of *Graus* '(feeling of) horror' two adjectival variants are of interest here - *grauslich* is preferred in Austria, and *gräuslich,* the umlauted form (today invariably showing dialectal unrounding of the diphthong), in Bavaria] *dial. colloq. (hässlich)* ugly, unsightly; *oft bleibt der ja wunderschön geschmückte Maibaum einige Jahre stehen, bis er halt „~" oder gar morsch geworden ist* often the maypole, beautifully decorated as it is, remains standing for a couple of years until, well, it isn't much to look at any more, or has even become rotten.

großkopfert *adj dial.* (1) *concr.* said of persons as well as animals: large-headed. - (2) *contp.* said of someone who has too high an opinion of his own importance: big-headed. - **Großkopferte** *m*, with *adj decl.*: -n/-n *dial., contp.* a rich as well as influential person (who therefore often has an inflated opinion of himself): (self-important) bigwig (*or* bighead), *AmE also* swellhead, conceited ass.

großkopfert

grüabig, **grüawig** *adj* [< a fusion of two compound elements, in StandG *ge-* + *ruhig*] *dial.* **1.** said of time spent in an unhurried atmosphere *(geruhsam)*: quiet, peaceful; *a ~er Tag* a day of restful peace; *an ~en Nachmittag verratschen* to spend a jolly good afternoon chatting. - **2.** said of an atmosphere, a person's home, etc. *(gemütlich)*: easy-going, cosy, homey; *da herin find ich's fei ganz ~* I feel as snug as a bug in a rug in here; *jetzt wird's erst richtig ~* things are really getting nice and cosy now. - **3.** said of a person's placid disposition *(gutmütig)*: good-natured, good-humoured, easy-going.

Grüabige, **Grüawige** *m* -n *dial.* (a person's) peace of mind; *in meinen vier Wänden hab ich meinen ~n* it suits me just about fine to be (*or*, I'm blissfully happy) within my four walls; *ich sag dir's [ich sag's enk], wir möchten unsern ~n habn* we want to be jolly well left in peace, I'm telling you; *der Bayer kriegt leicht einen Grant, wenn er seinen ~n nicht findet* a Bavarian soon gets his dander up if he doesn't find his bit of peace and quiet.

Grüabigkeit, **Grüawigkeit** *f* - jollification; *für den Bayern macht ~, also gemütlicher Spaß und Freude im Alltag, ein gut Teil seiner Lebensanschauung aus* to a Bavarian, jollification, in other words easy-going fun and enjoyment, forms a good part of his outlook on life.

grüß Gott *interj* [actually, an abridged optative, 'May God greet (and in doing so, also bless) you!'] **1.** a religious contact formula used to show the speaker's friendly attention to, or indeed affection for, a particular person or group: God bless (you), bless you: *grüß dich* [pl. *euch*, dial. also *enk*] *Gott!* bless you!; *grüß Gott beinand!* [last word, < *beieinander*] (1) when greeting two persons, often a (married) couple, brother and sister, etc.: (God) bless you both! - (2) when greeting more than two people, or indeed all those present in a big room: God bless you all! → **2.** a mundane, and usu. unspecific, greeting when entering a shop or office, or when approaching and wishing to speak to someone for the first time: hello [-ˈləʊ], *also* hallo, hullo.

Gschaftl *n* -s/-(n) [dim. of *Geschäft* 'business'] *colloq.* little job; *vor lauter ~n nebenbei kommt man zu gar keiner richtigen Arbeit* all those jobbing twiddlybits on the side keep one from getting down to real work. - **~huber** *m* -s/- *colloq.*, slightly *contp. (Wichtigtuer)* meddlesome person: Jack-in-office, busybody, fusspot, *AmE also* fuss budget; *du bist mir ein ~!* you're a regular fusspot || as a fictitious name: *Herr ~* Mr. Busyman, Meddlesome Mattie; *Frau ~* Mrs. Mixin. - **~huberei** *f* -/-en *colloq.*, slightly *contp.* fussiness, meddlesomeness.

gscheit, the syncopated *colloq.* variant of **gescheit 1.** *adj* (1) of a person: clever; *er ist sehr ~ in Mathe* he's very good *or* clever at maths (*AmE* math). - (2) of a person: capable, skilled; *können Sie mir einen ~en Doktor sagen?* can you tell me the name of a good doctor? - (3) said of one's hunger or thirst: enormous, great; *ich hab einen ~en Hunger* I'm (as) hungry as a wolf, I could eat a horse. - (4) of time, a tool, etc.: suitable, convenient; *wäre fünf Uhr eine ~e Zeit?* would five o'clock be a good time? - (5) of food: plain and substantial; *zum Kesselfleisch gehört ein ~es Bauernbrot* pork titbits should be eaten with hunks of good farmhouse bread. - **2.** *adv* (1) conveniently; *wie kommt man am ~esten (*dial., *am ~er[e]n) nach ...?* which is the best way to ...? - (2) seriously, in earnest; *sag ~, ist er wirklich verheiratet?* joking apart, is he really married? - (3) badly; *das letzte Gipfelstück scheint ein paar der Kletterer ~ hergenommen zu haben* the summit climb seems to have taken it out of some of the climbers. - (4) in negative sentences, describing, often reproachfully, an excess of speed or other activity: *wie nicht ~* like mad, *BrE also* like the clappers; *er hat dann wie nicht ~ herumtelefoniert* he went to work making phone calls like mad || → *busseln, pumpern.*

Gscheiterl, **Gscheitl** [dim. nouns formed from *gescheit*↑), **Gscheithaferl** [second el., < *Haferl*↓; thus, literally, 'one brimming over with conceitedness'] *n* -s/-(n) *colloq.* **1.** *hum.* said in praise, though sometimes in subtle mockery — capable person *(aufgeweckter [junger] Mensch)*: cleverboots *sg.*, cleverclogs *sg.*, clevershins *sg.*, smart boy [girl], wizard, *NorBrE also* cleversides *sg.*; *ja, der Hansi ist unser ~ - wenn wir den nicht hätten!* why, Johnny is our clevershins - what would we do without him? - **2.** slightly *iron.* or *contp.* someone who annoys others by claiming to know everything and trying to sound clever *(Alleswisser)*: know-all, smart aleck, smarty-pants *sg.*, smart-pants *sg.*, *BrE* clever dick, *AmE also* know-it-all, Mr. [Miss] Smarty, wise guy, wisenheimer; *er ist (und bleibt) halt ein ~* ah well, he thinks he has all the answers.

Gschịss *n* -isses (rare), or **Gschi̲e̲ß** *n* -es (rare) [the elided form of *Geschiss n*, < *geschissen*, p.p. of *scheißen vt/i* 'to shit(e)'] **1.** *vulg.* a bowel movement or its voided end product *([Ausscheidungs-]Produkt)*: shit; *das laufade* (less often, StandG *laufende*) *~ med.* diarrhoea *(Durchfall)*: the runs, the trots; *das laufade ~ haben* to have a sudden strong need to go to the toilet often: to be taken (*or*, be caught) short. - **2.** *fig., colloq.* a person's preoccupation, or hectic activity in connection, with a present or forthcoming event *(ängstliche Umständlichkeit)*: fuss (and bother); *warum denn ein ~ machen wegen so einer lächerlichen Sach'?* why make (*or*, kick up) a fuss about such a ridiculous thing?

gschlạmpert or **gschlạmpat** *dial. adj* **1.** also **schlạmpert** - lacking order and neatness *(nachlässig)*: sloppy, untidy; *a ~e Arbeit* a sloppy *or* slipshod piece of work || *prov.* a rhymed taunt establishing a causal relationship between slovenliness and obesity: *schlampert macht wampert* *"couldn't care nowt!" makes yer belly bulge out. - **2.** flouting the established practices of how marriages are contracted: living in sin || said of a man and a woman thus cohabiting in common-law marriage: *wir [die beiden] habm a ~s Verhältnis* we [the two] 're more or less married, we [the two] 're living together in unwedded bliss, *or* in holy bedlock.

Gschwẹrl *n* -s *dial., contp.* a set or clique, some or all of them distantly related, for whom the speaker has little respect: breed of pups, bunch, crew, gang, tribe; *ein ~ Gassenbuben* a bunch of guttersnipes (*AmE also* ... gutter bums); *das ganze ~ kann mir gestohlen bleiben* I can't be bothered with the whole lot (*or*, all this riffraff), *AmE also* I have no use for the whole kit and caboodle.

Gspu̲si ['kʃpu:zɪ], variously spelt **G'spu̲si**, **Gschpu̲si**, **Gespu̲si**, *n* -(s)/- [< *Gespons m hum.* 'bridegroom', 'husband' < L *sponsus* 'fiancé'] *colloq.*, often slightly *iron.* **1.** regular boy [girl] friend: flame, heartthrob; *ist sie dein ~?* is she your sweet thing (*AmE also* ... your cuddlebug)?; *der Hans ist ein verflossenes ~ von mir* Jack's an old flame of mine. - **2.** a sexual relationship between two people not married to each other, esp. one that lasts for some time: affair, steady flirt; *sie hat mit dem besten Freund ihres Mannes ein ~* she's having an affair with her husband's best friend; *die haben schon jahrelang ein munteres ~ (miteinand[er])* theirs has been a steady whirl for years; *er hat alle zwei Wochen mit einer anderen ein ~* he goes with a different girl every other week; *fang dir mit der kein ~ an* don't you go and give that one a whirl.

Gstạnzl [k-] *n* -s/-n *mus. (neckender Vierzeiler)* a popular rhyming couplet, broken into four lines in print, often improvised and usu. making teasing fun of someone: merry ditty (*or* jingle). - **~singen** *n* -s *mus.* communal singing of ditties (which, if strung together in a give and take, can readily become a lively contest of infectious banter and mirth):

Die Zwölfhäusler Menscher,
die ham an schen Gang,
mit oan Fuaß tean s' mahn
und mi'm andern heign s' zam.

*A Zwölfhäusl lassie
Has legs fine and gay:
One does the mowing,
The other makes hay.

H

ha̩ [hə] *dial. interj* **1.** a rather impolite interrogative utterance wishing someone to repeat what he or she has just said (corresponding to StandG *wie bitte?*): eh [eɪ]; *A: mir ist kalt! B: ~? A: kalt is ma, hab i gsagt!* A: I'm cold! B: eh? (*BrE also* y' what?) A: I said I'm cold! - **2.** a curt manner of asking someone to agree (corresponding to StandG *nicht wahr?*): eh, huh [hʌ]; *des taugt doch, ~?* that'll do, huh?

haa *interj* [< OHG *hweo* 'which way?'; related to E *how?*] low *colloq.* a rude way of demanding repetition of a word or phrase one has failed, or ostensibly failed, to understand: eh [eɪ]?, whazzat [< what's that]?

Hadern [-ɔ:-] *m* -s/- *colloq.* **1.** (1) *(Lumpen)* rag; *der Gassenbub kommt in ~ daher* the street urchin is dressed (all) in rags. - (2) *([Putz-]Lumpen)* cleaning rag; *hol mir einen Öl~* get me a piece of oily rag. - (3) *second comp. el.* of its former frequency, in that position, of denoting specific items of linen (e.g., *Hand~* towel; *Prang~* cuff, wristband; *Rüssel~* napkin), only two are left in actual use today; they, with a third one, all meaning 'handkerchief', can be arranged on a scale from light to blunt coarseness of expression: *Schneuztuch* nose-wipe(r), nose-clout; *Schneuzhadern* nose-rag, *AmE also* blower, blow-rag; *Rotzhadern* snot-rag. - **2.** *contp. (leichtes Mädchen)* loose(-living) woman: good-time girl, *NorBrE* flighty faggot.

Hafen [-ɔ:-] *m* -s/Häfen [< MHG *haven* 'large earthenware or cast-iron pot'] (cooking) pot; *irdener ~* earthenware *or* stoneware pot, crock || *colloq. phr.* (1) a vile remark on a person who squints badly: *der schaut mit einmal in neun Häfen hinein* he looks nine (*or* forty) ways for (*or* to find) Sunday. - (2) a piece of tongue-in-cheek consolation for an old maid: *jeder ~ findet seinen Deckel - auch ein alter, wenn er seine Löcher nicht weist* *there is (bound to be) a lid for every pot - even for one with holes in it, if the holes aren't showing.

Haferl [-a:-] *n* -s/-(n) [dim. of *Hafen*↑] *colloq.* **1.** (sturdy little) pot, sometimes made of enamelled metal, but most often of earthenware or porcelain: mug; *trink dein ~ Tee aus (*or *fertig)!* drink up your mug of tea || as a second compound element: **Kaffee~** coffee cup; **Milch~** milk jug; → *Nachthaferl.* - **2.** *colloq.* an imaginary mug, one of many such fictitious objects for which unsuspecting and gullible mortals, esp. children, are sent for as a practical joke: *geh, hol mir ein ~ Igelsamen* go and get (*or* fetch) me a pint of pigeon's milk (*or* a bagful of bumblebee feathers, *or, BrE also,* a yard of pump-water). - **3.** *prov.* (1) a consolatory wisdom telling us that everyone gets a mate in the end: *(ein) jedes ~ hat* (or *kriegt) seinen Deckel* every Jack must have his Jill, every Johnny will get his Joan. - (2) a graceful comment, usu. made in the presence of the mother concerned, on beauty being hereditary: *schöne ~(n) geben schöne Scherben* *the comeliness of the parent is mirrored in the offspring. - (3) a rather unfair tease according to which a small person is claimed to be more easily angered than a tall one: *kleine ~(n) laufen* (or *gehen) leicht über* a little pot is soon hot. - (4) a reproachful taunt directed at one who expects his wishes to be fulfilled without delay: *du brauchst ja bloß sagen „~" - nachher ist die Wurst auch schon drin!* *all you've got to do is command, "Pot, be filled!", and in pops the sausage for you. - (5) a considered opinion that, in a contentious issue, two quarrelers, often a married couple, are likely to share the blame: *der eine hat das ~ zerbrochen, der andere das Schüsserl* *one has gone and broken the pot, and the other one the dish; 'tis six of one and half-a-dozen of the other.

Haferl...: **~fest** *n* -(e)s/pl. rare: -e *hist. folklore* held until the 1970s at Ilzstadt, a northern suburb of Passau, along the banks of the River Ilz: "Potters' Parade", a popular one-day festival in August, originally organized by the members of that guild. - **~gucker** *m* -s/pl. rare: - *hum.* an inquisitive male, most often a member of the family, who takes a quick and rather stealthy look at what is being prepared by the cook: nosy lift-lid, (pot-and-pan) pokenose, (old) snoopie (among the saucepans), *AmE also* kitchen kibitzer. - **~schuh** *m* -s/usu. pl.: -e [hardly, as has once been suggested, < E *half-shoe*, but rather implying a jocular comparison to a *Haferl*↑] a sturdy walking shoe with a fringed tongue: brogue [brəʊg].

Haferlgucker

Haftelmacher *m* -s/- [first el., *Haftel n* 'hook', part of a two-piece clothes fastening the manufacture of which once required special care and attention to detail] *obs.* except in the *colloq. phr.* both preserving the occupational name, 'hook-maker', and honouring the ticklish nature of the man's work: *aufpassen* or *Acht geben (müssen) wie ein* ~ (to have) to keep one's eyes peeled *or* skinned; *wir müssen jetzt aufpassen wie die* ~, *dass wir die Ausfahrtstafel nicht übersehen* we now must keep our eyes peeled we don't miss the exit sign.

Hakelstecken, less correctly also **Hack(e)lstecken** *m* -s/- [first el., *Hakel n* 'curved end of a [walking] stick', used to retrieve objects or to suspend objects from] largely *hist.* **1.** walking staff (*or* stick), the frequent companion of a countryman, useful also as a retrieving device and a defensive weapon. - **2.** packstaff, slung over one's shoulder when carrying a burden suspended from its crooked end.

Hakelstecken

Halbe *f* -n/-n *bev. (eine halbe Mass [Bier])* half a litre (E *approx.*: a [sizeable] pint) of beer; *eine ~ um die andre trinken* to have one beer after another; *trinken wir noch eine ~?* shall we have another half?; *er (*dial. *der) sitzt stundenlang vor einer einzigen ~n* he can nurse his one pint a whole evening; *er (*dial. *der) hat schon einen (*dial. *an) Rausch, wenn er eine ~ Bier sieht* even the smell of beer fumes is enough to make him drunk.

Hallodri *m* -s/-(s) **1.** *contp.* a reckless, workshy, and morally depraved adult male: ne'er-do-well. - **2.** slightly reproachful, but usu. *hum.* (then often marked by downtoning attributes like *kleiner, na so ein,* etc.) for a trouble-making but usu. playful child: scamp, *BrE* scallywag, *AmE* scalawag.

handsam *adj* [a classic case of "false friends": G *handsam* and E *handsome* are made up of identical structural elements - *Hand*: hand, *-sam*: -some ('like', 'same') - but in composition their meanings differ widely, the latter among others denoting a 'good-looking' man, a 'strong-looking' woman, and a 'large' reward] *colloq.* **1.** of a for-mat, tool, etc. *(handlich)*: easy to handle, handy, convenient. - **2.** of a human being or an animal *(gut zu haben)*: easy to manage, manageable, docile, gentle.

hạntig *adj colloq.* **1.** said of food or drink that has a sharp, biting taste, e.g. asparagus or unsweetened coffee *(herb)*: bitter. - **2.** said of a person's gruffly uncooperative manner of speaking *(barsch)*: snappish, catty; *was bist du denn heute gar a so ~?* what on earth makes (*or* are) you such a crosspatch today?

Hạscherl *n* -s/-(n) *colloq.* **1.** usu. preceded by *armes* or *kleines* - pitiable child or woman *(bedauernswertes Kind oder weibliches Wesen)*: poor thing *or* creature; *ja mei, das süße kleine ~ hat ja hohes Fieber!* oh dear, the poor little darling has (*or*, is running) a high temperature; *die zweite Arie im „Freischütz" ist für die Agathe fürchterlich schwer zu singen, da kriegt das arme ~ grad vorher oft einen ganz trockenen Hals vor lauter Angst* the second aria in *Der Freischütz* is awfully hard to sing for Agatha; a few moments before, the poor soul's throat most often goes quite dry with fear. - **2.** sometimes with a slight note of irony or contempt - any human being who is to be pitied, even if only for her or his own naivety *(bedauernswerter [naiver] Mensch)*: poor wretch *or* devil, simple soul.

hạst mi?; less often, in formal address, **hạm S' mi?** *dial. interj* [< *hast du (haben Sie) mich verstanden?*] **1.** a neutral, or friendly, or downright impatient query whether the spoken message conveyed has been fully understood: d'you get me?, did you get me, *or* ... it? - **2. hạst mi?** only - a peremptory tag to an order calling a subordinate or a young person to attention (say, following a *dass mir das nicht wieder passiert!* 'I don't want this to happen again!', or *spätestens [um] zehne bist du zu Haus!* 'you'll be [at] 'ome by ten!'); or, in a blind fury, indeed lashing out at any one person: d'you read me?

ha̲tschen *v/i* [based on sound imitation] *colloq.*, often in self-pity - to cover a wearying distance on foot *([mühselig] lang marschieren)*: to trudge *or* tramp along, to foot(slog); *möchtest du uns wirklich zumuten, das greislich lange Stück zu ~?* would you really like to make us tramp that godawful long stretch of road? - **2.** to walk in an awkward way with small steps because (1) one's feet hurt: to hobble, to limp; or (2) one's gait is permanently afflicted: to limp.

Ha̲u̲sl *m* -s/-(n) *colloq.* *(Hausknecht, Hausmeister)* a boy or man, usu. big and muscular, who does practical work in an inn or hotel: houseman, *AmE also* houseboy, *BrE also* boots *pl.*

Hä̲u̲sl *n* -s/-(n) *colloq.* **1.** *emot.* (1) sometimes slightly self-deprecatory or *contp.* - *(Häuschen)* little house, cottage, *IrE also* houseen [-ˈiːn]; *wir haben immer davon geträumt, uns einmal ein kleines ~ am Land zuzulegen* we always dreamt of having a little cottage in the country some day; *wenn Sie mit meiner bescheidenen Übernachtungsbleibe vorlieb nehmen wollten, es ist halt nur ein ~* I wonder if you wouldn't mind putting

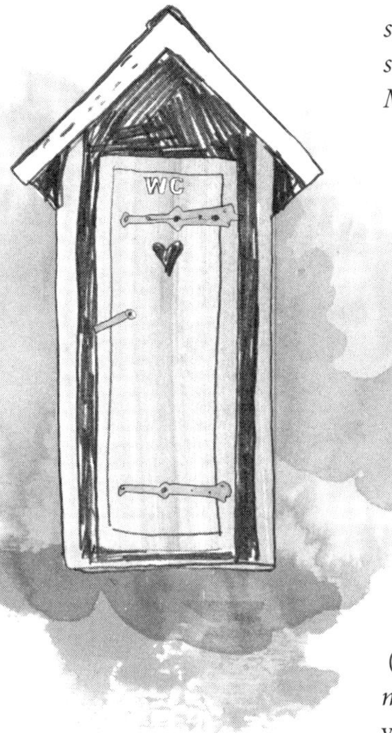

WC-Häusl

up with this modest night lodging of mine; it's no more than an apology for a house, I know; *das ist doch kein Haus, grad ein ~, wenn's hoch hergeht!* that's not a house, really; it's just a hut (*or* shack), at best. - (2) *fig.* in *phr.* with *aus dem ~* 'in a state of nervous excitement': *j-n (ganz) aus dem ~ bringen* to make s.o. go berserk; *aus dem ~ geraten* to go berserk; *ganz aus dem ~ sein* to be out of one's mind, to be all of a twitter (with joy, excitement, fear, etc.). - **2.** an outdoor toilet housed in a small, often wooden, structure *(Abort [im Freien])*: privy, *BrE* outside loo, Nessie, *AmE* outhouse, backhouse; *jeder weiß, was gemeint ist, wenn die Rede auf das verschwiegene Örtchen mit dem Herzausschnitt kommt - es ist das gute, alte ~ am Misthaufen* everybody knows what is meant when talk comes round to the hush-hush place that is marked by a little heart carved out of the wood - it's the good old privy on the midden; *wo geht's denn da zum ~ mit Luftspülung?* which is the way to the airy outside plumbing? - **3.** an indoor toilet *(Abort [im Haus])*: smallest room, *BrE also* loo, lavvy, *AmE also* john, can, pot; *ich muss aufs ~, nur klein* (I've) got to go to the loo (*AmE* ... the john), just number one; *musst du schon wieder aufs ~?* ([are] you) on the backdoor trot again?

Häusl... *colloq.*: **~papier** *n* -s toilet *or* tissue paper *(Klosettpapier)*: *BrE* loo paper, *AmE* bum fodder, bumwad; *wenn man auf einer Bergtour einmal „groß muss", langt auch ein Stückl Zeitung als ~* on a mountain tour, if the urge is felt, a bit of newspaper will be good enough for a behind-the-scenes activity. - **~schleicher** *m* -s/- *contp.* a person, usu. male, **1.** who goes with a soft, stealthy tread, as though afraid to commit himself on a point of issue *(Leisetreter)*: pussyfoot(er), mealymouth, *AmE also* flannelmouth; or **2.** who tries to win the favour of people of higher rank, esp. by praising them insincerely *(heuchlerischer Schleicher)*: creep, *esp. BrE* Uriah Heep.

Hauterer *m* -s/- *colloq.*, often *contp.* skinny person: (one [who is] all bones *or* ribs, *contp.* rattlebones, skinny-malink; said of an emaciated labourer considered unfit to do any heavy work: *mit dem alten ~ ist nimmer viel los* that old bag of skin (and bone[s]) is past making the fur (*or* the sparks) fly.

Hạx *m* gen. rare: -es/-(e)n *dial.* = *Hax(e)n*. - **Hạxe** *f* -/-n, *dial.* **Hạx(e)n** *f* -/- **1.** *zo. (Hachse)* (a quadruped's) lower leg. - **2.** *cul.* as an item of food, used in compounds only, to specify the customer's wish: *Kalbs*$\overset{x}{\sim}$ knuckle of veal; *Schweins*$\overset{x}{\sim}$ knuckle of pork, trotter. - **Hạx(e)n** *m* -(s)/- *dial., anat. (Bein)* (human) leg; *mei ~ tuat ma weh* me leg hurts; *(ja) mei, hat die ~!* (oh) my, ain't she got some legs! || *fig. phr.* graphically describing the fact that someone makes every possible effort to be helpful: *sich die ~ ausreißen* to bend over backwards, to lay oneself out, to break (*AmE also* to bust) an arm *or* leg *or* a gut.

hẹlfgott; to a relative or friend, also **hẹlfdirgott** *interj* to someone who sneezes *(Gesundheit!)*: [God] bless you!

Hẹlle *n* -n/-n *bev.* light (*or* pale) ale, *BrE also* lager; *ein (Glas) ~s, bitte!* one (glass of) light beer, please. || a word on measures, and a gentle warning: *wen es nach Bier lüstet, der verlangt als übliche Menge „eine Halbe" (1/2 l) oder „ein kleines ~s" (1/4 l); bei dessen Bestellung von männlicher Seite aber zucken die Gesichtsmuskeln einer urbayerischen Kellnerin freilich wohl etwas verächtlich zusammen* whoever hankers after beer, the customary measure asked for is "a half" (i.e., half a litre, or 0.88 pint) or "a small light" (i.e., a quarter of a litre, or 0.44 pint); if the latter order comes from the lips of a male, though, the facial muscles of a proper Bavarian waitress may well give a twitch of faint disdain.

Hẹndl *n* -s/-(n) *colloq.* **1.** (NorG *Huhn*) hen. - **2.** *cul. (Hühnchen)* chicken. - **~essen** *n* -s/- (NorG *Hähnchenschmaus*) chicken dinner. - **~friedhof** *m* -(e)s/...höfe *hum.* = *Gockerlfriedhof*↑.

Hendlfriedhof

Hẹrrgott *m relig.* **1.** -(e)s the Supreme Being who is worshipped as maker and ruler of the universe; speaking to, and of, Him under this compound name often tends to suggest added reverence, devout intimacy and confidence: the (*or* our) Lord (God), God; *der ~ weiß* *immer warum* our Lord God always knows (the reason) why; *der ~ wird's schon richten* the Lord will provide; *sollt's auch schlimm kommen, wenn der ~ bei uns ist, werden wir immer ein Auslangen finden können* if the Lord's with us, times won't ever be so bad we can't make a living for ourselves; *der ~ sei davor, dass unserm Vater was passiert!* God forbid that anything should happen to our father. || *phr.* giving vent to the speaker's feeling of mild surprise at how strangely some people behave (in the face of which, nevertheless, a true Christian should yet remain gentle and broad-minded): *unser ~ hat einen großen Tiergarten* it takes all kind of folk (*or*, all sorts of people) to make a world. - **2.** -(e)s/...götter *art* (1) figure of Christ; *einen ~ in der Nische überm Hauseingang, wär' das nicht was?* having a figure of the Lord to fit the niche [nɪtʃ] above the front door, wouldn't that be something? - (2) sg. only *loosely* crucifix.

Hẹrrgotts...: **~apotheke** *f* - *colloq.* "Nature's medicine cabinet," *i.e.* the popular wild herbs gathered and dried for medicinal purposes. - **~blume** *f* -/-n, **~blut** *n* -(e)s *bot. (Johanniskraut)* common *or* perforated St John's wort. - **~käferl** *n* -s/-(n), **~kü(c)hlein** *n* -s/- *ent. (Marienkäfer)* ladybird (beetle), *AmE also* ladybug. - **~ruh** *f* -/-en, **~ruhe** *f* -/-n *geog.* a popular name for many a scenic spot affording a panoramic view (e.g. the one above the town of Starnberg), where wayfarers would do well to 'rest and be thankful': "God's Rest". - **~schnitzer** *m* -s/- *arts (Kruzifix-, Andachtsbildschnitzer)* carver of crucifixes (and religious figures); *seit langem schon ist Oberammergau auch als Heimat der ~ weithin bekannt* Oberammergau has long been widely known also for its carvers of crucifixes. - **~winkel** *m* -s/- "God's corner" **1.** *relig.* often in a rural living room *(Andachtsecke [im Bauernhaus])*: a space provided with a crucifix and other religious objects, and devoted to worship, the figure of the Crucified leaning into the room in a protective attitude; *der ~ ist mit Palmkatzerln geschmückt, die der Priester am Palmsonntag geweiht hat* the God's Corner is decorated with pussy willows which were blessed by the priest on Palm Sunday. → **2.** *geog.* any outlook point of exceptional beauty; in the collocation *der ~ unserer Heimat* 'our country's God-blessed [-ɪd] corner' - an often-used metaphor for the awe-inspiring sweep of the Bavarian Alps seen in all their glory from a vantage-point due north in the Bavarian Foreland, esp. from the top of Hohenpeissenberg Hill, SW of Lake Starnberg.

Hẹrzepopperl, **Hẹrzipopperl** *n* -s/-n [second el., dim. of *Puppe*, in baby talk *Poppa* 'doll'] *apprec.* usu. preceded by *mei(n)* a doll or a small child one is very fond of: (my) ducky darling, lovey-dovey, popsy-wopsy.

Hẹrzkasperl [-ʃp-] *m* -s/-(n) *med. colloq.* the impersonation of a cardiac infarction *(Herzinfarkt)*, which suddenly lays low its victims, much like volatile

Kasperl↓ of pantomime fame who, when in the mood, strikes down his opponents with a slapstick: heart attack, coronary; *ihn hat der ~ geholt, er hat den ~ gekriegt* he's had a heart attack.

Heu *n* -(e)s **1.** *agr.* (1) hay, i.e. grass which has been cut and dried. - (2) in a narrower sense: the first crop of hay, usu. harvested in June. || phr. (1) ~ *machen* = *heuen.* - (2) *colloq. ins ~ gehen* to go haymaking; *wir gehen heute ins ~* we're haymaking today. - **2.** *fig. phr.* graphically exemplifying the fact that two persons are of divergent mentalities: *sie* (colloq., *die*) *haben das ~ nicht im gleichen Stadel* they don't talk the same language, they don't see eye to eye, they're not on the same wavelength, *IrE also* they don't dig with the same foot || if said by the speaker making his own point clear: he [she] is not my cup of tea.

heuen, *dial.* **haign**, **heugn** *agr. v/i* to make hay, *AmE also* to hay || *prov.* a piece of advice to use one's chances while conditions are favourable: *~ muss man, wenn die Sonne scheint* (or, in dialect, *wann's Heuwetter is*) make hay while the sun shines. - **Heuen** *n* -s = *Heumachen.*

Heu... *agr.*: **~ernte** *f* -/-n, *dial.* **Heuet** *m* -s/-e; *f* -/-e; **Heugert** *n* -s/-e **1.** hay harvest; *zweite ~* aftermath, second crop of hay. - **2.** *(Erntezeit)* haymaking time *or* season. - **~geige** *f* -/-n **1.** a high wooden structure with parallel bars (resembling the strings on a violin), for drying grass or clover: hay rack. - **2.** *fig., colloq.* and often *iron.* a tall, lanky person, usu. female: beanpole, lamppost, long drink (of water), *BrE also* beanstalk, *AmE also* clothes pole, string bean. - **~hupfer** *m* -s/- *colloq.* **1.** *zo. (Heuhüpfer)* grasshopper. - **2.** *fig., hum.* or *iron.* a tall and slender young man: skinnymalink, Harry Longlegs *sg.* - **~machen** *n* -s haymaking; *die Bauersleute waren schon beim ~* the farm people were already scything the hay crop down. - **~ochs** *m* -en/-en [actually, 'hay-eating ox'] low *colloq.* a stupid, strong fellow: bonehead, numskull; *er ist ein ~, wie er im Buch steht* he's all brawn and no brain(s). - **~raufe** *f* -/-n hayrack. - **~reuter** *m* -s/- *(Heureiter)* a tripod for drying hay and clover (cp. *Heugeige 1*): hay prop, rickstand. - **~schreck** *m* -s/-en *zo., colloq. (Heuschrecke) = Heuhupfer 1.* - **~stadel** *m* -s/- a small log structure away out in the meadows, to store hay for winter use: hay-hut, hay chalet. - **~wagen** *m* -s/- haywaggon (*AmE* haywagon), *BrE also* haycart. - **~wetter** *n* -s good weather for making hay || for its proverbial use, see under *heuen.*

Himmiherrgotzaggramentzefixallelujamilextamarschscheißglumpfaregtz *interj.* a string of uncouth dial. curses, run together for aural and visual effect, to be found on car stickers: = *goshalmightysakesaliveglory shovitshitpissandcorruption.

Hinter...: **´fotzig** *adj* & *adv*, low *colloq.* *(heimtückisch)* insidious: sneaky, sly; *das ist dir ein ganz ~er Kerl!* for your information, he's a sneaky slimeball!,

AmE I'm telling you, he's an underhanded jerk!; *auf ~e Art* in a sneaky manner, underhandedly. - **~fotzigkeit** *f* -/- low *colloq. (Hinterhältigkeit)* insidiousness: sneakiness, slyness; *vor dem seiner ~ musst du dich in Acht nehmen!* you need to watch out for his underhandedness. - **~tupfing** *n* -s/- *hum.* or *sarc.* an out-of-the-way, and therefore behind-the-times, village or small country town: *BrE* Little-Puddle-in-the-Mud, Much-Binding-in-the-Marsh, *AmE* Hickville (, U.S.A.), Podunk [pəʊˈdʌŋk], Timbuktu [ˌtɪmbʌkˈtuː]; *er ist in ~ zuhaus* he lives somewhere in the sticks (*or*, back of beyond). - **~türl** *n* -s/-n *colloq.* **1.** *(Hintertür)* backdoor; *der Einfachheit halber geh ich gleich durchs ~ raus* it's easier for me to go out the backdoor. - **2.** *fig. (heimlicher Ausweg)* loophole; *sich ein ~ offen lassen* to leave a backdoor open for oneself.

Hịrn... *colloq.*: **~batzerl**; more matter-of-factly, **~batzl** *n* -s/-(n) [the gestural roundedness of one finger and the thumb forming a Q, and the follow-up catapult motion combine to suggest the heavy lumpiness of a small projectile, which is at the semantic basis of *Batzl*↑, the second element of the compound] *body language* a playful or reproachful flick aimed at the forehead of a (usu. young) person with one's bent forefinger or middle finger; the finger is tensed against the inner top joint of the thumb, and then released with some force *(Stirnknips)*: finger flick, finger nudgie. - ≗**brandig** *adj* = *hirnverbrannt.* - **~kastl** *n* -s/-(n) [second el., dim. of *Kasten* 'chest'] sometimes *hum.* the human skull as housing man's intelligence: brain-box, *AmE also* old bean, think tank, upper story; *ja geht denn das gar net in dein ~ 'nein?* can't you ever get this into your thick skull? - ≗**rissig** *adj* outrageously foolish: crack-brained; *ein ~er Vorschlag* a lunatic proposal; *der tut ja ganz ~ NorBrE* he's going on as if he were cut in the head. - **~schmalz** *n* -es another concrete visualization of something impalpable - *Schmalz* 'lard', 'grease' (cp. *Irxenschmalz*↓, *Muskelschmalz*↓), in simple folk belief, obviously being a proper nourishment for brawn a n d brain *(praktische Intelligenz)*: gumption, what it takes (to get along), *AmE also* milk in the coconut; *~ haben* to have a head on one's shoulders, to have (plenty of) stuff on the ball. - ≗**verbrannt**, *dial.* ≗**verbrennt** *adj* [literally, 'having one's brains destroyed by fire'] stupid: cockeyed, crazy; *ist das wieder eine von deinen ~en Ideen?* is this another one of those cockeyed (*AmE vulg. sl. also* half-assed) ideas of yours?

hochnasig, *dial.* **hochnasert** *adj, colloq.* & often *contp.* arrogant *(hochmütig)*: stuck-up, uppity, uppish; *~ sein* to be on one's high horse; *die ≗e red't nicht einmal mit alten Freundinnen, seit sie eine so reiche Partie gemacht hat* she's too stuck-up to speak to her old friends ever since she's managed to marry a fortune. - **Hochnasigkeit**, *dial.* **Hochnasertheit** *f* - *colloq.* & often *contp.* arrogance *(Hochmut)*: stuck-uppishness.

hochnasig

Hochwasserhosen *f -/- garm., hum.* or *iron.* trousers shorter than the fashion: trousers (*AmE* pants) at half-mast, *AmE also* high-water pants; *er hat (eine) ~,* or *er hat Hochwasser* his trousers (*AmE also* pants) are at half-mast.

Hochzeitlader *m* -s/pl. rare: - *folklore* = *Hochzeitslader*↓.

Hochzeits... *folklore* [these compounds still testify to the presence, though now on the wane, of two quaint prenuptial customs in rural areas]: **~lader** *m* -s/pl. rare: - *(Hochzeitsbitter)* bride's messenger; *der ~, niederbayerisch „Prog(r)oder" genannt, geht mit geschmücktem Hut und Stock herum und bittet dabei mitunter an die zwölf Dutzend Gäste zur Festlichkeit* the bride's messenger, known as "proctor" in Lower Bavaria, festively adorned with hat and wedding staff, duly makes the round, at times bidding some twelve dozen guests to attend the celebration. - **~schmuser** *m* -s/pl. rare: - *colloq. (Heiratsvermittler)* marriage broker: matchmaker.

hocken, *dial.* **hocka** *v/i colloq.* & *dial.* to sit (often for an unconscionable time): to be glued to one's seat; *die Bierdimpfl ~ vor ihren Massen und stehn grad zwischenrein zum Bieseln auf* the (*or* those) old beer guzzlers refuse to budge from behind their mugs, and they do so only betweentimes to get out and pee; *die sind fei ~ blieben, bis der Wirt den Spruch „Habt 's ihr Herrschaftn keine Bettn daheim?" rauslassen hat* they stayed put (*or*, sat tight, *AmE also* sat on their tails), mind, until the landlord came up with his spiel, "Time, gentlemen, time, it's a lovely night outside!"

Hofbräuhaus *n econ.* **1.** -es in Munich, since 1583: Ducal and Royal Brewery, now a state enterprise and the most famous of all beer cellars in town - whose very presence, according to a local song, is a solid assurance that *Gemütlichkeit*↑ "will never die out in Munich." → **2.** -es/...häuser Court Brewery Inn, any of the more or less spacious beer temples in other towns of Bavaria where devotees of the barley juice can regularly meet in great numbers.

Holler *m* -s/- *bot.* **1.** a small wild tree with white flowers and black berries *(Holunder[baum, etc.])*: elder; *gemeiner* or *schwarzer ~* common or black-berried elder, *scient.* Sambucus nigra. - **2.** = *Hollerbeeren pl.*↓; *den ~ von den Stielen lösen* to remove the elderberries from their umbels || in *comps.*: **~baum** *m* -(e)s/...bäume *bot.* elder(berry) tree. - **~beere** *f* -/-n *bot.* elderberry. - **~blüte** *f* (1) -/-n elder flower, elder blossom. - (2) - elder-blossom time; *zur ~* in elder-blossom time. - **~blütentee** *m* -s/-(s) *bev.* elder(-flower) tea; *~ ist gut gegen Erkältungskrankheiten und Blasenleiden* elder-flower tea is good for (*or*, beneficial in cases of) coughs and sneezes as well as bladder trouble. - **~busch** *m* -(e)s/...büsche *bot.* elder(berry) bush, elder(berry) shrub. - **~koch** *n* -s/pl. rare: -(s) *cul.* elderberries stewed with apples and plums. - **~küchel**, often *dial.* **~küachl**, **~kiachl** *n* -s/usu. pl.: -(n) *bak.* elder blossoms dipped in pancake batter, fried and served with a sprinkling of powder sugar. - **~mus** *n* -es/-e *cul.* elderberry sauce, a refreshing dish made by boiling elderberries, sugar, and some flour. - **~saft** *m* -(e)s/pl. rare: ...säfte *med.* elderberry juice. - **~schnaps** *m* -es/...schnäpse *bev.* (1) elder(berry) brandy. - (2) elder-flower brandy. - **~sekt** *m* -(e)s *bev.* elder-blossom champagne, *colloq.* elder-blossom bubbly. - **~staudn** *f* -/- *dial.*, **~strauch** *m* -(e)s/...sträucher *bot.* = *Hollerbusch.* - **~suppe** *f* -/-n *cul.* elderberry soup. - **~tee** *m* -s/-(s) *bev.* = *Hollerblütentee.* - **~wein** *m* -(e)s/-e *bev.* (1) elder(berry) wine. - (2) elder-flower wine.

Hopfen, *dial.* **Hopf** *m* -s/no pl. *bot.* hops || some current proverbial lore of the Hallertau, north-west of Landshut, the third-largest hop-growing area in the world: (1) the delicate plant, which is trained to climb along the slanting wires of trellises some 30 feet high, is

Hopfen

often subject to mildew, blight, and other diseases, the prevention of which keeps farmers busy from early April until late August, when harvesting begins: *der ~ will täglich seinen Herrn sehen* *the hops want to see their master every day, *hop flowers want attendance danced upon them every day. - (2) besides, world market prices tend to fluctuate and may play havoc with man's "best laid schemes": *der Hopf ist ein Tropf* *hops are wayward crops.

Hopfen...: **~anbau** *m* -(e)s hop cultivation, hop growing; *wollten wir den ~ in England und in Bayern miteinander vergleichen, dann sollten wir Kent und die Hallertau ausgiebig durchstreifen* if we were to make a comparative study of hop growing in England and in Bavaria, we should be well-advised to go on an extensive ramble through Kent, and the Hallertau, respectively. - **~pflücker** *m* -s/- hop-picker, *BrE also* hopper. - **~schmuser** *m* -s/- *econ., colloq. (Hopfenaufkäufer)* buyer-up of hops (usu. acting merely as the wholesale trader's assistant, who is engaged in the verbal preliminaries [hence, *Schmuser*↓] of the transaction). - **~stange** *f*-/-n **1.** *bot.*, largely *hist.* a slender pole of spruce-wood, up to some 16 feet tall, for training a hop-seed along: hop-pole. - **2.** *colloq.*, often *hum.* or slightly *sarc.* tall, lanky person: beanpole, beanstalk, lamppost; *das ist dir eine zaundürre ~!* there's a gangling lathlegs for you!, *NorBrE also* he [she]'s all legs and wings. || → *zaundürr*. - **~zupfen** *n* -s *agr., colloq.* and *obsolescent* (since now often no longer done by hand) hop-picking: hopping. - **~zupfer** *m* -s/-, **~zupferin** *f* -/-nen *agr., colloq.* and *obsolescent* hop-picker: hopper.

hoppala *interj* [< *hoppa*, the beginning of a famous jog-along knee song which makes the 'horseman' tumble down (or, as an English ditty of that genre has it, go 'bumpety-bump') + the echoic nursery suffix *-la*] in adult speech only **1.** a little gasp of surprise when stumbling, dropping something, or making a mistake; and used in lieu of an apology when accidentally brushing past or bumping into a person: whoops, oops(-a-daisy)! - **2.** a sympathetic catchphrase to a child that has knocked its head or falls over: boomps-a-daisy!

Hörndlbauer *m* -n/-n [first el., *dim.* of *Horn* 'horn', one of a pair, on the heads of cattle] *agr., colloq. (Viehzüchter* [opp. *Körndlbauer*↓]) cattle *or* beef farmer.

Hosentürl *n* -s/-(n) [second el., dim. of *Tür* 'door'] *colloq. hum. (Hosenschlitz)* fly (of [the] trousers): shop door || *phr.* (1) in a warning to a male friend or relative, seeing that his trousers are unbuttoned: *du hast das ~ offen!, das ~*

steht [dir] offen! your shop door is open, your secret interests are in evidence, *AmE also* (depending on the number of fly buttons undone:) it's one [two, *etc.*] o'clock (at the waterworks), Johnny's out of jail. - (2) in a witticism given rise to by Prince Luitpold, the aged Regent of Bavaria, 1821-1912, who during a shooting party happened to reveal an awkward sartorial irregularity, which a junior hunting assistant tried to deal with in his own way: *Königliche Hoheit, halten zu Gnaden, wie wär's, wenn wir jetzt alle unser ~ zumachen?* Your Royal Highness, with your gracious permission, what about all of us now having a go at getting our shop doors shut?

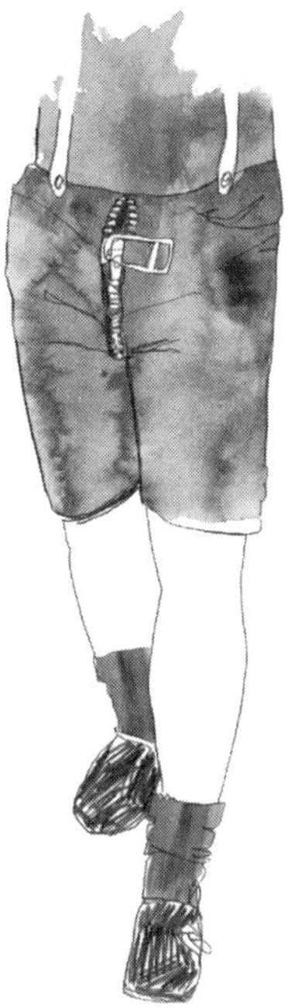

Hosentürl

hudeln *v/i colloq.* **1.** to act in a hasty manner *(übereilt agieren)*: to rush (through) things; *nur nicht ~!* never hurry!, no good thing is done in a hurry!, keep your hair (*AmE also* hat) on!, what's the rush?, we mustn't run before we can walk!, *IrE* fine day, no hurry!, *specif.* we'll come to that all in good time! - **2.** to scamp *(nachlässig arbeiten)*: to botch things; *so etwas Gehudeltes!* what a botched piece of work!

hundig, hundselendig *adv* [ex the proverbial *Hundeleben*, or 'dog's life' (with its frequent vagrancy, and rejection by human beings), many such quadrupeds were condemned to lead in past centuries] *colloq.* said of, and more often even by, a person who is in a wretched state of health: miserable [miserably]; *seitdem ich mir den Husten geholt hab, geht's mir ganz ~* ever since I caught this cough, I've been feeling like death warmed up.

Hundling *m* -s/-e, less often **Hundlinger** *m* -s/- *colloq.*, said in contempt, yet occasionally with an admixture of admiration for somebody who is clever in cheating *([durchtriebener] Spitzbube)*: tricky customer, slyboots *sg.*, *AmE also* slick *or* smooth article, con artist, sharp operator; *schau zu, wie du mit dem zurechtkommst, das ist ein ~!* be careful how you deal with him, he's a tricky customer (*or*, ... he's a sharp one).

hupfats Wasser [*hupfats* < StandG *hüpfendes* 'effervescent', i.e. containing tiny balls of carbonic gas that float to the surface] only in: *(ein,* dial. *a) ~ ~* *dial.* & *colloq.* any drink that contains bubbles of gas - if **1.** non-alcoholic, carbonated water *(Sprudelwasser)*: soft bubbly, bubble water, fizz water; **2.** if alcoholic, sparkling wine *(Schaumwein, Sekt)* or French champagne *(Champagner)*: bubbly, fizz.

hupfats Wasser

hupfen *v/i* [the unumlauted form of StandG *hüpfen*] *colloq.* to hop || *phr.: das ist gehupft wie gesprungen* (1) the real difference, after everything has been considered, is negligible: it's six of one and half a dozen of the other, it's Tweedledum and Tweedledee. - (2) which alternative shall be preferred is of no consequence to me: it makes no never-mind to me, *AmE also* it doesn't make a diff of bitterness to me.

Hupfer *m* -s/- *colloq.* **1.** *(Hüpfer)* leap, skip, bounce; *mein Herz hat einen ~ gemacht* my heart leapt (*or*, missed a beat); *zum nächsten Telefonhäusl sind ja grad ein paar ~ über die Straße* (why,) the nearest phone box is just a short hop across the street. - **2.** often slightly *contp.* a young man who is no longer a boy but is not yet really a man *(unreifer Bursche)*: stripling, youngster; *was will denn der? das ist ja noch ein junger ~!* what does he want? he isn't dry behind the ears yet.

I

Ibidum, also **Binisodum** *n* -s [two self-incriminatory sentence nouns the meaning of which though is likely to remain dark to any non-dialect speaker: < StandG *ich bin dumm* 'I am stupid', *bin ich (doch) so dumm!* 'ain't I stupid, really!'; their pseudo-L form no doubt sounds more acceptable through the presence of many medicinal plant names ending in *-um*, e.g. *Basilikum, Nasturtium, Origanum, Triticum,* and *Vaccinium*] *hum.* two names of fictitious medicines a gullible person is sent for as a practical joke: (bottle of) pigeon's milk, bumblebee oil; *ich hab so Schädelweh - geh spring in die Apotheke und hol mir ein ~!* I've such a headache - could you pop (*BrE also* nip) round to the chemist's (*BrE; AmE* drugstore) and get me some noggin powder (*or* pills)?

Idioten...: **~hang** *m* -(e)s/...hänge, **~hügel** *m* -s/-, **~wiese** *f* -/-n *skiing* a gentle practice ground for near-beginners *(Übungshang für Skianfänger)*: nursery slope, fool-proof slope.

Irxen, Irxn, in the northern Upper Palatinate **Öißn** *f* -/- *dial.* *(Achsel[höhle])* shoulder, armpit; *unter* (or *in) der ~* under the armpit. - **~schmalz** *n* -es/no pl.

colloq., often *hum.* **1.** muscular energy, *colloq.* elbow grease, *AmE also* axle grease; *da brauchst schon ein ~ dazu!* it'll take (you) some elbow grease to do that!, *AmE also* that'll take some axle grease!; *die Burschen des Dorfes machen es sich zur Ehre, den Maibaum nach Urväterart, nur mit „~", unter Verzicht auf technisches Gerät, aufzustellen* following the tradition of their forefathers, the young men of the village consider it an act of honour to put up their maypole relying only on pure brawn and elbow grease, thus shirking the use of any technical tools. - **2.** *fig.* said of a dialect or slang that is marked by vitality and virile strength: pep, go; *das Bairische hat ein ~* (the) Bavarian (dialect) is full of vim and vigour.

i-Tüpfel *m* & *n* -s/-, **i-Tüpferl** *n* -s/-(n) *colloq.* dot over the (letter) i || a perfectionist's dream of happiness regarding things to be done by, and for, and around, him: *alles muss bis auf das letzte ~ genau stimmen* everything has to be right and proper down to the last T (*or*, ... to a T); *da darf kein ~ fehlen* not one jot or tittle must be missing.

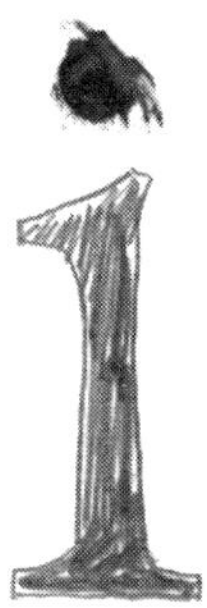

i-Tüpfel

J

Jagertee *m* -s/pl. rare: -s *bev.* "huntsman's tea," **1.** *rather rare* tea, rum, wine, and spices, a brew made up by deer-stalkers in a wintry mountain cabin. - **2.** an industrial alcoholic tea concentrate, containing also herb and fruit extracts as well as sugar, to be mixed with hot water in a ratio of 1 to 2 (or 3); *der ~ darf als das ‚Nationalgetränk' der Skifahrer und Bergwanderer gelten, in den Alpen fehlt es im Winter auf keiner Getränkekarte* "huntsman's tea" may be looked upon as an absolute favourite with skiers and mountain hikers, it is a must on every list of Alpine beverages in wintertime.

Jahrtag *m* -s/-e *dial.* the anniversary of a person's death *(Todestag)*: day of (s.o.'s) death, deathday; *morgen um halb neun is die Mess für'n ~ von der Mutter* tomorrow at half past eight (*BrE dial. often*, at half eight) 'll be the memorial (*or* commemorative) service for mother's deathday.

ja mei [ˌjɔːˈmaɪ] [*mei*, the scant remains, altogether lacking in directedness, of a former appeal to Deity, < *mein Gott!*] *dial. interj* expressing either indifference or good-natured resignation in the face of the complicated way the world goes (usu. to be verbalized more fully in what follows), but often also indicative of the speaker's reluctance to do something about it - which might benefit others, esp. his interlocutor: oh dear!; ~ ~, *da kann man nix machn!* oh dear, there's nowt [naʊt] to be done about it!

jẹggerl, often expanded into **u̲i̲ jẹggerl** *interj* [a dim. corruption of *Jesus m*] an expression of gentle surprise: oh dear! - **jẹssas** *interj* [another, but much less downtoning corruption of the same word] an expression of considerable surprise, signalling annoyance but also pleasure and admiration: *BrE* dear oh dear!, dear dear!, lordy!, gee-whizz!, *AmE* gee!, geez(e) *or* jeez(e)!, jeepers (creepers)! - **Jẹssmar(i)andjo̲sef**, **Jẹss-Mar-and-Jo̲sef** *interj* [lit., an invocation to the Holy Family] full-bodied rallying cries for help giving vent to one's strong feelings, be they of profound shock, contempt, etc.: Jesus, Mary and Joseph! - **JẹssasandJo̲sef**, **Jẹssasmari̲a** *interj* invocations including one sainted parent: Jesus and Joseph!, Jesus and Mary!

jo̲ [joː - a very close vowel, formed with pointed lips and the back part of the tongue raised high towards the palate] *dial. particle* contrasted with *naa* 'no' - (1) expressing friendly and lively agreement, affirmation, etc. *(gewiss)*: oh aye [ɑɪ]; and (2) serving, often reinforced by reduplication, to dispel one's interlocutor's doubt laid into a question with a negative element *(schon; doch [doch]; und ob)*: (why,) of course; I do [am, can, will, etc.]; I'll say; and how.

Jo̲del *m* -s/- & Jö̲del [< *jo*, an Alpine shout from hill to hill, drawing attention to the shouter, but also done for mere joie de vivre; thus *jodeln*, and *johlen* 'to bawl', once simply verbalized that distinctive loud cry] *mus.* = *Jodler 1.* - ~**n**

Jodler

vt/i mus. to sing or warble with interchange of falsetto and the natural voice, in the manner of Alpine people: to yodel, to yodle, to jodel.

Jodler *m* -s/- *mus.* **1.** a melody or brief musical phrase inarticulately sung with interchange of the ordinary and falsetto voice *(Jodelruf)*: yodel(l)ing song; *if brief*, yodel(l)ing cry. - **2.** one who yodels: yodel(l)er, yodler, jodler, yodelist. - **Jodlerin** *f* -/-nen *mus.* girl yodel(l)er; *sie ist in der Jugend eine großartige ~ gewesen* she was a fine one for yodel(l)ing in her youth.

Josefi *m* gen. sg. [< L *Josephus*] *R.C.* St Joseph's Day (March 19), honouring the husband of Mary, the mother of Jesus - an important national holiday of Bavaria; *zu ~* on St Joseph's Day. - **~tag**, also *Josephitag m* -(e)s/pl. rare: -e = *Josefi*.

juchazen [the natural, undiphthongized form of StandG *jauchzen*; < *juchhe* 'yoohoo'] *dial. v/i* to shout with joy and delight: to yoohoo; to (give a short) yodel; *und es juchazt der Bua, wann er d'Liab hat im Sinn* and the lad shouts yoohoo when there's love in his mind.

Juchhe *n* -s/pl. rare: -s [< the shout of triumph, in E *yoohoo*, given by mountaineers upon reaching the peak] *colloq.*, often *hum.* **1.** *theat.* the seats high up at the back of a theatre *(die oberste Galerie im Theater)*: gods; *am ~* (a seat) in the gods, *AmE also* (a seat) with the gallery birds. → **2.** the top storey of a house, often a garret under a slanting roof: *im ~ wohnen* to live at nosebleed height.

K

Kaiser *f* -/- *colloq.* — short for **Kaisersemmel** *f* -/-n *bak. (Brötchen mit [fünf windradförmigen] Einschnitten)* a crisp white bread roll with windmill-shaped crust ridges, said to have been invented by Emperor Frederick III in 1487: "Emperor's roll", round (Vienna) roll; *fünf Kaiser bitte; die kosten im Sonderangebot ja eins zwanzig, gell?* five Emperor's, please; they're one twenty as a bargain offer, aren't they?

Kalbs...: **~haxe** *f* -/-n, *dial.* **~hax(e)n** *f* -/- [second el., → *Hax*] **1.** *husb.* calf's foot. - **2.** *cul.* knuckle *or* shin of veal. - **~schäuferl** *n* -s/-(n) [second el., dim. of *Schaufel* 'shovel' (ex the shape of the bone)] *cul.* shoulder of veal, boiled or grilled. - **~vögerl** *n* -s/-(n) [second el., dim. of *Vogel* 'bird' (ex the vague resemblance of the meat dish, in its final shape, to the plump brown body of a little bird)] *cul.* a thin flat piece each of veal cutlet and bacon, with a layer of sliced carrots, onions, gherkins, etc., rolled up and held in place by a skewer or toothpick *(Kalbsroulade)*: stuffed veal cutlet, veal bird.

Kammer *f* -/-n *archit.*, often in *hist.* contexts - a small room, esp. bedroom, in a(n old) farmhouse, either for a junior member of the farmer's family or for one of the maidservants and farmhands: chamber || *dial.*, specifically: *Menscher*~̈ maidservant's room.

Kạmpel, *dial.* **Kạmpl**, **Kạmpe** *m* -s/-(n) [a dim. formation < **1.** *Kamm m* 'comb'; and **2.** *Kämpe m obs.* or *hum.* 'old campaigner'] *colloq.* **1.** comb [kəʊm]; *wo hab ich denn meinen ~ hingelegt?* where did I put my comb (, I wonder)? - **2.** nearly always preceded by a positive attribute - (1) a man who impresses through a combination of bravery, style, and self-confidence: dazzler; *er ist ein fescher ~* he cuts a dash. - (2) *ein lustiger ~* a cheerful person, usu. male: a glad lad, a happy duck. - **kạmpeln**, *dial.* **kạmpln**, **kạmpen** *colloq.* *(kämmen)* **1.** *v/t* to comb [kəʊm]; *geh (und) kampel ihn!* go and comb his hair || *prov.* expressing confidence, and recommending resolute action, where circumstances look favourable: *kurze Haar san bald kamplt!* a short horse is soon curried. - **2.** *v/refl* to comb one's hair; *kampel dich, bevor du weggehst!* comb your hair before you go out.

Karfreitagsratschen *f* -/- [last el., 'a simple mechanism that makes a repeated loud noise'] **1.** *R.C. relig.* "Good Friday clapper", a wooden rattle used by *Ratschenbuben*↓ on the last three days of Holy Week, when it is customary for the church bells to remain silent. - **2.** *contp.*, also **Regimẹntsratschen** *f* -/- a formidable gossip: great blabbermouth before the Lord; *if female, also* Dame Gossip in person.

Kas or **Kaas** *m* -es (rare)/- *dial.* **1.** *comest.* the curd of milk *(Quark)* separated from the whey *(Molke)* and prepared in many ways as a food *(Käse)*: cheese; *magst (du) an ~?* (d' you) wan' some cheese? || in *phr.* of praise and warning, and when describing certain human moods and reactions: (1) man's rhymed delight in a simple good snack: *Brot und ~, wia guat schmeckt das!* *bread and cheese are sure to please. - (2) a recommendation to make cheese round off a four- or five-course meal: *a ~ is fei der Magnschluss, der alles andre schlagn muss* *for topping up tummy cheese surely tastes yummy. - (3) another dietary recommendation as to which time of day is best for eating cheese: *da ~ is in da Früah a Dorn, z' Mittag a Eisn - und auf d' Nacht a Blei* cheese is gold in the morning, silver at noon - and lead at night. - (4) *contp.* said of a person known for volubility but little substance: *bei dem muaß auf an ~ a Brüah hin* he sputters lots of foam but little beer. - (5) as a conciliatory gesture, expressing the opinion that bygones are bygones, and not worth worrying about; also, signalling the speaker's readiness to forget, and possibly also forgive, something bad

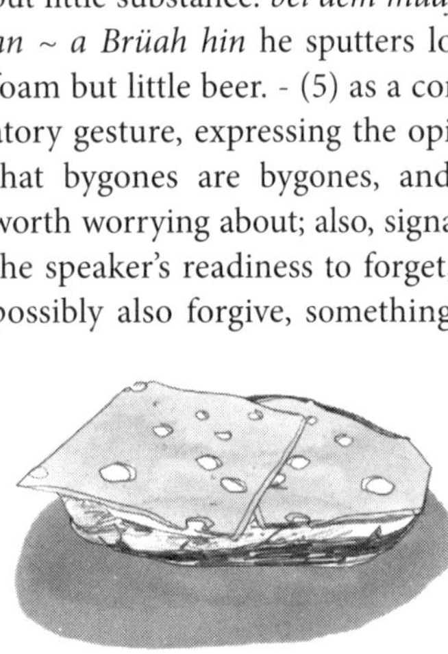

Kas

that has been done to him: *für mi(ch) is der ~ g'gessen* that's (all) water under the bridge, if you ask me. - **2.** *colloq.*, often *contp.* (1) something without any use or value *(wertloses Zeug)* - (a) *concr.* junk, *AmE also* chunk of cheese; *wirf den ~ weg!* throw that junk away! - (b) *abstr.* trash, tripe; *was heut Abend im Fernsehen kommt, is a großa ~* there'll be a lot of trash on TV tonight; *was liest denn (du) so an ~?* why d'you read such tripe? - (2) nonsense *(Unsinn)*: bunkum, twaddle, *AmE also* hooey, noodle soup; *er hat an gscheitn ~ dahergredt* he talked a lot (*or*, a load) of hogwash; *red do(ch) koan ~!* don't talk rubbish (*or*, such drivel)! don't give me that baloney!

Kasloabl, Kaasloabe *n* -s/-(n) [second el., dim. of *Loab* (StandG *Laib*) *m* 'loaf'] *comest., dial.* small-sized whole cheese, wheel-shaped || *fig.*, in a simile describing a person's complexion that, from fear or shock, has gone extremely pale: *er is weiß wordn wia a ~* he went white as a sheet.

Kasperl [-ʃp-] *m* -s/-n **1.** *theat.* (1) the principal male character in a puppet show, known for his humorous fights with his wife and for other acts of clowning: Punch. - (2) a figure of mirth at funfairs and in carnival time: merry-andrew. - **2.** *colloq.* a male person whose silly behaviour makes him a laughingstock: figure of fun, *AmE* oddball, wacko; *er ist halt einfach zum ~ geworden, keiner nimmt ihn mehr ernst* he's become just a figure of fun, and no one takes him seriously any more. - **3.** *colloq.*, said with indulgent humour — a child who, in the presence of adults, likes to engage in somewhat grotesque horseplay: (little) monkey; *jetzt kannst du aber schon langsam aufhören, du ~!* now that's about enough of your antics, you little monkey (*or*, ... you little show-off).

Kasperl [-ʃp-] ...: **~puppe** *f* -/-n *theat.* hand puppet. - **~theater** *n* -s/- **1.** *theat.* (1) puppet-theatre. - (2) puppet show, *BrE* Punch-and-Judy show. - **2.** *fig. contp.* a series of acts of inefficiency and empty pretence which those in authority, esp. politicians, make themselves guilty of in the eyes of the public: sustained farce of silly acting; *das ist ja ein ~, was uns die Großkopferten da vorspielen!* those bigwigs are just a bunch of clowns trying to pull the wool over our eyes.

Kini *m* -(s)/- *dial.* *(König)* king **1.** a popular reference to one of the Bavarian rulers of the Wittelsbach line, and with especial affection to King Ludwig II, also known as "Fairy King" (on the throne, 1864-1886). - **2.** in the games of skittles and bowling, the pin at the centre: kingpin.

Kini

Kịrchweih *f* -/-en *relig.* = *Kirta(g)*↓. - **~baum** *m* -(e)s/...bäume *folklore* in the Cham area, at Kemnath, Lupburg, and elsewhere: kermis pole, a symbol of harvest thanksgiving, decorated with fir-twig wreaths and many gay ribbons, put up in a village square or in front of an inn. - **~bursch** *m* -en/-en *folklore* "kermis attendant", one of a group of village lads officiating at a village fair; the duties include putting up the *Kirchweihbaum*↑ on the Saturday before the event. - **~fest** *n* -(e)s/-e *relig.* = *Kirtag 1.* - **~gans** *f* -/ ...gänse *gastr.* kermis goose, the mouth-watering centre of attention, especially if roasted nice and crisp, for any native kermis celebrant. - **~krapfen** *m* -s/- *gastr.* at Waldkirchen, and elsewhere: kermis doughnut.

Kịrta *m* -s/- Bavarian Forest *dial.*, **Kịrtag** *m* -(e)s/-e *colloq.* [< *Kirchtag* 'church anniversary'] **1.** *relig. (Kirchweihfest)* church dedication day, celebrated annually on the name day of the patron saint; also known as *der kleine* ~, to distinguish it from *Allerweltskirtag*↑. → **2.** *folklore (Jahrmarkt)* kermis, kermess, kirmess, an annual fair or festival held on the patron saint's name day, with games, merrymaking, etc.; formerly the feasting went on for some time, as is testified by this old rhyme: *A richtiga ~, der geht bis zum Irta, / und tuat a si schicka, geht's weita bis Migga* *Our kermis will last until Tuesday is past, / and if in a frenzy, we'll go on through Wednesday. || *prov.* (1) a popular saying (found in many languages) that folly often results from the absence of a person in authority: *ist die Katz aus dem Haus, haben die Mäus'* ~ when the cat's away the mice will play. - (2) an impatient warning that omnipresence is not an attribute of man: *man [ich] kann nicht auf zwei Kirtagen tanzen* you [I] can't be in two places at once (*or*, ... dance at two weddings in one day) || euphem. *phr.* two instances in which the headword is a mere shield for something crude or awkward, the first implying the Goethean *Götzzitat* (corresponding to E "[he can] kiss my arse"), and the second referring to a woman's menstrual period: (1) *er kann mich in den ~ laden!* he can take me out on the town. - (2) *sie hat den* ~ the curse has struck again, she's having friends to stay (*or*, visitors).

Klạmm *f* -/-en *geol.* a deep narrow passage with steep rocky sides usu. made by a stream which runs through it *(Felsenschlucht [mit Wasserlauf])*: gorge, *NorBrE* ghyll [gɪl], *AmE also* canyon *or* canon; *wild zwängen sich die Wasser der Partnach durch die* ~ the torrents of the Partnach rush through the narrow mountain gorge.

Klạmpfn [-pfm] *f* -/- *dial.*, rarely **Klạmpfe** *f* -/-n **1.** *constr. (Klammereisen)* cramp(-iron), clamp. - **2.** *mus.* guitar *(Gitarre)*: tickle-box, *AmE also* belly fiddle, git-box, git-bucket.

Klạpperl *n* -s/-(n) [< obsolete *Klapp*, an echoic noun suggesting a quick and repetitive movement, each time accompanied by a short explosive sound, + *-erl*] *colloq.* **1.** *tech.* a simple mechanism, with a hammer-like object, that makes a repeated loud noise: (1) (a child's [etc.]) rattle; *einem Buziwackerl macht ein ~ die süßeste Musik, und die Eltern klettern dabei die Wände hoch* for toddlekins a rattle is the sweetest music ever, enough to drive parents up the wall. - (2) *R.C.* (an altar boy's) clapper; *am Karfreitag bleiben alle Kirchenglocken stumm - sie sind, so heißt es, „nach Rom geflogen" -, und auf den Altarstufen treten hölzerne ~n an die Stelle des Ministrantengeläuts* on Good Friday, all church bells remain silent - they are said to have "flown to Rome" -, and on the altar steps wooden clappers take over from the servers' sets of little bells. - **2.** *hum.* or *iron.* a garrulous person's tongue: clack, clacker, clapper, gabber; *ihr ~ geht* (or, *das ~ geht ihr) in einem fort* her tongue goes clackety-clack; *hör dir nur an, wie im Saal unten die ~n gehen!* just listen to the mass of clacking tongues in the hall below. - **3.** *garm.*, usu. *pl.* a light open shoe for summer wear, with a thick flat bottom (thus making for inevitably loud progress): (1) if made of wood, and with a leather band to hold it on the foot: clog; (2) if completely made from one piece of wood: clog, sabot; (3) if made all of rubber, and held on by the toes and loose at the back: *BrE* flip-flop, *AmE* thong. - **4.** *tech. (kleines [Metall-] Blättchen)* a small flat thin part of metal or other material that either hangs down to cover an opening (e.g., a keyhole), or that falls open on an electrical impulse (e.g., from the room number of a hotel switchboard): flap.

Kl̩etze *f* -/-n rare; = StandG for the next. - **Kl̩etzen** *f* -/- *dial. cul. (Dörrbirne)* dried pear.

Kl̩etzen...: **~bene** *m* -s/-e(n) *contp.* a dull person *(Langweiler)*, giving the appearance of being possessed of a dry and shrivelled mind: bore, *AmE also* droop goop, (cold) molasses *sg.* - **~brot** *n* -(e)s/-e *bak.* & *folklore* a type of bread containing dried fruit, esp. pears, plums, figs, apricots, and apples, and garnished with blanched almonds and raisins *(Früchtebrot)*: fruit loaf; *an Weihnachten stellt man das ~ auf den Tisch, das Überbleibsel altheidnischer Festbrote* at Christmas fruit bread is served, which is a relic of pagan ceremonial breads. - **~kopf** *m* -s/...köpfe *dial., contp.* = *Kletzenbene*↑.

Kl̩upperl *n* -s/-(n) *dial.* **1.** *tech.* a small wooden or plastic instrument for holding wet washed clothes on a clothesline to dry *(Wäscheklammer)*: *BrE* (clothes) peg, *AmE* (clothes)pin. → **2.** *pl.* only - one's fingers: divers, fives, muck-forks *(all three pl.)*; *mi' frierts an meine ~n* my fingers are like icicles, *or* ... are falling off me with the cold.

Kn̩ackwurst *f* -/...würste *comest. AmE* knockwurst, a short plump pork sausage, spiced and smoked.

Kni̲e... *colloq.*: **~schnackler** *m* -s/- [cp. *schnackeln*] *med.* knee-ache caused by walking downhill for a long time: sore knees, aching knees; *(den) ~ kriegen [haben]* to get [to have] sewing-machine leg; *nach dem Abstieg (vom Berg) hab ich einen richtigen ~* my knees just feel like jelly after walking down the mountain. - **~schwamm** *m* -(e)s, **~schwammerl** *n* -s/- **1.** = *Knieschnackler*. - **2.** numb legs due to a sudden shock: *ist es ein Wunder, wenn ich vor lauter Aufregung den Knieschwamm* (or, *Knieschwammerl) hab?* I'm not a bit surprised that my knees have gone all rubbery with excitement.

Knọ̈cherlsulz *f* -/-en *cul.* a pickled preparation made from pigs' feet, a beer-garden delicacy that goes well with fried potatoes: chopped pig's knuckles in brawn.

Knö̱del *m* -s/- **1.** *cul. (Kloß)* dumpling, shaped by hand (cp. *Nockerl 1*), the mainstay or at least strongly supporting feature of many a substantial Bavarian dinner, whether sweet or meaty; samplings are, from A to Z: *Aprikosen~* apricot dumpling; *Erdäpfel~* potato dumpling; *Fleisch~* meatball, *BrE also* faggot; *halbseidene ~* dumpling made of boiled potatoes and potato flour; *Leber~* liver dumpling; *Nieren~* tiny dumpling filled with minced kidney; *Semmel~* bread dumpling; *Servietten~* large bread dumpling tied in a napkin and boiled in saltwater; *Tiroler ~* bread dumpling with bits of bacon, ham, or smoked sausage, chopped herbs and the odd caraway seed; *Zwetschgen~* plum dumpling. - **2.** *fig.*, in *colloq. phr.* (1) in slight mockery, to a young boy who is not strong enough yet to perform a certain physical task: *da(zu) musst du noch mehr ~ essen!* you've got to eat dumplings (*AmE* ... eat your carrots) for strength! - (2) reproachfully, to one who speaks little or nothing: *hast du einen ~ im Mund* (or, coarsely dialectal, ... *im Mäul)?* has the cat got your tongue?, *AmE also* d' you have a bone in your throat? - (3) lump in one's throat, i.e. a feeling of pressure caused by emotion: *es ist mir kein Wort rausgekommen, ich hab einen ~ im Hals gehabt, und Tränen in den Augen* I couldn't get out a word, I had a lump in my throat, and there were tears in my eyes. - **3.** *colloq.*, slightly *contp.* silly person *(Dümmling)*: silly (billy *or* goose); *du bist ein ~, das hättest du ihm doch gleich sagen können!* you were a silly, you could have told him right away.

Knö̱del...: **~brot** *n* -(e)s *bak. (würfelig geschnittene Semmeln)* pre-cut white-roll cubes, for use in making bread dumplings. - **~friedhof** *m* -(e)s/...höfe *hum.* paunch, *hum.* pot-belly, corporation, bay window, bread *or* dinner basket; → *Gockerlfriedhof.*

kọppen, *dial.* **kọbbm** *v/i colloq.* **1.** to belch *(rülpsen)*: to burp, *AmE also* to backfire; *während der Mahlzeit zu ~ (so sagt man, boshaft witzelnd) sei eine*

Knödel

Ehrenbezeugung für den Gastgeber und für die Köchin ripping off (*or*, letting fly) a burp should be taken as a compliment to the host and to the cook, somebody's tongue-in-cheek claim has it. - **2.** to rise in anger and challenge to a fist fight *(aufbegehren)*: to square up; *möchst (du) ~?* (you) squaring up?, (you) spoiling for a fight?

Kọpperer *m* -s/- *colloq.* an eructation *(Rülpser)*: burp; *hat unser Dimpfl im Biergarten ein schönes Quantum stark kohlensäurehaltigen Gerstensafts inhaliert, verschafft er sich ganz natürlich mit ein paar ~n Luft; auf besonders gelungene Exemplare macht er seine Umwelt mit erhobenem Zeigefinger aufmerksam* in the beer garden, a liberal downing of very fizzy John Barleycorn invariably has our frothblower duly come up with a series of burps; if particularly successful, he raises a forefinger to make those around him acknowledge the feat.

Kọrndl... [dim. of *Korn* 'grain']: **~bauer** *m* -n/-n *agr., colloq.* (*Getreidebauer* [opp. *Hörndlbauer*↑]) grain (-growing) farmer, cereal grower, *BrE also* corn (-growing) farmer. - **~fresser** *m* -s/- *diet., hum.* or *contp.* vegetarian: cereal freak.

Kọtze *f* -/-n; more often, *colloq.* **Kọtzen** *f* -/- **1.** *(grobe Wolldecke)* thick woollen blanket. - **2.** *garm. (einteiliger Überwurf mit rundem Kopfloch)* poncho.

krạchledern *adj* [< the creaky sound given off by old leather trousers, resonantly stiff for long wear, when slapped by their proud wearer; note also the - by now obsolete - word *lederkrachen*, which describes the sound made when the crackling, i.e. the hard brown skin of cooked pork (a delicacy highly prized by Bavarian gourmets!) is broken] *colloq.* **1.** with reference to long or short nether garments, much favoured in Upper Bavaria: made of tough leather. → **2.** *fig.* (said to be) typifying the wearer of such regional garment, but also his way of life and his diction - (1) unsophisticated *(urwüchsig)*: homespun; *unser Gebirgstrachtenverein hat etwas dagegen, wenn man uns als ~e Gaudiburschen abtut* our society for the continued use of traditional Alpine costume refuses to be passed off as a bunch of peppy thigh-slappers; *die deftige, ~e Seite der bayerischen Liebe* the crude pungency of love among Bavarians. - (2) uncouth *(ungehobelt)*: unpolished; *es fällt einem Nichtbayern manchmal schwer, die ~e Ausdrucksweise der Einheimischen zu schlucken* a Bavarian's unpolished way of putting things is sometimes hard for an outsider to swallow. - **Krạchlederne** -n/-n *colloq.* **1.** *f* *(Lederhose*↓*)* leather shorts (*AmE also* pants). - **2.** *m* (1) *(Lederhosenträger)* leather-trousered man, *BrE* chap in leather shorts, *AmE* guy in leather pants; → (2) *(grobschlächtiger Mensch [vom Land]* uncouth (country) yokel, local yokel.

Kra̠mer *m* -s/- *obsolescent* **1.** *(Kleinhändler)* small shopkeeper, grocer. → **2.** (1) *gen. (Ladengeschäft)* small general store, grocer's; *beim ~* at the grocer's. - (2) *contp.* a nondescript grocery:

tatty little shop; *das ist ein ~ und nicht ein Kaufhaus - dass ich nicht lach'!* that's a tatty old general store, and at best an apology for a department store.

Krạmpf *m* -(e)s/- [actually, 'cramp', the sudden contraction of a muscle, which makes movement difficult] *dial.*, usu. said in disdain: **1.** something that should not be taken seriously: stuff and nonsense; *was die Leut da erzähln* (or *verzähln), ist ja ein ~* (or, *san ja ~)* it's all stuff and nonsense what the people are saying. - **2.** an unnecessary delay caused by a person's whim; *kimm scho(n), jetzt mach koane ~!* don't make any fuss (*or*, pull yourself together) now, get going.

krạmpfeln *vt/i* [< *krampfen* (now rare) 'to tighten the muscles - here, of one's hand - over an object, as if from a sudden cramp' + *-eln*] *colloq.* to filch (usu. something of small value): to swipe, *BrE also* to pinch; *da hat mir (doch) so ein Depp den Spitzer (ge)krampfelt!* (why,) some jerk's gone and swiped my pencil sharpener.

Krạmpfhenne *f* -/-n, usu. *dial.* **Krạmpfhenna** *f -/- contp.* a fashionable, wealthy, or society woman who talks a lot in a pretentious manner: *esp. AmE* (highfalutin) cackle-broad.

Kr<u>au</u>t *n* -s/- **1.** *bot.* cabbage (*~ anbauen* to grow cabbage); *Blau~ (Rotkohl)* red cabbage; *Sauer~* sauerkraut, sourcrout, sourkrout; *Weiß~ (Weißkohl)* white cabbage; *ein kleines ~ (Rübenkraut)* beet (*or* turnip) tops *pl.* (*or* greens *pl.*). - **2.** *colloq. phr.* (1) expressing a very low opinion of an idea, suggestion, effort, etc. which, if carried out, will hardly bring about an improvement of the lamentable status quo: *das macht das ~ auch nicht fett!* that won't help matters any, that is much of a muchness. - (2) a more or less grim resolution to take deep offence, or indeed to have no more contact, social, business, or otherwise, with a person: *einmal hätte sie mit ihrer Gschaftlhuberei meinen Eltern bald das ~ ausgeschüttet* her fussiness just about made my parents reach a parting of the ways with her one day; *der hat mir das ~ ausgeschüttet!* his name is Mud with me!, *AmE also* he's on my ditch list (*or*, stink-list)! - (3) an exemplification, by humorous hyperbole, of frugal living: *besser eine Laus aufm ~ als (wie) gar kein Fleisch* better a bone in the faraway hills than nothing to gnaw on at all.

Kr<u>au</u>t...: **~acker** *m* -s/...äcker *agr.* field of cabbages, cabbage field. - **~salat** *m* -(e)s/pl. rare: -e *cul.* dressed shredded cabbage, cabbage salad, coleslaw. -

Krautstampfer

~scheuche *f* -/-n, *dial.* **~scheuch** *f* -/-n or **~scheuchn** *f* -/- **1.** *agr.* an object, usu. the figure of a man in old clothes, set up to frighten birds away from a cabbage crop: scarecrow, *AmE also* bird scarer (in a cabbage field). → **2.** *contp.* an ugly or unpleasant woman, esp. one who is old: hag, harridan. **~stampfer** *m* -s/- **1.** *agr.* a heavy tool for pounding white cabbage, duly sliced and salted, in a tub or barrel to make sauerkraut: cabbage pounder (*or* ram, *or* tamper). → **2.** usu. pl. *contp.* a woman's ungainly fat legs: tree trunks, stumps, pile drivers, keg-legs, elephant legs, *AmE also* ham hocks; *schau dir (nur) die ~ an, die die hat!* (just) look at her pair of (great big) elephant hooves! - **~wickerl** *n* -s/-(n) *cul. (Weißkohlroulade)* "cabbage roll", stuffed cabbage, i.e. minced (*AmE* chopped) meat and onions wrapped in savoy or white-cabbage leaves, gently browned and stewed.

Kraxe *f* -/-n, much more common in its dial. form, **Kraxn** *f* -/- **1.** (a) a wooden framework for supporting a porter's bags and boxes, a pedlar (*AmE* peddler)'s wares, a grapepicker's basket, etc. *([Rücken-] Traggestell)*: carrying-frame. - (b) a porter's etc. load to be strapped onto the carrying-frame: pack, basket etc. (to be) carried on the back. - **2.** usu. **lange** ~ *iron.* (a) a tall, lanky person: beanstalk, broomstick, clothes pole, long drink (of water); (b) a nickname for such a person, often used in direct address, *also*: Bonylegs, Longlegs *sg.* - **3.** *colloq.*, often *hum.* or *iron.* a dilapidated vehicle: old crock, boneshaker, rattletrap, jalopy. - **4.** *contp.* a meaningless written marking: scribble, hen scratch; *mit solchen ~n tust du dich fei schwer* my, such scribbles are (*or*, such a scrawl is) indeed hard to make out.

Kraxelei, Kraxlerei *f* -/- *mount., colloq. ([langwieriges] Klettern [in den Bergen])* climbing, climb; *mein Bergfex hat grad seine ~ im Schädel* my mountain freak can think of nothing but his climbing; *mei, das war dir fei eine ~ das letzte Stück bis zum Gipfelkreuz* gee, that was some climb the last stretch to the summit cross, I can tell you.

kraxeln *v/i colloq. (klettern)* **1.** *mount.* to climb (using both the feet and hands); *am Wochenende kraxelt er gern in den Bergen* he likes to do a bit of climbing in the mountains at the weekend. - **2.** *mount.* to climb with difficulty: to slog; *wir sind geschlagene fünf Stunden ge-*

kraxeln

kraxelt, bis wir endlich oben waren we slogged up the mountain for three unhallowed hours until we got to the top at last. - **3.** to climb about in an undisciplined way: to clamber, to crawl; *meine Kinderliebe sinkt in den Keller, wenn ich sehe, wie deine Fratzen über meine neuen Möbel* ~ my love of children is chilled to the core at the sight of your brats clambering about over my new furniture.

Krạxenträger, much more common in a dial. form, such as **Krạxntrager** or **-droga** *m* -s/- **1.** *hist., com.* one who carries his merchandise from place to place on a frame strapped to his back *(Hausierer)*: pedlar (*AmE* peddler) carrying his wares on his back. - **2.** *mount.* a man taking provisions and other supplies on his carrying-frame to high-lying shelter huts and dairies *(Lastenträger)*: porter, bearer; *bedächtig und gleichmäßig geht's bergan - schau nur unserm ~ zu, wie der das macht!* it's the heavy, steady tread that makes you gain heights - just watch our porter's way of walking!

Krạxler *m* -s/- *mount., colloq. (Bergsteiger)* mountaineer, (mountain) climber; *ein begeisterter* ~ a mountain freak. - **Kraxlerei** *f* -/-en *colloq.* = *Kraxelei.*

Kren *m* -(e)s *bot., NorBavG (Meerrettich)* horse-radish; *wir haben Frankfurter mit ~ gehabt* (or *gegessen)* we had frankfurters and horse-radish.

Kren...: ~fleisch *n* -(e)s *cul.* fat boiled beef and (*or* with) horse-radish. - **~weiberl** *n* -s/- *colloq.* a female hawker of horse-radish: horse-radish girl.

Kroatzbeer *f* -/-n; *StandG,* rare, **Krạtzbeere** *f* -/-n [first el., the stem form of StandG *kratzen* 'to scratch,' < the prickly armour of the wild bush bearing that fruit] *bot. dial. (Brombeere)* blackberry, bramble. - **Kroatzbeerschnaps** *m* -es/...schnäpse *bev.* blackberry brandy. - **Kroatzbeerstaudn** *f* -/- *bot. dial. (Brombeerbusch)* bramble *or* blackberry bush.

krowotisch, krawọttisch *adv* [a *dial.* corruption of *kroatisch* 'Croat', 'Croatian' - a name encapsulating reminiscences of acts of violence long past, committed by Croatian constabulary in northern Bavaria during the War of the Austrian Succession, 1742-45] *dial.* by sheer force, energetically - as in the lusty invitation to resolute physical action, either jointly or by the speaker only, say when an unwieldy piece of furniture is to be lifted and moved: *(iatz) pack ma's ~ o!* it's brutal strength that does it - here we go (*or*, now or never)!

Kụchel, often *dial.* **Küachl**, **Kiachl** *n* -s/-(n) *bak.* a light cake sporting a bulging roundness but thin in the middle, cooked in hot fat and served with a sprinkling of powder sugar - a staple delicacy at rural festivities: Bavarian doughnut.

Kuh *f* -/Kühe, *dial.* **Kua**, **Kou** *f* -/Küa, Kia *zo., agr.* cow || *colloq. phr.* **1.** similes - (1) said by one unexpectedly encountering Stygian darkness (an experience made, we know, by Tom Thumb *[Däumling]* in the fairy tale after having been swallowed by a black cow): *da is 's finster* (or *dunkel) wie in einer ~* it's as dark (in here) as the inside of a cow (*sometimes with the hum. extension ...*, tail down and eyes shut), *BrE also ...* as the Black Hole of Calcutta. - (2) said of one completely bewildered: *dastehen wie die ~ vorm Scheunentor* to be surprised as a calf looking at a new gate. - (3) *contp.*, hitting out at mental inertia and ignorance: *von Kunst (usw.) so wenig Ahnung haben wie die ~ vom Kalender (und der Ochs vom Sonntag)* not to know one's bum from one's elbow about art (etc.). - (4) adversely commenting on a person's clumsiness: *sich anstellen wie eine ~ beim Mistbreiten* (or *Schlittenfahren)* to be as awkward as a cow with a musket (*or* ... a cow on crutches, *or* ... a cow on skates). - **2.** proverbs - (1) a warning about the consequences of belated action: *mach nicht das Tor zu, wenn die ~ schon aus dem Stall ist!* it is too late to lock the stable when the horse has been stolen, it's no use shutting the stable door after the horse has bolted. - (2) a reminder that there are circumstances under which also very noticeable differences tend to be evened out: *bei (*or *in der) Nacht sind alle Kühe schwarz* all cats are alike grey in the night.

Kuh beim Schlittenfahren

Kụrbe *f* -/-n, *dial.* **Kụrben**, **Kụrm** (through assimilation), **Kịrm** (through unrounding) *f* -/- *(Flechtkorb)* (wickerwork) basket.

L

la̲bern *v/i contp.* to talk continuously in a low dull voice: to drone on, *BrE also* to rabbit on; *das is' fei einer, der über seine Probleme labert und kein End findet* he is a right one to drone on and on about his problems.

lạck *adj* slightly *contp.* **1.** of beer: *(abgestanden, schal)* stale, flat; *eine Mass Bier, die länger herumsteht, schmeckt ~* a mug of beer left standing for some time tastes flat. - **2.** of an unmarried woman who is no longer young: old-maidish; *sie schmeckt ~* she's no spring chicken.

Lạckl, less often **Lạckel** *m* -s/- *colloq.* **1.** *contp.* a man who uses his strength or power to hurt or frighten other people *(aggressiver Mensch)*: bully; *ein grober ~* a rough customer, *AmE also* a roughneck. - **2.** a large heavy male *(Klotz)*: hulk, man mountain; *ein ~ von einem*

Mann a hulk (*if used appreciatively*, a hunk) of a man, *AmE also* a big bundle *or* package. - **3.** *contp.* a stupid awkward man or boy: oaf.

Lahmarsch *m* -(e)s/...ärsche [in this figure of speech, known as *pars pro toto* (or *synecdoche*), some part deputizes for the whole: a man without impetus is seemingly incapable of getting up from his comfortable sitting position] *vulg.*, always *contp.* a person who is intellectually, emotionally, or aesthetically boring, tedious, tiring, or colourless: *BrE* lame arse, *AmE* lame ass, drag, slack ass. - **~ig** *adj vulg.*, always *contp.* boring (in all the above shades of meaning): *BrE* lame-arsed, *AmE* lame-assed, slack-assed.

Lalle *m* -/- [an onomatopoeic noun, supported by *lallen*, the StandG verb form, to describe someone who speaks indistinctly since allowing his tongue to hang loose - which is exactly what the related E *to loll* must have once meant] *dial.* stupid person *(Trottel)*: dolt, *AmE also* tommy noddy.

Laugen... *bak.*: **~brezen** *f* -/- (hardly ever **~breze** *f* -/-n or **~brezel** *f* -/-n [see *Brezen*]) "brine-treated pretzel", a shiny brown pretzel dipped in a solution of soda ash and sprinkled with fine salt before baking; *~ kann ich zum Bier nur wärmstens empfehlen, sie müssen allerdings knirschfrisch sein* I warmly recommend salt pretzels with beer, but only if they are crackle-fresh.

Lauschlappen *n* -s/usu. pl.: - *anat., hum.* or *contp.* a person's ears: ear-flaps, listeners, tabs, *AmE also* flappers, wattles

Lauschlappen

|| a warning and a comment: *halt deine ~ offen!* keep your ear-flaps open!; *der hat seine ~ runter* he's got cloth-ears, *AmE also* ... flannel *or* rubber ears.

Leber... *gastr.*: **~käs**, *dial.* **~kas** [-kɑ:s] *m* -es/pl. rare: -e, **~käse** (the StandG form, which is very rare) *m* -s [first el., < *Laib* 'loaf' (because it is offered for sale in long cube-like loaves at butchers' and grocers' shops)] meat loaf; *der ~ besteht aus durchgedrehtem Rind- und Schweinefleisch, sogenanntem Brät* a meat loaf consists of finely ground beef and pork, or what is known as 'sausage meat' || *fig.* in a piece of abusive speech imputing utter stupidity: *dem hat man ja das Hirn raus- und ein Stück warmen ~ hineinoperiert!* they must have gouged his brains out and filled the cavity with blubber (*or*, ... with fat [cheese, mush, sawdust])! - ~**knödel** *m* -s/- liver dumpling, made of minced (*AmE* ground) liver, bread and onions, cooked and served in soup; *~suppe f* -/-n liver-dumpling soup.

Lederhose *f* -/-n an article of Bavarian men's wear: "lederhosen" **1.** if leaving the knees free *(Kurze)*: leather shorts. - **2.** if reaching below the knees *(Bundhose)*: *BrE also* leather breeches, *AmE also* knee pants.

Leich *f* -/-en *colloq.* **1.** (dead) body, corpse. - **2.** *dial. also* **Leicht** *(Begräbnis)* burial, funeral; *(Trauerzug)* funeral procession: (1) *auf die ~ gehen* to go to the funeral; *gehst du (mit) auf die (*or, *mit der) ~?* will you be at the funeral?; *wie viel Leut sind bei der ~ gewesen?* how many folks were at the burial? || with reference to Old Bavarian ceremonial obsequies, for which people have often taken their ghoulish delight since the Biedermeier Age: *eine schöne ~* a lovely funeral; *er hat eine schöne ~ gehabt* he had a lavish funeral, *AmE also* ... a fine send-off. (2) *fig.* & *prov.*: *der Herr Geheimrat hat ein Gesicht gemacht, als wenn er mit einer ~ geht* *the Privy Councillor pulled a face as though he were one of the chief mourners at a funeral || pleasing circumstances can work wonders to a strained atmosphere: *bei einer schönen ~ kann man sich sogar übers Sterben unterhalten* *a lavish funeral is as fine a setting as any to talk about dying || a warning that difficulties tend to multiply, or a dryly humorous observation that somebody trying to swat flies, ants, etc. is duly faced with an even increasing number of the tribe on the scene: *eine bringst du um und hundert kommen auf die ~* kill one fly [ant, etc.] and ten others come to the funeral.

Leichtrunk *m* -(e)s/-e *folklore (Umtrunk nach einer Beerdigung)* funeral social (with drinks all round).

letschert; less often **lätschert** *adj colloq.*, always with a pejorative connotation **1.** said of a person lacking in energy *(kraftlos)*: feckless, listless, lackadaisical; *der ~e Heini, der kriegt ja nie einen richtigen Posten!* that feckless fellow, he'll never land a decent job. - **2.** said of a person's expressionless face *(ausdruckslos)*: dull, *AmE also* dead-pan. - **3.** said of vegetables, etc. without sufficient taste to be pleasing *(nach nichts schmeckend)*: insipid; *mei, die gelben Rüben sind heut aber ~, Mama!* my, the carrots are a tasteless lot today, mum. - **4.** said of meat, sausages, etc. lacking firmness *(fade)*: flabby, flaccid; *die Weißwurst darf das Zwölfuhrläuten nicht hören, sonst wird sie ~* a white sausage is bound to go flabby if it lives long enough to hear the noonhour bell strike. - **5.** said of enervating air *(schlapp [machend])*: soft and anything but bracing; *so eine ~e Luft!* that air makes me all go limp!

Loawidoag [-ɔʌ-] *m* -s/-(e) *dial. ling.* the keyword [< StandG *Laibchenteig m* 'dough to make round bread rolls from'] of a popular pronunciation test for non-Bavarians, capitalizing on the double occurrence of a diphthong largely unfamiliar beyond the white-and-blue pale (cp. *Oachkatzlschwoaf*) - the insider's quiet little triumph of easily wrapping his tongue round those vowels, and thus making himself "readily understood by everybody", is also reflected in a *Schnadahüpfl*:

Wannst halt „Loawidoag" sagst,
woaß glei jeda, was d' magst;
„Brötchenteig", kruzifix!,
sagt fei unsaoans nix.

"Loawidoag" is well kent,
And folks know what is meant;
"Brötchenteig", though, oh hell,
Doesn't ring any bell.

Luller *m* -s/- [< *lullen*, an imitative formation, in regional use meaning 'to suck'] **1.** a rubber teat for sucking, put in a baby's mouth to keep it quiet: *BrE* dummy (*NorBrE* & *IrE also* dumb-teat, soother), *AmE* pacifier. - **2.** the mouthpiece of a nursing bottle: *BrE* teat, *AmE* nipple.

Lüngerl *n* -s/-(n) [dim. of *Lunge* 'lung'] *gastr.* also *[das] Saure ~* a typical mid-morning snack at an inn, and once a favourite entrée at traditional peasant weddings and funerals, hence also known as **Voressen**: calf's lungs *pl.* (*or* lights *pl.*) and heart, boiled in a stock of allspice, pot-herbs, one bay leaf, vinegar, and then cut into a light roux [ru:], and stock poured on, though boiling continues (to the addition of a little sugar and pepper and sour cream for seasoning); served with bread dumplings, the dish is a gourmet's delicacy, and often a full meal in its own right.

M

Magen *m* -s/- or Mägen - in a crudely *hum. phr.* expressing intense hunger: *mir hängt der ~ schon bis zu den Kniekehlen* (I'm so empty) I can feel my (*or* me) backbone touching my (*or* me) belly button, *NorBrE* my stomach thinks that my throat is cut, I'm hungered to the hole of the heart, *ScotE* ma belly's like to cut ma throat. - **~tratzer** *m* -s/- [second el., < *tratzen*↓, here: 'to tease' or, alternatively, 'to whet s.o.'s appetite'] *colloq.* **1.** often *contp.* a ridiculously small amount of food or drink: smidgin, smidgen; *das ist alles? das ist ja grad ein ~!* is that everything? why, that wouldn't keep a sparrow alive. - **~tratzerl** *n* -s/-(n) [a dim. of the former] *colloq.* **1.** *hum.* used in a friendly invitation to have a small amount of food or drink before a meal, just to increase the desire for the main affair: wee appetizer. - **2.** rare, slightly *contp.* = *Magentratzer*.

Maibaum *m* -(e)s/...bäume *folklore* maypole, a tall pole in an open place and symbol of reawakened life, richly decorated with wreaths and ribbons and emblems of the local trades; *Tanz um den ~* maypole dance. - **~aufstellen** *n*

-s setting up the maypole (usu. on the market-square). - **~feier** *f* -/-n on May 1: May Day Celebration, with a procession and dances round the maypole. - **~klettern**, *dial.* **~krax(e)ln** *n* -s climbing the maypole, a competitive event among village youths on May Day. - **~stehlen** *n* -s robbing the maypole, one of the many expressions of village rivalry practised by youths one night in May; if successful, the trophy must be bought back with a heavy ransom of beer.

Mạndl, less often **Mạnndl** *n* -s/-(n) [< *Mann* 'man' + *-l*, with intrusive *d* (as in *Hendl*↑ 'chicken' < *Henne*) - structurally corresponding to the NorG dim. form *Männchen*] *colloq.* **1.** (1) slightly *iron.* or *contp.* — an adult male, slight, of middling or small size, often timid and not healthy-looking: (a) featherweight, half-pint, half portion, *AmE also* minus quantity, snip of a person; (b) if married: apology for a husband. - (2) without such pejorative connotations, for pure sex distinction (thus referring to human beings as well as to animals [opp.: *Weibl* 'female']): male; *es ist ein ~* it's a he || *phr.* as an expression of utter bewilderment, excitement or disappointment: *jetzt weiß ich's nimmer - bin ich ein ~ oder ein Weibl?* I'm all in a dither now - am I on my head or on my heels? (*or*, ... - am I coming or going?) - **2.** *zo.* said of hares, rabbits, marmots, and dogs: sit-up position (with front legs raised, paws at an angle); *ein ~ machen* to sit at attention. - **3.** *agr.*, now somewhat obs. — a harvesting feature, observed immediately after cutting the grain *(auf dem Feld zum Trocknen aufgestellte Getreidegarben)*: stook [-u:-], *NorBrE also* hattock, stack stowk [-ɔ:-], [-əʊ-], i.e. several sheaves stood against each other like a pyramid, to facilitate further drying in the harvest field before removal to the farmstead; *acht bis zehn Garben gehen auf ein ~* eight or ten standers (= standing sheaves) make up a stook.

Mạnner... *dial.* [< the unumlauted plural form of *Mann*: StandG *Männer*]: **~leut** *pl.* men in general; male

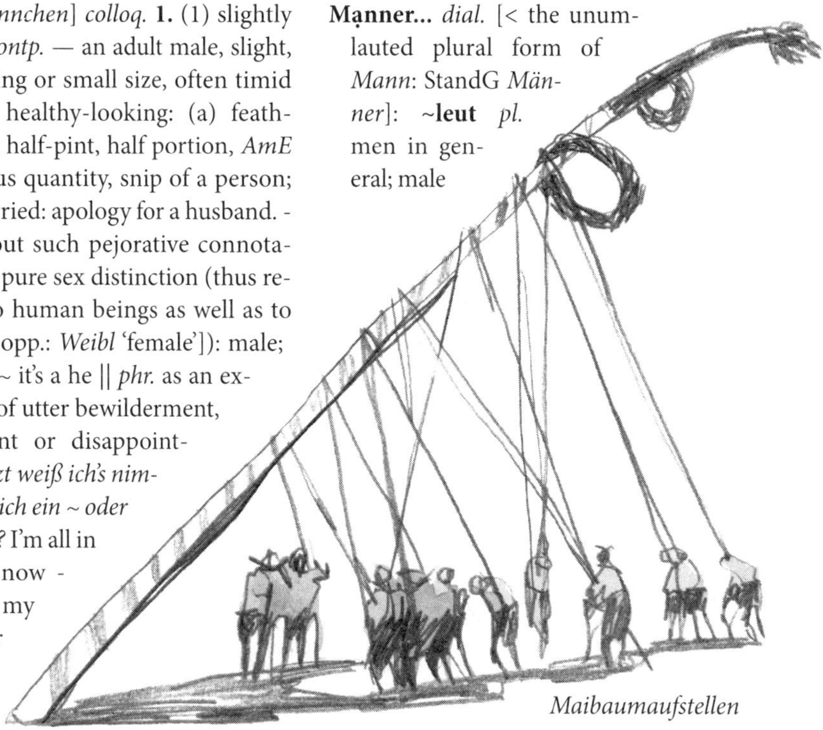

Maibaumaufstellen

members of the family: menfolk *pl.; wenn es darauf ankommt, helfen ja doch alle ~ zusammen* when it matters, menfolk are sure to stick together; *was, heute allein? wo sind denn deine ~?* why, you're by yourself today? where are all your menfolk? - **~seite** *f* - [opp. *Weiberseite*] **1.** *eccles.* the right-hand section in a country church (when looking down the nave towards the altar), indicative of a seating arrangement according to the sexes, now no longer strictly adhered to: men's side, epistle-side. - **2.** *bak.* the bulgy side of a bread loaf: top crust.

Mạnnsbild *n* -(e)s/-er *colloq.*, often *emot.* a male person: feller, *AmE also* guy; *ein gestandenes* or *kerniges* ~ a he-man; *BrE also* a big strapping chap, *AmE also* a regular guy; *gestandene ~er können nicht immer ein und dieselbe Ansicht zu allen Fragen haben* he-blooded fellers surely can't see eye to eye with one another on all matters all the time; *sie weiß, wie sie mit ihren ~ern umzugehen hat* she knows how to cope with (*or* handle) her menfolk (*AmE also* menfolks); *die ~er können mich alle gern haben!* stuff those men, one and all!

Märchen...: **~könig** *m* -s/-e *sobr.* "Fairy-Tale King," "Dream King," epithets for King Ludwig II of Bavaria (1864-86), who often retired into a world of his own, for his eyes to feast on castle splendour, and his ears in raptures over Wagner's music. - **~schloss** *n* ...schlosses/...schlösser *sobr.* fantasy castle, a frequent epithet for Neuschwanstein, but also for Herrenchiemsee, both of them built at the bidding of King Ludwig II.

Maria und Josef *interj* a R.C., usu. female, person's shout of unpleasant surprise or even horror (as if feeling the need, at that moment, to invoke divine assistance): Holy Mary and Jesus (*or*, ... and Joseph)!; *ja, ~, wie schaust denn du aus! Deine Kleider sind ja ganz verdreckt!* Holy Mary and Jesus, what a sight you are, with muck all over your clothes!

Mạss *f* -/Masse (after numerical data: - [e.g. zwei Mass]; *dial.* pl. also: Massen) the customary term used when handling beer **1.** one litre (*BrE* = [somewhat less than] two pints, *or* one quart [cp. *Quartl*↓]) of beer; *eine ~ trinken* to have a large beer; *gehen wir eine ~ stemmen!*

zünftige Kellnerin

let's be off and tip a large beer! || a conciliatory move, yet one with a selfish afterthought: *du hast schon ganz Recht; und wer Recht hat, der zahlt eine ~* you're quite right as it is; and the one who is right (*or*, whoever is right) has to buy me (*or*, treat me to) a beer. → *Radlermass.* - **2.** the customary nominal measure for Bavarian habitués when ordering their beer in a pub - in English-speaking countries, rather: pint (= 0.568 l); *keiner von den Spezln da möchte am Abend auf seine ~ verzichten* there's none of those lads here would like to miss their nightly pint. - **3.** = *Masskrug*↓; *eine zünftige Kellnerin kommt mit fünf bis sechs ~ Bier in jeder Hand daher* a proper barmaid comes along swinging five or six steins of beer in each hand; *er hat einen tiefen Schluck aus seiner ~ gemacht* he took a deep draught from his mug (of beer); *die Fertigkeit, eine ganze ~ Bier ohne Absetzen auszutrinken* the skill of drinking (*or*, draining) an entire mug of beer without taking a pause for breath (*or*, without taking it from the lips).

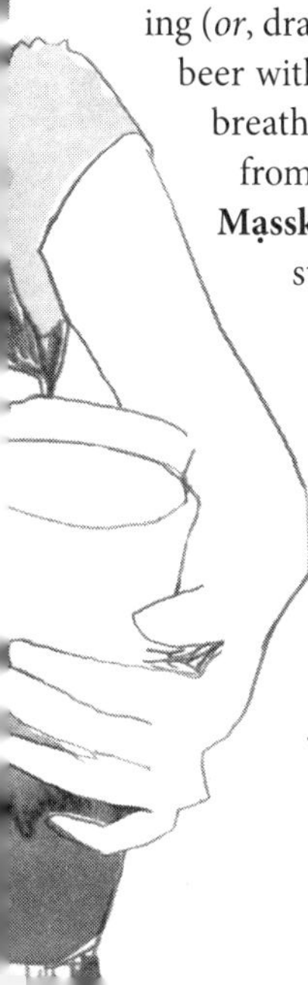

Mạsskrug *m* -(e)s/...krüge stoneware (*or* earthenware) mug, - if with a lid: *BrE* tankard, *AmE* stein -, commonly holding about a quart of beer || *phr.*: *er hat den ~ genommen und auf einen Zug geleert* he took the mug and drained it at one gulp; *j-m einen ~ am Schädel zerschlagen* to break a beer mug over s.o.'s head; *er ist so klein, dass man ihn in einen ~ hineinstecken könnte* he's so small you could hold him in the palm of your hand (*or*, ... you could put him in your pocket) || a *prov.* warning against Demon Drink (with *BavG* and *IrE*, as it were, "comparing notes"): *wo der ~ übergeht, (da) bleibt der Verstand stehen* thirst is a shameless disease.

Maul..., *dial.* **Mai...** 'mouth': **~tasche** *f* -/usu. pl.: -n, *dial.* **~taschn** *f* -/- *cul.* a Franconian delicacy, each piece of which is made up of two thin squares of noodle dough, with spinach and grated cheese (or other fillings) in between, the edges "sealed" with egg-white, the whole then boiled in salt water and appropriately garnished: pasta ['pæstə] square. - **~trommel** *f* -/-n *mus.* a small Alpine musical instrument held between the teeth and played by striking a piece of metal with one finger *(Brummeisen)*: Jews'-harp, Jew's-harp, Jews' (*or* Jew's) trump, *less often* guimbard.

mäuserlstad *pred. adj* [first el., dim. of *Maus*, '(sweet) little mouse'; second el., → *stad*] *colloq.* of persons *(mäuschenstill)* (as) quiet as a mouse; *die Klasse ist ~ gewesen* there was a dead silence (*or*, there wasn't a murmur) in the classroom, it was so quiet in the classroom (that) you could have heard a pin drop.

Mẹtte *f* -/-n, *dial.* **Mẹtten** and, by sineresis, **Mẹttn** *f* -/- **1.** *R.C.* midnight mass (*or* vespers *sg.*), esp. the one following Christmas Eve. - **2.** *R.C.* & *folklore*, also

Pumpermette(n) a church service held in Holy Week, initiated by churchgoers who made clanging noises and beat drums (cp. *pumpern*↓) to voice their bitterness against the betrayal by Judas Iscariot. -**3.** *fig.*, often *dial.* obstreperous noise: hullabaloo; *macht's koa so a ~!* stop making such a racket (*or*, ... kicking up such a row [raʊ])!

Mịlli *f* - *dial.* *(Milch)* milk; *eine ~* some milk. - **~bauer** *m* -n/-n **1.** (rich) dairy farmer; → **2.** *hist.* *~ mit der Ziehharmonikahosen* "Lord of the Dairy Manor with the crumpled trousers," the nickname for King Ludwig III of Bavaria, 1912-18, which originated from the fact that he was an agricultural expert, of rustic manners and appearance, and supplied the Capital with milk from his Wittelsbachian estate at Leutstetten, NNE of Starnberg.

Mịnga, conventionally spelt **Mịnka** *n* -s (rare) *place-name* a *dial.*, and often *hum.*, form of endearment for the Bavarian capital, *München*: (good old) Munich; *muaßt d' wieda af ~* (or, *wieda a ~ nau)?* up to Town again?

mi̱r san mi̱r [ˈmiːə san ˈmiːə] *dial. phr.* [< StandG *wir sind wir*: on the dialect pronunciation of that personal pronoun (always denoting the *nominative* of the first person *plural*, never the dative of the first person singular!), the lips form a closure, [m-], strengthening the body of the word on which the emphasis falls; a parallel instance in English would be the oblique pronominal form *me* (felt to sound more adequate than the consonantless diphthong *I*) in the common colloquial interjection, *it's me!*, G 'ich bin's!'] **1.** *interj* a truculent assertion of self-esteem uttered by a clique, e.g. a group of drinking cronies to snub others suspected of wishing to sit down at their table - an attitude of verbal rejection that might well lead to spluttered tongue-lashings like *Do hocka de do, de allawei do hocka!* 'There's for them that's always sits there!' (→ *Stammtisch 1*). - **2.** *attrib.* used as an adjunct before an abstract noun in order to describe rather than actually verbalize a group of people's defiant self-assertion: *ihre ~-~-~-Haltung* or *Mentalität* their "we-are-as-we-are-and-so-shall-we-be" attitude *or* mentality.

Mọrds... an initial morpheme in nominal compounds, meaning '(unusually)

Minga

great', in the senses 'big', 'grand' or 'grave', *colloq.*: **~gaudi** *f* - [see *Gaudi 1*] hilarious fun; *bei unsrem Klassentreffen gestern Abend hat's eine ~ gegeben* we had a whale of a time at our class reunion last night. - **~radi** *m* -(s)/-(s) **1.** *bot.* a white vegetable, *Raphanus sativus*, if of the uncommon size of a turnip (cp. *Radi 1*): giant *or* king-size radish. - **2.** *fig.* a sharp reprimand: good dressing-down, proper telling-off; *die Lehrerin hat uns einen ~ gehalten, weil wir wieder zu spät gekommen sind* the teacher gave us a sound tongue-lashing for being late again. - **~schädelweh** *n* -s *med.* violent headache: splitting *or* blazing headache.

Mụckser *m* -s/pl. rare: - [by sound imitation; basically related to G *muhen* and E *to moo*] *colloq.* a soft low continuous sound of half-suppressed anguish or protest: murmur, mumble; *ohne einen ~* without a murmur || a stern warning for a child to keep quiet: *ich mag jetzt keinen ~ mehr hören!* I don't want to hear another squeak (*ScotE also* cheep) out of you!

Mụffelkopf *m* -(e)s/...köpfe *colloq.* = *Grantler*↑. - **mụffeln** *v/i colloq.* to smell unventilated *(abgestanden riechen); es muffelt in dem Zimmer, weil die Fenster schon wochenlang bummfest zu sind* it smells very musty in this room (*or*, this room smells very musty) because the windows have been shut tight and fast for weeks. - **mụfflig**; with a dial. ending, also **mụfflert** *colloq. adj* said of a room, box, clothes, old manuscripts, books etc. marked by an unpleasant smell as a result of having been shut up for a long time, esp. when not quite dry: musty, fusty, stuffy.

Mu̲hackl, less often **Mu̲hachl** *m* -s/- [< *Muh* 'moo,' the long, loud sound a cow or ox makes + *Hachl, Hackl n* 'flax-comb,' 'flax-hackle'] *dial.* **1.** a rough and stupid person, usu. male: lout, *AmE sl. also* (big) lug, dumb-cluck, dumb-clunk. - **2.** a person awkward in movement or action: clumsy oaf, *BrE also* clumsy clot, *AmE also* lumbering ox, stumblebum; *du ~, (du) hast mir jetzt den Kaffee ausgeschüttet!* you clumsy oaf, you've knocked over my coffee.

Mü̲hlhiasl *m* -s [first el., < *Mühle* 'mill,' since the bearer of the nickname, it is believed, was once employed as a monastic miller by the Praemonstratensians of Windberg; second el., a dim. of *Mathias* 'Matthew'] *hist. folklore* "Matt of the Mill," a secondary name for (scholars incline to think) Matthias Lang, Apoig nr. Hunderdorf 1753-1806 Rabenstein nr. Zwiesel, whose gloomy prognostications about this world going to rack and ruin have earned him the sobriquet *Waldprophet* 'Forest Prophet'; interestingly, for instance, his secondsightedness foresaw the advent of the railway when he warned his countrymen against "an iron dog barking its way through the forest."

Mụ̈nchner Kịndl *n* -s *colloq.* "Little Child (*or*, Kid) of Munich" **1.** *her.* the armorial device chosen by the Municipality of the Bavarian capital - a child clad in an ecclesiastical garment roughly resembling a monk's habit, his arms raised as in blessing; the figure recalls the first settlement in the area of Benedictines from the Tegernsee, who became powerful under Reinald of Schäftlarn, a dwarf monk, about the year 1100, but it may also symbolize the *Christkindl*↑, in this version probably holding in his hands a Bible and the keys of St Peter. - **2.** *hum.* a native of Munich, often an attractive female: Munich lassie [lad]; *mit Ingeborg Hallstein war ein ~ zur Primadonna geworden* Ingeborg Hallstein, the First Lady of the Munich Opera, was a local lassie who has made good.

Mụskelschmalz *n* -es [a standardizing approximation to dialectal *Irxenschmalz*↑] *hum. colloq.* = *Irxenschmalz; da musst du schon mit beiden Händen zupacken, und wie! - ohne das nötige ~ geht da nichts* you've got to grab things with both your hands, and how! - nothing doing without a good bit of elbow grease.

N

Nạchbar *m* -n (*or, rarely,* -s) /-n, **Nạchbarin** *f* -/-nen || *colloq. interj* an Old Bavarian's easy-going, often broadly vernacular, way of addressing a person he happens to find himself together with, say, on a bench at a beer festival or during a bus ride: *Herr Nachbar* good sir; less often: *Frau Nachbarin* dear ma'am; *könnten S' a bisserl umeruckn, Herr Nachbar, dass ma uns aa hi(n)hockn können?* would you mind edging over a bit, good sir, so that we might park our anatomies as well?

Nạcht... *colloq.*: ~**haferl** *n* -s/-(n) *(Nachttopf)* = *Potschamberl*↓. - ~**licht** *n* -(e)s/-er **1.** *(Nachtmensch)* a person who likes to stay awake most of the night to read, work, etc.: night bird, (night) owl, stay-up. - **2.** *(Nachtschwärmer)* a person who spends the night in enjoyment: bird of the night, night-lifer, *BrE also* stop-out, *AmE also* stay(er)-out(er), sundodger; *er ist ein ~* he makes a night of it, *AmE also* he's a dirty stay-out.

Nạcka [short for dial. *nackert* 'naked', 'in the nude'] ...: ~**bäzi**, ~**bezi** *n* -s/- [second el., a nursery word for 'little lamb'. - ~**frosch** *m* -(e)s/...frösche *hum. colloq.* a young child skipping about, etc. "with no more clothes on than a frog" *(Nackedei)*: little bare monkey.

nạckert or **nạckat** ['nɔkat] *adj, dial.* [< StandG *nackt* 'naked'] *colloq.* & *phr.* **1.** *comest.* *~e Bratwurst*, or simply *≈e*, also known as *Gschwollene* or *Wollwurst* skinless frying sausage (made from finely ground calf's meat *[Kalbsbrät]*); *beim Zubereiten werden die ~en Bratwürste kurz in Milch gewendet und in der Pfanne abgebräunt, dazu passt dann ein Kartoffelsalat* in processing, the skinless sausages are briefly dipped in milk and browned in the pan; the customary side dish is potato salad. - **2.** an old simile (yet still well-winged) harking back to past centuries when schoolmasters, often scoffed at as *Gmoafresser*↑, ranked desperately low on the prestige and income scale: *mi friert wiar an ~n Schuilehra* I'm frozen to the marrow. - **3.** a *prov.* wisdom, according to which dire indigence acts as a perfect safeguard against being made a victim of theft or robbery: *einem ~n Mann kann man nicht in die Taschen greifen* (or, ... *nichts aus den Taschen ziehen)* you cannot get feathers off a frog.

nạrrisch *dial.* [< StandG *närrisch*] **1.** *adj*, also **nạsch** mad, foolish *(verrückt)*: crazy; *ja, sag amal, bist du ~ wordn?* I say, have you become crazy or something? - **2.** *adv* immensely *(unendlich)*: no end; *i hob mi über das Gschenk ~ gfreit* I was over the moon about the present I got; *i hob di ~ gern* I love you with all my heart.

nạtzen [-ɔ-] *v/i* Lower Bavarian *dial.* to take a short sleep *(ein Schläfchen machen)*: to (take *or* have a) nap, to take forty winks. - **Nạtzerl** [-ʌ-] *n* -s/pl. rare: - Lower Bavarian *dial.* a short sleep, esp. during the day *([Mittags-]Schläfchen)*: nap, forty winks; *der Vati macht nach dem Essen immer ein ~* Dad always takes *or* has a nap (*or*, has forty winks) after lunch, an afternoon nap is a must for Dad.

Nẹrverl *n* -s/-n *colloq.*, often slightly *contp.* a very nervous person: *BrE* jitterbug, *AmE* nervous Nelly; *ja, bist denn du ein ~?* why, have you got the jitters (*or*, the fidgets)?; *seitdem sich die Tochter mit einem „von" verlobt hat, ist sie ein ganzes ~* she's been all of a twitter since her daughter got engaged to one who's a handle to his name.

Nesthockerl

Nẹsthockerl *n* -s/pl. rare: -(n) [second el., < *hocken*↑ 'to squat, i.e. to sit with the knees bent and the legs drawn fully up under the body', + dim. *-erl*] *colloq.* the youngest of a group; actually, the last of the fledglings in a bird's nest to learn to fly *(Nesthäkchen)*: baby of the family; *ja der Hansi ist unser ~, er geht noch in den Kindergarten* Johnny is the baby of our family, he still goes to kindergarten.

Nịckel, *dial.* **Nịgl** *m* -s/-(n) [the abbreviated or affectionate forms of *Nikolaus* 'Nicholas', a once popular Christian name in Southern Germany - in English corresponding to *Nichol* and *Nick*] *colloq.*, rare **1.** a small fairy that plays tricks on people: (hob)goblin. - **2.** a bad-mannered child: (little) brat, little nuisance *or* pest || → *Bos*$\overset{x}{\sim}$, *Not*$\overset{x}{\sim}$.

niederlegen *v/refl* to lie down - *colloq.* only as a rhetorical imperative in a phr. expressing great surprise: *da legst d' di' nieder!* well, I'm (*or* I'll be) blowed!, well, blow me (down)!, *NorBrE also* by the 'eck!; *da legst d' di' nieder und stehst nimmer auf - a Preiß als Chef vom boarischen Wörterbuach!* well, I never - a Prussian heading the team of our Bavarian Dictionary - you can knock me down with a feather!

nịx *indef. pron.* [< *nichts*, by elision (as so often) of the middle of three consonants] *colloq.* nothing: *dial.* nowt [naʊt] *phr.* **1.** said as a warning, or in resignation: *aus ~ wird ~* you can't get blood out of a stone. - **2.** a warning, deliberately employing the double negative, that past events often remain to some extent inexplicable (and future ones unpredictable), that one should not go by rumours, or that the speaker is reluctant to divulge his opinion or knowledge of the matter under discussion: *~ Gewisses weiß man nicht!* or, in broad Bavarian, *~ G'wiss woaß ma net!* it's nowt you never know for sure! - **3.** an apologetic plea for what has just been, or is about to be, said: *~ für ungut!* no offence!, no hard feelings!

Noagerl ['nɔagɑl] *n* -s/-(n) [< *neig-*, the stem of *neigen* 'to incline', 'to tilt' (since the glass or mug in question is tilted for closer inspection, to see how much liquid is really left at the bottom) + dim. suffix *-erl*] *dial.*, often slightly *contp.* or *iron.* dregs, esp. of beer: backwash, tail-

Noagerl

end; *was, auf das ~ kommt's dir an?* what, you can't even polish off that little bit?; *vielen Dank, aber das ~ kannst du dir behalten!* thanks a lot, but you can keep your backwash!

Nọcken *f* -/- *contp.* a stupid and unenterprising person (the word tending, because of its grammatical gender, to be a little more often applied to a female): dope, *AmE also* dummy, dingbat, *BrE also* (great) lump; *das ist dir fei eine fade ~!* there's a lump on a log for you (I [can] tell ye)!

Nọckerl *n* -s/-(n) **1.** (1) *cul.* a (necessarily) irregular-shaped lump of dough, made with eggs, that - like its mates - is dropped from a spoon or cut slantwise from a board into boiling water *(Mehlklößchen [aus Eierteig])*: small dumpling || in word combinations: (a) *Grieß-*

nockerlsuppe semolina-dumpling soup; (b) *Salzburger ~ pl.* a frothy delicacy, actually indigenous to the City of Salzburg, Austria, but appreciated also in neighbouring Bavaria, either as a dessert or as a main dish: sweet soufflé omelette (*sg.*) Salzburg style. - (2) *fig. colloq.* in a sententious phrase conveying the futility of overabundance in worldly riches (according to which a person who enjoys all the luxuries of life may be inclined to spend his excess money on a hobby, give to charity, etc.): *goldene ~(n) kann man nicht essen!* *you cannot eat golden dumplings; how can you use any more money than what you've already got? - **2.** *colloq.* an epithet bestowed with gently raised eyebrows or in amused humour on a young woman for an act of gaucherie or unprovoked touchiness *(Gänschen)*: silly billy *or* goose; *so ein ~, das hab ich ja gar nicht gemeint!* what a silly (goose), I didn't mean that at all.

notig *adj, dial.* [< StandG *nötig*] **1.** lacking money *(arm)*: pinched (for money); *es ist verflucht schwer gewesen, sich in diesen ~en Zeiten durchzufretten* it was damn hard to make both ends meet in those awful times. - **2.** *contp.* hating to spend money *(geizig)*: cheese-paring, tight-fisted; *so a ~a Hund, a ~a!* he's a damn skinflint, and I don't mean maybe!

Notnickel, *dial.* **Notnigl** *m* -s/-(n) [see *Nickel*] *colloq.* a person who dislikes spending or giving money *(Geizhals)*: penny-pincher, skinflint, screw, *AmE also* nickel nurser, tightwad.

O

Oachkatzlschwoaf [ˈɔʌχkʌtsl̩ʃwɔʌf], in StandG *Eichkätzchenschweif* 'squirrel bushytail'. This triple compound, redolent of its upland dialect subsoil, bristles with difficulties for the innocent speaker from Anglo-Saxon countries, but also from non-Bavarian lattitudes of Germany. He is unacquainted with the vowel sequence [-ɔʌ-] at either end (heard also in *Loawidoag*↑, StandG *Laibchenteig*, the basis for a 'round rye

Oachkatzlschwoaf

bread roll sprinkled with coriander or caraway seeds'), and he also has to master the two consonant clusters plus the syllabic diminutive consonant [-l] in the middle. Our overseas visitor, thus stymied, may reciprocate by posing tongue-twisters of his own, such as "The sixth sheikh's sixth sheep's sick" and "The Leith police dismisseth us" - which, incidentally, are said to have been used to test the sobriety of a person suspected of drunkenness. Now, gentle reader, can you do justice to all the four with equal ease? If so, well done - you deserve a putty medal with a string to it!

Obatzte [ˈoːbɑtste] *m* -n/-n; as a term of reference more often used with the indefinite article, *a Obatzta* [ɑ ˈoːbɑtstə] (sometimes spelt with the standard ending, *Obatzter*) [< StandG *Angebatzter*, p.p. of *anbatzen* 'to add to with a short flick of the wrist'] *dial., gastr.* "cheese clump", cheese mix, a prepared spread made from the combination of gervais and camembert cheeses, butter, egg yolk, pepper and other spices, as well as half an onion, finely chopped; for better spreading, a smidgin of beer can be helpful; *zu unserem ~n gehören Salzstangen oder ein deftiges Vollkornbrot* the perfect partners for our "cheese clump" are salted breadsticks or a few slices of heavy coarse-grained bread.

Obstler *m* -s/- **1.** *bev.* a brandy distilled from the fermented juice of apples, pears, plums, etc., or of a blend of such juices *(Obstbranntwein)*: (1) *gen.* fruit brandy. - (2) *specif.*, apple brandy; *AmE also* applejack; pear brandy; plum brandy, slivovitz (*or*, slivovic, slivowitz). - **2.** *com.* a dealer in fruit *(Obsthändler)*: fruit trader, *BrE also* fruiterer. - **Obstlerin** *f* -/-nen *com.* a woman selling fruit: (1) *(Obstverkäuferin)* (woman) fruit-seller. - (2) *colloq. (Obstfrau)* fruitwoman.

Ochs *m* -en/-en *colloq. (Ochse)* ox/*pl.* oxen **1.** a strong but sullen draught animal shown in lusty folk speech to be a bundle of muscular energy and a voracious eater, as when (1) describing a woman's irresistible attractiveness to a male: *ein Frauenhaar ist* (or *zieht) stärker als sieben ~en* one hair of a woman draws more than a hundred pair of oxen, or (2), in dialect hyperbole, ridiculing the paltry amount of food offered to a very hungry person: *das is ja grad (so), wie wenn ein ~ ein Veigerl fraß* seems to me, that's just about enough to feed a bird on (*or*, ... to keep a sparrow alive). - **2.** *fig. contp.* a clumsy, stupid fellow: ox, ass, dope, *BrE also* twit.

Ochsen... *cul.*: **~augen** *n pl.* [since reminiscent of the animal's round big eyes] *([zwei] Spiegeleier)* "ox eyes", i.e. (two) fried eggs, *AmE sl.* Adam and Eve, bride and groom || a waiter's instruction to the chef: *zwei ~!* two eggs sunny-side up! - **~braterei** *f* -/-en *gastr.* esp. at the October Feast in Munich: "ox roastery," beef barbecue stand, *i.e.* a temporary fairground restaurant serving meat of oxen roasted on the spit in an open furnace. - **~fiesel** *m* -s/- [second el., 'sinew'] *dial. (Ochsenziemer)* **1.** the penis of a bull: bull's pizzle (formerly used as an instrument of flagellation). - **2.** the strip of leather made from a cow's (etc.) hide and used as a whip: cowhide, oxhide, horsewhip, *AmE also* bull whip || said of a sinewy young person: *flachsig wie ein ~* (as) wiry as a whip. - **~maulsalat** *m* -(e)s *cul.* "ox snout salad," of pickled ox snout meat combined with vinegar, oil, spices and onions.

Odel or **Odl** [ˈo:-], rarely **Adel** [ˈɔ:-] *m* -s *agr. dial. (Jauche)* liquid manure, *BrE dial.* cowpiss, muck-water; **~grube** *f* -/-n cesspit, cesspool, *BrE dial.* yeddle-hole, mucky pond.

odeln, **odln** *v/i agr. dial.* **1.** to distribute stable urine from a mobile tank *(jauchen)*: to spread cow piss; *zweimal im Jahr wird geodelt - im Auswärts, wann die Felder noch, und im Herbst, wann sie wieder brachliegen* the fields are drenched with cow piss twice a year - in spring, before sowing; and at the back-end, after harvesting's done. - **2.** to reek of stable urine *(nach Jauche stinken): mei, da odelt's ja!* ee, there's a stench of cow piss in the air.

Ohrenhöhler *m* -s/- [< from the supposition that it enters people's ear-holes] *ent. (Ohrwurm)* earwig: *BrE dial.* lugwig, twinge, twitch(y)-bell, (s)kutchy-bell, forky-tail.

Ohrwaschel *n* -s/-(n) *colloq. (Ohr[muschel])* (external) ear; *mach deine ~ auf!, wasch dir deine ~ aus!* prick up your ears!, open up those ears of yours!, wash *or* clean out your ears!; *meinst du, ich hock' auf meinen ~n?* do you think I'm sleeping (*or* sitting) on my ear?, *AmE also* ... I'm cloth-eared (*or* flannel-eared)?; *ich zieh' dich gleich am ~!* I'll give your ears a good pulling!, I'll tweak your ear in a minute!; *du bist noch viel zu grün* (or, *noch nicht trocken) hinter*

odeln

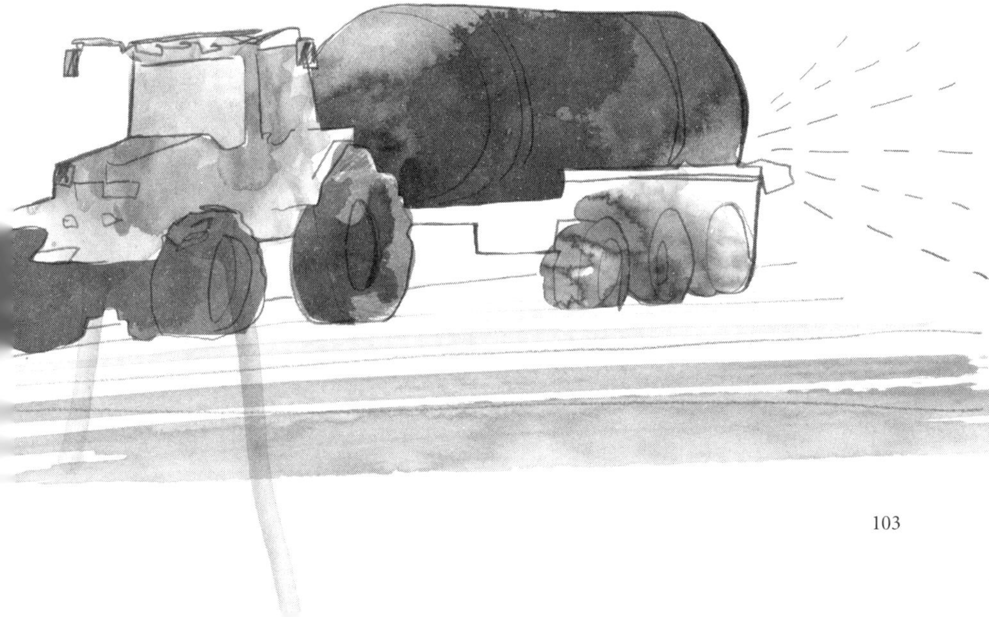

die ~ you're still too wet behind the ears *or* about the gills; *der Wind reißt einem ja die* ~ *weg* that wind's strong enough to rip your ears off; *der hat so abstehende* ~, *dass er bei Sturmwarnung im Haus bleiben muss* his ears stick out like a taxi with its doors open; *ihm zieht's das Maul auseinander, dass ihm beinahe die* ~ *hineinfallen vor lauter Vergnügen* [Ludwig Thoma] he's getting such a kick out of it that his ears nearly disappear behind the wide expanse of his grin.

Oktoberfest *n* -(e)s/-e *folklore* October Feast, October Fair, October Festival - **1.** on the Theresienwiese, Munich: an enormous fair, and the time of much merrymaking complete with a costume procession, horse races, side-shows, beer tents, open barbecues for roasting venison, oxen and chicken, observed every autumn for a fortnight beginning at the end of September; it originated with a popular celebration arranged by King Maximilian I for the wedding on October 12, 1819, of his son, the future King Ludwig I, to Princess Therese of Saxe-Hildburghausen. → **2.** any of the 170 or so beer festivals celebrated on the Munich model in Europe and elsewhere, especially in the United States, some such festival cities being Vienna, Paris, London, Toronto, Montreal, Melbourne, Sydney, Brisbane and Adelaide.

o lẹck [by rigorous curtailment, to make the phrase socially acceptable, < *leck mich am Arsch* 'kiss my arse'] *interj* a polite curse, or an expletive expressing mild surprise or disappointment: dang it!, blow it!, *AmE also* (oh) fudge!

ọzapft is 's *interj* [< StandG *angezapft ist es - es* referring to the first barrel of beer ceremoniously opened at a beer-broaching festival] the triumphant shout of *fait accompli* prescribed for the dignitary who duly swings the mallet *(Bierschlegel)*, drives the spigot *(Zapfhahn)* in place, bespatters himself (more often than not) unmercifully in the act, and at last cheers the audience, his pristine mugful of frothy delight held high: the barrel's tapped!

Note: Such moments are relished throughout the year whenever crowds of Bavarians forgather in glee, say, at the broaching of the Lenten beer, or of the especially strong "May bock" and, of course, at the Munich October Festival where, on the opening Saturday late in September, the lord mayor draws the first litre of beer at the stroke of twelve noon.

ozapft is's!

P

Pạpp *m* -(e)s/pl. rare: -e *colloq.* **1.** a thin mixture of flour and water, used for sticking paper together or onto other surfaces *(Kleister)*: (starch-flour) paste. - **2.** frozen snow clinging to the sole of one's boots *([Schnee-]Klumpen)*: lump(s) of snow.

pạppen *vt/i colloq.* **1.** *v/t ([auf-]kleben)* to stick, to paste; *wie viel pappt man denn auf einen Brief nach Neuseeland?* what's the postage you slap (*or* smack) on a letter to New Zealand? - **2.** *v/i (fest [und klumpig] haften)* of snow under one's boots, etc.: to lump, to form lumps, to become lumpy; *der Schnee pappt so fest, ich geh wie auf einem Kothurn* the snow's so lumpy on the soles I seem to be walking on stilts.

pạsst scho *interj* [< *es passt schon* 'it is correct (as it is [, forget it!])'] *dial.* at a restaurant or similar establishment, a customer's friendly, or sometimes also slightly pompous, verbal gesture to the waitress not to return the small cash the customer is due to receive after proffering a large coin or bank note (whose value somewhat exceeds the sum stated on the bill): that's all right (, keep the change)!

Patrona Bavariae

Patro̲na Bava̲riae *f* - *relig.* the honorific title in Latin of Holy Mary, the mother of Christ: Our Lady the patron saint of Bavaria; *Zehntausende Bayern strömen anfangs Mai zum Fest der ~ ~ nach Altötting* in early May, Bavarians by the tens of thousands flock to Altötting for the feast of their lady patron saint.

Pfạnnenkuchen, **Pfạnnkuchen** *m* -s/-, *dial.* **Pfạnnakuacha** *m* -/- **1.** *cul.* pancake, *AmE also* crepe || *phr.* a provocative query, uttered as a friendly banter or in slight annoyance, when somebody always leaves doors open: *habt ihr einen ~ (*or, *einen [Stroh-]Sack) daheim (vor der Tür)?* are there no doors in your house?, why can't you put the wood in the hole?, were you born in a barn *or* in fields (*or, ScotE,* ... brocht up in a cairt-shed)? - **2.** pl. only, *vulg.* pendant breasts *(lappiger Hängebusen)*: droopers, super droopers.

Pfạnnenkuchen..., often also *dial.* **Pfạnnakuacha...**: **~gesicht** *n* -(e)s/pl. rare: -er *colloq.*, used slightingly, a large, expressionless face: deadpan (expression), frozen face, poker face. - **~suppe** *f* -/-n *cul.* clear beef broth garnished with fine strips of pancake.

Pfeiferl *n* -s/-(n) [dim. of *Pfeife* 1. 'whistle', and 2. '(water) pipe', 'spout'] *colloq.* **1.** (tin) whistle. - **2.** *euphem.* a child's penis: peenie, whistle; cp. *Zipferl 2.* - **~wasser** *n* -s/pl. rare: - [a refined speaker's variant for what others would bluntly refer to as *Soachwasser* 'piss water'] *hum.* or mildly *contp.* any non-alcoholic drink, esp. carbonated water (naturally held in contempt by 'a real man' *[ein gestandenes Mannsbild]*, who in Bavaria doubtless plumps for beer): gargle, gullet wash, mouthwash, wishwash.

pfeilgrad *adv* [< *pfeilgerade* '(as) straight as an arrow'] *colloq.* used in the sense of *pfeilgeschwind* '(as) swift as an arrow (*or*, as lightning)', and from there to other semantic widenings, all generally connoting emphasis and specificity: **1.** directly, right away, without a second thought; *er hat gefragt, was ich gemacht hab, und ich hab's ihm ~ gesagt* he asked what I did, and I told him off the cuff (*or*, without blinking an eye). - **2.** really (and truly); *mir fällt jetzt ~ nicht ein, wie das Buch heißt* I cannot for the life of me remember the title of the book. - **3.** the very [+ noun]; *heut bin ich doch ~ dem Menschen über den Weg gelaufen, den ich nie hab treffen wollen* I came across the very person today I never wanted to meet.

pfẹnningguat *adj, dial.* anything concrete or abstract in everyday life (from a garment to a social event) that deserves full praise; anything - to give the compound elements in their present-day acceptation their due - that looks "as *good* as a shiny bright new penny": fabulous, first-rate, nice and good, stunning, tip-top, *BrE also* cracking, *AmE also* mighty good; *a ~a Janker* a snazzy Alpine jacket.

pfiat (*di[ch]*, pl. *euch* or *enk*; in formal address, *Eahna* [< StandG *Ihnen*]) **Gọtt** [first word, < *behüt'*, the optative of *behüten v/t* 'to protect,' 'to watch over'] *dial. interj* a friendly farewell: **1.** if filled with innate godliness: God save you kindly! - **2.** if such pious thought has paled into a formality: good-bye, *AmE also* good-by [= a contraction of 'God be with you (ye)'].

Pfịnsta, less often **Pfịnstag** *m* -(s)/- *rural dial. (Donnerstag)* Thursday.

Pfloutsch *m* -s/-(n) [< OBav interj *pflatsch*, a word imitating the dull sound of a heavy, flat-faced object striking a solid surface; cp. E *thud*] *dial., contp.* or jokingly self-incriminatory -

(1) an ungainly person *(unbeholfener Mensch)*: butterfingers, *BrE also* clumsy clot. - (2) an awkward, lazy, or inept person *(behäbiger Mensch)*: slouch, *AmE also* lubber, lumbering ox, lummox, lump. - **pfloutschert** or **pfloutschat** *adj, dial.*, said disparagingly of persons lacking physical coordination or skill *(unbeholfen, ungeschickt)*: clumsy, gawky || said in humorous self-accusation: *heut is, mir scheint('s), (Sankt)* [x]*Valentinstag ... i stell mi fei richtig ~ o* [o:]*!* I seem to have the falling sickness today ... acting a real butterfingers! - **Pfloutschn** *f -/- dial.*, usu. *contp.* a clumsy or stolid female = *Pfloutsch*↑; also (analogous to the entry under *Pfloutsch 2*): *AmE* lumbering cow.

[x]Pronounced [f-], which makes the pun on G *fallen* (lassen) 'to drop (things [by chance and without any deliberate intention])' abundantly clear.

Plạ̈rrer *m* -s/- [< dial. *plärren* 'to shout'] **1.** *dial. (lauter Ruf, Schrei)* shout; *einen ~ machen* or *tun* to give a shout; *ich mach'* or *tu' an ~, wenn ich soweit bin* I'll give you a shout when I'm ready; → **2.** *dial.*, often in annoyance *(Schreihals)*: shouter, loudmouth. - → **3.** in Franconia and Bavarian Swabia *(Tummelplatz, Volksfest)*: fair ground; occasionally used as a local place-name, e.g. in Nuremberg, Hersbruck, and Augsburg. - **plạ̈rrgoschert** *adj contp.* strident: loud-mouthed.

plạttert *adj, dial.*, slightly *contp.* bald *(glatzköpfig)*: *sarc.* barefooted on top of the head, sunny side up. - **Plạtterte**

plattert

m -n/-n *dial.*, slightly *contp.* bald-headed man: *colloq.* baldy, *sarc.* bald coot, cue ball || *joc.* a facetious piece of "remedial" advice for one seized by sudden hiccups or a fit of sneezing: *denk an drei ~ und halt die Luft an!* *just (try to) think of three baldies and hold your breath!

Plẹmpel *m* -s/- [< *plampen* (of a liquid) 'to swash heavily from side to side'] slightly *contp.* stale beer: slipslap, slipslop, slops, dishwater, bilgewater.

Pọstkastl *n* -s/-(n) *colloq.* a box in a post office, street, etc., in which letters can be posted: letterbox, postbox, *AmE also* mailbox, mail drop, *BrE also* pillar box; *wo ist denn da bittschön das nächste ~?* where is the nearest letterbox, please?

Potschạmberl *n* -s/-(n) [dim. of F *pot de chambre*] *colloq.*, often *hum.* chamber pot *(Nachttopf)*: chamber (of commerce), piddle potty, *BrE also* geogra-

Potschamberl

phy (under the bed); *ich weiß in der Nacht vielleicht nicht genau, wo man bei euch hingeht, wenn man hinausmuss, so wäre mir in meinem Kammerl ein ~ schon ganz recht unterm Bett, bittschön* at night, when I feel like wandering (you know where), I might perhaps have my problems with the geography of your house; so I wouldn't mind having a little geography under the bed, please.

Prạngertag *m* -(e)s/pl. rare: -e [< *prangen* 'to be festively garbed' - said with reference to Mother Nature, then in the prime of the spring season, but especially to the prettily dressed young girls attending the religious ceremony described here, to the houses gaily decorated with branches and sprigs of light-green birch wherever the procession passes and, not least, to the impressive pageant of *Prangstangen*↓] "Glory Day" **1.** *eccles.* & *folklore (Fronleichnam)* Corpus Christi Day, celebrated with great splendour by R.C. communities, the central feature being the Corpus Christi Day procession, during which wreaths and garlands, brass bands, bell-ringing and gun-salutes are much in evidence. - **2.** *fig.*, often *joc.* a day to show one's festive garb, for any reason whatever: *sich wie zum ~ herausputzen* to dress in one's best clothes: *colloq.* to titivate oneself, to put on one's best bib and tucker (*AmE also*, ... best duds); *ja, ist denn heute ~, dass ihr euch so schön herausgeputzt habt?* why (*or*, I say), what kind of red-letter day are we having today that you are so spruced up (*or*, decked out) for? - **Prạngstange** *f* -/-n *eccles.* & *folklore (Prozessionsstange)* "glory pole", one of the ornate poles carried in church processions.

Prạtzen, **Prạtzn** [-ɑ-] *f* -/often pl.: - *dial.* [actually, an animal's foot that has nails or claws] **1.** coarsely *hum.* (1) a human hand: paw, mitt; *geh und wasch dir die ~!* go and wash your dirty paws!; *die Zigaretten gehören mir, lass die ~ davon!* these are my cigarettes, get your mitts off them! - (2) said to a card-player: *ich wünsch dir a ~ voller Trümpf* I wish you a fistful of trump cards. - **2.** shrilly *contp.* - a female's warning not to be handled roughly in a sexual way: *(nimm) die ~ weg!* (take your) paws off (me)!; having hands trouble? stop mauling me! - **3.** low *colloq.* (usu.) a (male's) large, heavy hand: paw, mauler; *der hat ja richtige ~!* he's got hams (*AmE*

Pratzen

also mutton chops) for hands; ~ [pl.] *so groß wie Abtrittsdeckel* maulers the size of (*or*, as big as) manhole covers.

prątzln, **brątzln** [-ʌ-] *v/t* [< to use (as is known of a young cat) one's little paw (*Pratzl*, a dim. based on the prec. entry) in order to play with, and unwittingly annoy, a much smaller animal] *colloq.* **1.** to make playful fun of someone *(necken)*: to pull s.o.'s leg; *er fühlt sich von den Stammtischbrüdern gepratzlt* he feels he's been made the butt of a leg-pull by his drinking cronies. - **2.** to cheat *(betrügen)*: to pull a fast one on s.o.; *nach altbayerischer Volksüberlieferung ist es ein Leichtes, den Boandlkramer, der einen ja von dieser Welt weglocken möchte, zu ~: Man muss grad die Uhr verstellen, und der Engstirnige lässt sich belehren, er habe die rechte Minute für den Sensenschlag versäumt* according to an Old Bavarian popular tradition, it is easy to pull a fast one on the Grim Reaper wishing to lure you from this world: just by twiddling the hands of your clock you make the narrow-minded fellow believe that he missed the right minute for the proper swing of his scythe.

Preiß, the *dial.* pronunciation and spelling of **Preuß** *m* -en/-en *colloq.*, often with a negative bias: (so-and-so) Prussian; *er ist ein ~* he's a Prussian (, mind you; *or*, what [else] do you expect?); *diese ~en* (well,) those Prussians; *dial.: da siecht ma halt wieder de ~n* Prussians will be Prussians, that's like them all over || a semi-malicious little invitation to fellow-Bavarians: *Heidaufdnachtwernpreissnabgschlacht / werpreissnfleischmogsoikummadedog!*
*Folks, tonight is butchering night / if you love Prussian meat drop in for a treat!

Preißensau *f* -/...säue low *sl.* always an invective (cp. *Saupreiß*): Prussian swine, *AmE also* Prussian son-of-a-bitch.

Prẹsssack *m* -(e)s/pl. rare: ...säcke *gastr. (Schwartenmagen) BrE* jelly brawn,

AmE headcheese, head souse, hog maw, i.e. meat from the head (and feet) of pigs, pressed into a cheese-like mass after suitable seasoning and boiling; the word is often qualified by the attributes *schwarzer* or *weißer*, according to whether blood, liver, kidneys, and other entrails (causing the dark red colour) have been added or not.

prịtscheln *vt/i colloq.* **1.** v/i *(plätschern)* (a) said of a brook: to babble; (b) said of a fountain: to splash. - **2.** *v/i* to rain hard *(stark regnen)*: to come down in buckets; *es pritschelt schon den ganzen Tag* it's (*or*, the rain's) been bucketing down all day. - **3.** *v/i* also **aus**~, **daneben**~ to miss the mark when pouring a liquid *([Flüssigkeit] verschütten)*: to spill (some [drops], etc.); *haltaus, du pritschelst ja!* whoa, you're spilling things! - **4.** *v/i* to cause an amount of water to fly up into the air with loud noise by hitting or disturbing the water *([im seichten Wasser, in der Badewanne,* etc.*] planschen)*: to splash *or* splatter (water) about *or* around. - **5.** *v/t* to adulterate *([Wein,* etc.*] panschen)*: to water down.

pritscheln

prịtschen *v/i dial.*, often *contp.* to reveal a secret, usu. with gossipy eagerness *([Vertrauliches] weiterplaudern)*: to blab, to snitch, to tell tales (out of school), *AmE also* to squeak, to turn on the leaks. - **Prịtscher** *m* -s/- *dial.*, often *contp.* a person who informs about other people's secrets, wrong actions, etc.: telltale; *sie ist ein ~ - was du ihr heute anvertraust, weiß morgen die Stadt* she's a telltale - what you confide to her today she'll shout from the housetops tomorrow.

Progroder *m* -s/- *folklore* = *Hochzeitslader*↑.

pụmperl... [first el., ≚ *n* 'little pump,' *sl.* for 'heart'] *colloq.*: ~**gesund** *adj* thoroughly healthy *(kerngesund)*: as fit as a fiddle, as sound as a bell, *AmE also* as healthy as a horse; *schau mich fei an mit meinen sechzig Jahren, ~ wie eh und je!* just have a look at me, sixty years old, and as hale and hearty (*or*, as sound in wind and limb) as ever. - ~**munter** *adj* cheerful and active *(quicklebendig)*: as chirpy as a bird, *BrE* sprightly, bright-eyed and bushy-tailed, *AmE also* as chipper as a sparrow, as fresh (*or* crisp) as a brand-new dollar.

pụmpern *v/i colloq. (stark klopfen)* to thump, to hammer; *sein Herz hat vor Aufregung gepumpert* his heart was thumping (away) (*or*, hammering [away]) with excitement || venting one's anger in blasphemous dialect speech: *Kruzifix noch einmal, wer pumpert denn da ans Hoftor wia net gscheit?* who the devil is pounding on (*or*, against) the (yard) gate like mad (*or*, like a madman)?

Q

Quadrat... [the word, as a mathematical term meaning 'squared,' here acts as a colloquial intensifier] *dial.* **~latschen** *f pl.* large feet, or big heavy strong shoes: clodhoppers *pl.*, beetle-crushers *pl.* - **~ratschen** *f* -/- [cp. *Ratschen 2*] *contp.* an excessively talkative person: big windbag, prattlebox, *AmE also* bunch of hot air; *des is dir Eahna fei eine ~* his [her] tongue wags like a lamb's tail, mind. - **~schädel** *m* -s/- *colloq.*, often *contp.* a male's massive square head, whose dimensions are popularly interpreted as being symptomatic of the persons's pigheadedness: great big tin can, *BrE also* great bonce, noddle, *AmE also* pumpkin; *des will einfach net in seinen* (or, more colloq., *sein'n*) *~ 'nein!* that just won't sink into his big fat skull.

Quartl *n* -s/-(n) [< L *quart(us)* 'fourth' + SouG dim. suffix *-l*] a liquid measure, the fourth of a litre or *Mass*↑ (= 0.44 UK pints, or 1.76 UK gills): "quarter"; *drei ~(n) hist.* three quarters of a litre (= 1.32 UK pints), a set mark on the liquid-measure scale once popular with that section of Bavarian froth-blowers that had to, or simply wanted to, economize - tendering their one-litre family mug and placing an order of "three quarters", hoping, often quite rightly so, that the landlord would comply by filling her up to the brim.

Quetschn *f* -/- [< *quetschen v/t* 'to press forcibly together'] *mus., dial.* an accordion (with a keyboard) or a concertina (a small hexagonal accordion, with keys to be pressed at each end) *(Ziehharmonika)*: squeeze-box, *BrE sl. also* squiffer.

Quetschn

R

Radi *m* -(s)/- *bot. (Rettich)* radish.

Radieserl *n* -s/-(n) *bot. (Radieschen)* (red) radish; *ein Bund ~* a bunch of radishes || *colloq.* said in grim humour of somebody lying dead and buried: *die ~(n) von unten anschauen* (or *wachsen sehen)* to push up (*BrE* the) daisies, to turn one's toes up to the daisies.

Radi... *colloq.*: **~frau** *f* -/-en *(Rettichverkäuferin)*: (streetside) radish vendor, radish-girl, *BrE also* radish-wife. - **~kopperer** *m* -s/- low *colloq.* radish burp, a noisy belch caused by the gourmet's sizeable intake of radish and beer; *einen ~ lassen* to give (*or* let out) a radish burp. - **~schneider** *m* -s/- *tech.* radish-slicer, a special blade attached to a metal spindle which, when revolved, transforms the radish into a long, accordion-like spiral. - **~weib** *n* -(e)s/-er in brusque speech, for *Radifrau*↑: radish-woman. - **~weiberl** *n* -s/-(n) **1.** in affective speech, for *Radifrau*↑: dear ([*or* sweet] old) radish-lady; **2.** *hum.* in Carnivaltime, as part of the Lusticania pageant, one of the court girls who is flashily dressed as a radish vendor: snazzy radish trouper.

Radler *n* -s/- [with the gender transferred from *Bier*], short for **Radlermass** *f* -/...masse (after numerical data: - [e.g., zwei Radlermass]; *dial.* pl. also: Radlermassen), or **Radlerhalbe** *f* -/-(n) *bev.* half beer and half lemonade, reputed to be splendidly refreshing and considerably less potent than beer neat - a drink for "knights of the wheel" (and other devotees of the mixture): (one litre of) *cyclists' special (*or*, ... *cyclists' delight), *BrE* shandy.

Ramerl, **Rammerl** *n* -s/-n *colloq.* **1.** *cul.* the hard residue clinging to the bottom or rim of a pan after baking and frying *(Back-, Bratrückstand)*: sticky crust. - **2.** *cul.* the hard usu. brown outer section of roast potatoes, sweet yeast dumplings, etc. *(Angebräunte)*: crusty bit(s). - **3.** thick mucus *(verhärteter Nasenschleim)*: nose blob.

Rannen *f* -/- *bot. (rote Rübe)* beetroot, *AmE also* beet.

Rapunzel *f* -/-n, **Rapunzelsalat** *m* -(e)s *bot. (Feldsalat)* lamb's lettuce, corn-salad.

rass *adj, dial. (beißend)* **1.** causing a burning sensation in one's mouth: sharp, pungent, hot-tasting; *der Kas [Radi] da is mir zu ~* this cheese [radish] tastes too hot for my liking. → **2.** said in awe, or with amused criticism, of a chronically ill-tempered woman: waspish; *mei, die hat aber ein rasses Mundwerk, das is fei ganz a Rasse!* my, that woman's got a rare sharp tongue, she has a vicious tongue in her head!

Ratsch *m* -es/pl. rare: -e [< *ratschen 1*] *colloq.* **1.** *(gemütliche Unterhaltung [im vertrauten Kreise])* a friendly informal conversation: chat; *komm doch auf* *einen gemütlichen ~ herüber, so was um neun - meine Leut sind dann alle aus dem Haus* do come over for a cosy chat, let's say about nine - my folks will all be gone by then. - **2.** rare — gossip: chatter stuff; *das ist alles nur ~, an dem ist nichts dran!* it's all tittle-tattle (*AmE* prittle-prattle), there's nothing in it.

Ratsch

Ratsche *f* -/-n, the rare StandG variant of the next; **Ratschen** *f* -/-, [see the verb↓] *colloq.* **1.** a baby's toy; or an apparatus, in juvenile hands, that makes a repeated loud noise, e.g. in order to communicate to others a liturgical message (→ *Ratschenbub*) or one's participating glee over the events in a football stadium: clapper, rattle. - **2.** often *contp.*; if female, also **Ratschenweib** *n* -(e)s/-er (1) a talkative person: chatterbox; *das ist dir eine Ratschen, da kommt kein anderer zu Wort!* what a prattler that man [woman] is - no one else can get a word in! - (2) if indiscreetly loquacious: blabbermouth; *das alte Ratschenweib schnüffelt allerweil bei anderen herum - kein Wunder, dass es über so vieles Bescheid weiß* the old tattler's always poking her nose into other people's business - no wonder she's so well informed.

ratschen *vt/i* [< *ratsch*, an interjection formed through sound imitation of the long sharp tear when quickly made into cloth, paper, etc.] *colloq.* **1.** *v/t* also **herụnterratschen** to perform s.th. quickly, often mechanically: to rattle off *or* through (a poem, a prayer [e.g. the clapper-boy jingle given at the end of the next entry]). - **2.** *v/i* (1) to use a baby rattle. - (2) to use a clapper; *die Buben freuen sich schon darauf, am Karfreitag durch den Ort ~ gehen zu können* the lads are already looking forward to the chance of jangling their clappers through the place on Good Friday. - **3.** *v/i* (1) to talk in a friendly informal manner: to chat, to chitchat, to have a chinwag, *AmE also* to chew the fat (*or* the rag), to shoot the bull (*or* the breeze); *er ratscht ganz gern, ist aber ein lieber Mensch* he's a friendly, chatty sort of person. - (2) to be an exaggerated talker: to wag the tongue; *es haben schon zu viele geratscht, als dass die Sache noch vertraulich bleiben könnte* too many tongues have been wagging for the matter to remain confidential any longer.

Ratschen...: **~bub** *m* -en/-en *R.C. relig.* one of a group of altar boys "rattling" the street scene with their *Karfreitagsratschen*↑ every daylight hour between Maundy Thursday and Easter Sunday: clapper boy; *da nach frommen Glauben die Kirchenglocken nach Rom geflogen sind, laden jetzt ~en die Gläubigen zum Gebet ein* since, according to pious belief, the church bells have flown to Rome, clapper boys now invite the faithful to pray - this is the first of two couplets chanted by them before resuming the jangling:

Wir ratschen, wir ratschen
den Englischen Gruß,
den jeder Christgläubige
beten jetzt muss.

*We clapperdeclap
Ave Mary all day,
which every good Christian
is now bound to pray.

Ratschkathl *f* -/-n [second el., a dim. variant of *Katharina* 'Catherine' > 'Cathy'] *hum.* or *contp.* = *Ratsch(e) 2* (but restricted to females).

Ratz *m* -es/-e, *dial.* -(en)/-(e)n **1.** *zo.* (1) *(Ratte)* rat. - (2) *(Hamster)* hamster. - (3) *hunter's jargon*, also: *Mummel*~↑ *(Iltis)* polecat. - **2.** *phr.* in a *colloq.* simile describing deep and peaceful sleep: *er hat geschlafen wie ein ~* he slept like a top (*or*, like a log); *ich kann schlafen wie ein ~* I could sleep without rocking, I could sleep on a clothes line.

Ratz

Rauchbier *n* -s/-e *bev.* a speciality of Bamberg, Upper Franconia, and the surrounding area: "smoked beer," deriving its flavour from a specific method of processing malt on a large grid *(Tara)* over a beechwood fire; the idea of having roasted malt as a primary ingredient is said to have struck monastic brew-masters who were once faced with the question of reusing grains that had been partially destroyed through fire.

Rauhnacht *f* -/...nächte [first el., either < *rauh* 'rough,' a quality referring to the riotous behaviour of the Season's mummers in fantastic disguise; or < *Rauch m* 'smoke' (related to and synonymous with ScotE *reek*) which, by an old Alpine tradition invoking the Lord's New Year's blessing, comes from smouldering bushes of juniper and other herbs used to fumigate the rooms and stables of farmhouses with between Christmas and Epiphany] **1.** *folklore* demons' night, *i.e.* one of several nights in mid-winter, esp. those preceding St Andrew's Day (November 30), Christmas, St Thomas's Day (December 29), New Year, Epiphany (January 6, known in English as "Twelfth Night"), when the souls of the departed, popular belief has it, reinforced by witches, goblins, elves, and other mischievous spirits, are let loose on this earth to harass the living; the air then can only be cleansed by "smoking out" or otherwise dislodging the Wild Hunt *(die Wilde Jagd)*, which abhors the presence of fearful ugliness and obstreperous noise. → **2.** *eccles.*, pl. only - the twelve nights of Christmas, *hist.* Twelfthtide, *i.e.* the time between the birth of Jesus and His manifestation to the Gentiles in the persons of the Magi (['meɪdʒaɪ] *die Heiligen Drei Könige*).

raunzen *v/i colloq.* **1.** to keep complaining in an unhappy way *([anhaltend brummig] nörgeln)*: to moan, to bellyache, to have the grumbles; *etwas machen, ohne zu ~, wär' das net was?* to do a job without grumbling (*or*, without a grumble), wouldn't that be something? - **2.** to complain in a sad, annoying voice about something *(weinerlich klagen)*: to whine, *AmE* & *AustralE also* to whinge [wɪndʒ]. - **Raunzer** *m* -s/- *colloq.* one who keeps complaining in an unhappy way *(Nörgler)*: moaner, bellyacher. - **Raunzerei** *f* -/-en *colloq.* *(Nörglerei)* moaning, bellyaches *pl.; deine ewige ~ geht mir schön langsam auf den Wecker* or *Geist!* your moaning and groaning, mind you, is really getting on my wick; *hör auf mit der ~ und mach weiter mit der Arbeit!* stop bellyaching and get on with the job. - **Raunzerl** *n* -s/-(n) *colloq.* a quietly complaining child who feels obviously miserable (gently encouraged or teased by a sympathetic adult): whiney little tot, my niggly baby.

Reherl

Regensburger ['reŋgʃ-] *f* -/- *cul.* "Regensburg Knockwurst," a short and plump pork sausage, highly seasoned and smoked, resembling a small type of South German or Austrian *Knackwurst*, or an American knockwurst; *~ werden in Ketten gebunden* Regensburgers are linked in chains.

Reherl ['re:-əl] *n* -s/-(n) [actually, 'little roe' (with the dim. suffix *-erl*), the tertium quid being the fawn, i.e. light yellowish-brown, colour common to the young deer and to the mushroom] *myc.* *(Pfifferling)* chanterelle, egg-mushroom.

Reiber... [< *Reiber m* 'grater' (= a simple kitchen appliance with a metal surface full of sharp-edged holes)] *cul.*: **~datschi** *m* -(s)/-(s) *(Kartoffelpuffer)* potato pancake ([like the next item] made from grated raw potatoes). - **~knödel** *m* -s/- *(Kartoffelkloß)* potato dumpling.

Rein *f* -/-en, less often **Reine** *f* -/-n *cul.* one of variously shaped middle-sized, shallow cooking utensils - **1.** with two handles *(Kochtopf)*: (cooking) pot; **2.** with one straight handle *(Pfanne)*: saucepan; **3.** round or rectangular *(Bratpfanne)*: frying pan, *AmE also* skillet.

Reindl, less often **Reindel** *n* -s/-n [dim. of above] *cul.* small saucepan.

Reinheitsgebot *n* -(e)s *brew.* a set of rules laid down by law in 1516, and rigidly observed to this day, according to which Bavarian brewers are held to use barley, hops, and water only when making their beers: beer purity ordinance, *or* regulations *pl.*

resch *adj* **1.** *bak.* of rolls and bread *(knusprig)*: crisp(y), crunchy. - **2.** *colloq.* said of a lively female, often a businesswoman or a waitress, down-to-earth and good at repartee: sharp and crusty.

Ribisel *f* -/-n **1.** *bot.* the small, edible, acid, round fruit or berry of certain wild or cultivated shrubs of the genus Ribes *(Johannisbeere)*: currant - *Rote* ~ red currant, garnet berry, *scient.* Ribes rubrum; *Schwarze* ~ black currant, quinsy-berry, cassis, *scient.* Ribes nigrum; *Weiße* ~ white currant, *scient.* Ribes album. - **2.** *phr.* (1) *concr.* *~(n) brocken* or *zupfen* to pick currants. - (2) *fig.* a blame laid on overly zealous statisticians who are suspected of fixing their roving eyes on items unworthy of recording: *~(n)* or *Ribiselsträucher* (or, dial., *Ribiselstaudn*) *zählen* to (tend to) count currant bushes || here is a disclaimer by a President of the Bavarian Board of Statistics and Data Processing in Munich: *es ist wiederholt behauptet worden, wir in Bayern zählen mit Hingabe auch die Zahl der Ribiselsträucher, schön kleinweis, ja sogar die Beeren - das stimmt aber nicht* it has repeatedly been maintained that we Bavarians are happily engrossed with counting currants, ticking off bushes one by one, or indeed even their berries - but in fact this is a myth. - **3.** in *comp.*: **~gelee** [ʒəˈleː] *n* -s/-s *gastr.* red currant jelly. - **~marmelade** *f* -/-n *gastr.* red currant jam. - **~saft** *m* -(e)s/...säfte *bev.* red *or* black currant juice. - **~strauch** *m* -(e)s/...sträucher, *dial.* **~staudn** *f* -/- *bot.* currant bush *or* shrub [see also above, under 2 (2)].

Ribisel

Rindviech; with the odd dial. spelling **Rimbfich** *n* -s/-er, dial. -a *dial.* **1.** *breed.* (1) *sg.* -s cow; bull; ox. - (2) *pl.* <a> only in collocations like *zehn Stück* (or, dial., *Stucker*) ~ ten head of cattle. - <b> -er; *wie viel ~er hast d' da im Stall?* how many cattle have you (got) there in the (*or*, yer) shed? - **2.** low *colloq.* [ex sense 1, with reference to the genetically dull and indifferent look and drowsy motion of the bovine race (proverbially encapsulated in such comparisons as G "er ist stur wie ein Ochs," "sie ist eine blöde Kuh," E "he's as dull as an ox," "she's a silly cow")] *contp.*, sometimes *hum.* an extremely stupid person: blockhead, ass; ~ *du!* you blithering idiot!; *ja mei, ~er gibt's alle Dam lang!* ah well, blockheads are ten a penny (*AmE* ... a dime a dozen).

Rịpperl *n* -s/-(n) [dim. of *Rippe* 'rib'] *cul.* *([Kasseler] Rippenspeer)* cured, smoked pork spareribs.

Rohrnudel *f* -/-n [not to be confused with *Dampfnudel*↑], in the Bavarian Forest also **Ofenknödel** *m* -s/- *bak.* a popular delicacy, arranged with a dozen or so of its "mates" in a pan and baked in the oven: (sweet) yeast dumpling, often filled with cherry or plum jam, plum purée, and other centres.

Rọssbollen *m* -s/- [second el., < *Bolle (f)* and *Bollen (m)* 'onion'] **1.** *vet. med.* (1) a general proof of sound equine digestion: *(Pferdekot)* (round) horse dung, horse dropping, *colloq.* horse apple; *er hat frische ~ aufgekehrt, um damit seine Rosen zu düngen* he swept up some newly dropped horse dung to manure his roses with. - (2) if such proof is found in the roadway: *colloq.* alley apple, road apple. - **2.** *fig. colloq.* a countryman's elaborate description of a downpour: *da hat's dir geschüttet, dass die ~ nur so gehupft sind* it was surely raining cats and dogs (*AmE also* ... bull frogs and heifer yearlings, *or* pitchforks with the tines on both ends).

Rọtz *m* -es, *dial.* **Rooz** *m* low *colloq.* *(Nasenschleim)* nasal mucus: snot || *phr.* (1) *den ~ wegschnalzen* to blow one's nose with the fingers: to sling a snot. - (2) a *hum.* evidence that, as far as the treatment of nasal waste is concerned, the rural method is much to be preferred to the urban one: *am Land schmeißn die Leut den ~ weg, und die in der Stadt schiabm eahm ein* country folk sling their snot away, townsfolk pocket it; *nachdem die Mutter ihrem Lauser ordentlich den Hintern versohlt hat, hat er ~ und Wasser geheult* after mother had given her little nuisance a good hiding he blubbered out his misery from eyes and nose.

Rọtz...: [this far from polite element (see above) lends colour to the overall concept: each of the following compounds pictures a child (occasionally also, with added venom, an adult) who is very untidy and shockingly misbehaved] low *colloq.*: ˣ~**besọffen** *adj* extremely drunk: soused to the ears *or* gills, stinking drunk, tight as Dick's hatband. - ~**bua** *m* -buam/-buam [< *Bub m* 'boy,' 'lad'] *dial.* snotty-nosed kid. - ~**löffel** *m* -s/- [*Löffel* 'spoon' here denotes a young culprit's ears which get pulled, or clouted, by way of punishment; the compound carries more acidity than the preceding one] cheeky snot-nosed brat. - ~**madl** *n* -s/-n [*Madl* 'girl,' 'lass'] *dial.* snotty-nosed little miss.

Rübe *f* -/-n *agr.* one of several root vegetables: (1) *gelbe ~ (Möhre, Mohrrübe)* carrot. - (2) *rote ~ (Beete) BrE* beetroot, *AmE* beet; *roter ~nsalat* beetroot salad.

rụntergerissen *p.p.* [< *(he)runterreißen* 'to tear off', with regard either to a piece of cloth where, if ripped to equal shreds, one fragment differs very little from the other; or to a tear-off calendar, in which the individual sheets look speciously identical to the casual eye] *colloq.* only used in phrases that speak of a striking resemblance in appearance or disposition - **1.** generally, not necessarily restricted to one's next of kin: *j-m ~ gleichschauen* (or *gleichsehen*) to be the dead (*or* the spitting) image [actually, < the spit and image] of someone, ... the very spit (*or* the dead spit) of someone. - **2.** with reference to a parent and child: *der Bub schaut* (or *sieht*) *dem Vater [der Mutter] ~ gleich*, or, for short, *~ der Vater [die Mutter]!* the lad is a chip off the old block, his father [his mother] will never be dead while the son is alive.

S

Sạch [-ɔ-] *n* -s [a dial. variant of StandG *Sache* f 'thing', 'object'] *colloq.*, often *apprec.* **1.** (1) *(Besitz)* possessions, property || prov.: *willst dein ~ haben recht, mach dein'n eignen Knecht!* if you want a thing done well, do it yourself. - (2) *(Bauernhof)* farm(stead); *er hat a schöns ~* he can call a large farm his own. - **2.** *euphem. ([ansehnlicher] Busen)* (beautiful) bosom: *sie hat a schöns ~* she's got big brown eyes. - **3.** *(Aufgabe, Arbeit)* task, job; *er hat sein ~ können* he knew his stuff (*or*, his onions).

sạcklzemẹnt, or **Sạcklzemẹnt** *interj* [literally, 'sack of cement' - a harmless-sounding (and indeed semantically vapid) corruption of and stand-in for *Sakrament n* [-ˈment] 'sacrament', a word within the sainted aura of the Church and hence taboo for other uses; in low colloquial and vulgar speech, however, *Sakrament*! brazenly holds its ground as an expletive, and so do *damn!* and *Jesus Christ!* as the English non-euphemistic equivalents here listed] said in considerable, yet controlled annoyance: dang it all!, oh fudge!

sạkra *interj* [a euphemistic shortening of *Sakrament* (cp. the prec. entry); here and elsewhere, a solemn affirmation by the holy Host can lightly be turned into a blasphemy, flippantly thoughtless of origin though it may be] **1.** a mild imprecation: dang it! - **2.** a word of surprise, and possibly also of appreciation: well, I'm damned!, I'll be damned!

S<u>au</u> *f* -/Säue, *dial.* Säu [saɪ]; in the sense of 'wild boar': -en **1.** *zo.* (**I**) the female (domestic) pig: sow. - (**II**) (a) wild boar; (b) the female wild pig: wild sow, sow. - **2.** *fig. vulg.* person of unclean habits or appearance, e.g., a slatternly housekeeper: dirty pig, *Ozark AmE* sow. → **3.** *fig. vulg.* person of immoral habits or language: filthy(-minded) pig. - **4.** *fig. vulg.* a strong invective used in the heat of an argument; swine, dirty rotten pig; *du besoffene ~* you drunken pig (*or* sot). - **5.** *phr.*, all robustly *colloq.* unless otherwise indicated: (**I**) *prov.* (a) the *hum.* avowal of a non-vegetarian: *die Erdäpfel sind mir lieber, wenn sie zuerst die ~*

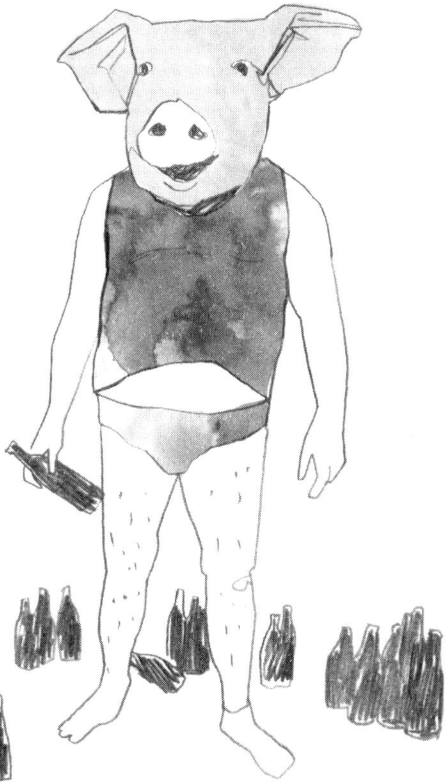

besoffene Sau

gefressen hat; Kartoffel sind am besten, wenn sie zuerst durch die ~ getrieben werden *potatoes taste better to me (*or*, taste best) after they've been eaten by the pig, and the pig has become pork. - (b) *iron.*, said to a person who eats anything and everything: *dich wenn wir nicht hätten, dann müssten wir uns eine ~ halten!* if you weren't around (*or*, if we didn't have you), we'd have to keep a pig, *AmE* ... we'd need a garbage disposal. - (c) a couplet of dialect rhymings that warns against the consequences of getting into bad company: *wer sich mischt unter die Klei* [dial. for *Kleie* 'bran'], *den fressen die Säu!* lie down with the dogs and you get up with the fleas! - (d) a warning not to give unnecessarily, e.g. to a rich person: *einer fetten ~ schmiert man nicht den Arsch* you don't stuff a fat pig (*or* sow) in the tail. - (e) the callous maxim of a libertine or confirmed bachelor: *solang man das Schweinerne pfundweis kriegt, solang kauft man keine ganze ~* you don't have to buy a cow just to get a glass of milk (*or*, merely because you are fond of milk), *AmE* why buy a cow when milk is so cheap?; if I can get it by the piece, why should I buy a whole pig (*AmE* hog)? - (f) a proverbial distinction between a good housewife and a lazy one: *in der Früh bettet die Frau, auf der Nacht die ~* *a good wife makes the beds at dawn, a sloppy one when day is gone. (**II**) *in metaphors and hyperboles*: (a) said in indignation over undue noise, smell, etc.: *das kann (ja) keine ~ aushalten!* I wouldn't ask a dog to put up with that! - (b) said in disgust about inferior food: *das kann (ja) keine ~ essen* or *fressen!* not even a pig would touch that! - (c) a comment on the triviality of a certain matter: *keine ~ fragt danach* nobody gives damn about it, nobody gives (*or* cares) a hoot; *später fragt dich keine ~ mehr danach, was für Noten du in der Schule gehabt hast* later on it doesn't make the least scrap (*or* a blind bit) of difference what marks (*AmE* grades) you got in school. - (d) a *hum.* or *sarc.* admission of having an excessive amount of something: *von dem [denen] haben wir so viel, dass wir die ~ damit füttern können* we've got so much of it [so many of them] we don't know where to put it [them] all; *in München gibt's so viele Maier, dass wir die ~ damit füttern können* there are so many Maiers in Munich we don't know what to do with them all. - (e) said in disgust when faced with great disorderliness: *da schaut's (ja) aus, dass es einer Sau graust* this place looks like it's been hit by a bomb, this place isn't fit for pigs, not even a pig (*or* a tramp) would stay in this place, *ScotE* this place is a sicht to seiken a sou frae its supper. - (f) a strongly worded criticism of someone's handwriting: *das kann (ja,* or *doch) keine ~ lesen!* that handwriting looks like hen tracks (*or* chicken tracks), ... as if a spider had walked across the page! - (g) to do something unusual and exuberant; *die ~ rauslassen* **1.** to afford oneself a rare luxury, *colloq.* to splash out, to splurge; *heut Abend gehen wir in ein feines Lokal, und dann lassen wir die ~ raus* we'll go to a posh restaurant tonight and really live it up (*AmE* ... and live high off the hog) for a change. **2.** to be an enthusiastic performer, e.g. on the piano, *colloq.* to let it rip. - (h) a comment on someone's unnecessary sensitiveness: *was schreit sie denn? ich tu doch keiner ~ was!* what's she upset about? I didn't even lay a finger on her (*or* I didn't touch a single hair of her head, *or* I didn't even come anywhere near her)! -(i) *unter aller ~* low *colloq.* very bad *or* badly; *schau dir mal die Arbeit an, die ist doch unter aller ~* just look at this piece of work, it is an absolute mess (*BrE* a complete shambles); *das Theaterstück gestern Abend war unter aller ~* the play last night was a complete waste of time; *das Kantinenessen war heute unter aller ~* the food at the canteen today wasn't fit for pigs. - (j) a *low colloq.* description of one's anger and loss of self-control: *da werd ich zur ~* that really drives me up the wall. - (k) *vulg.* a curtly obscene refusal to co-operate: *meinetwegen könnts der alten ~ hinteinfahren* (or, *fahrts der alten ~ hintein)!* as far as I'm concerned, you can go stuff yourselves! **(III)** *in similes*: (a) *bluten wie eine ~* to bleed profusely, *colloq.* to bleed like a pig; *fressen wie eine ~* to eat ravenously, *colloq.* to eat like a pig, to stuff one's face, *BrE* to scoff one's food; *grunzen (*or *schnarchen) wie eine ~* to snore like a pig (*or* hog); *schwitzen wie eine ~* to perspire profusely, *colloq.* to sweat like a pig; *ich schwitz (ja) wie eine ~* I'm sweating like a pig (a bystander's *sarc.* rejoinder: *jeder schwitzt, wie er kann,* or *wie sollst [du] denn sonst schwitzen?* that doesn't surprise me, that's the way you were made, *or* how else would you be sweating?); *stinken wie eine ~* to have an unpleasant smell, *colloq.* to smell like a pig, to stink like a polecat, to stink to high heaven; *iron.* said of one whose reputation is very low: *der hat ein Ansehen wie eine ~ im Judenhaus* he's about as popular as pork to (*or* with) a Jew. - (b) *juv. sl. wie d' ~* a popular cliché used to emphasize a variety of situations: *ar-*

beiten wie d' ~ to work like a dog (*or* horse); said of an irresponsibly fast driver: *fahren wie d'* ~ to drive like a bat out of hell, *Lancs dial.* to drive like a scalded moggy [= cat] (yet speed and skill are virtues in *Schi fahren wie d'* ~ to be really something on skis, *AmE* to ski like you wouldn't believe); said of one's shirt, collar stud, etc.: *kratzen wie d'* ~ to scratch like hell (*or* fury); *regnen wie d'* ~ to rain like hell (*or* the devil), and, describing such an occurrence with dramatic crudity, *jetzt schifft's wie d'* ~ it's now raining like a cow pissing on a flat rock; *saufen wie d'* ~ to drink like a bloody fish; said of a plant, etc.: *wachsen wie d'* ~ to grow like a weed, to sprout (*or* shoot) up like nobody's business.

Sau...: **~bär** *m* -(e)n/-(e)n [second el. not related to *Bär* 'bear', but < OHG & MHG *ber* 'breeding boar'] **1.** *zo. (Eber)* boar, male swine. - **2.** low *colloq.* an emotional word used in critical condemnation: (1) a dirty fellow, often a child or young person, torn clothes sometimes offending the eye even further: scarecrow, *BrE also* mudlark, *AmE also* (nasty) bum. - (2) a man with a marked predelection for bawdiness: smuthound, *AmE also* muck spout, porn lover. - **~bub** *m* -en/-en, *dial.* **~bua** *m* -m/-m strongly *emot.*, usu. in an expletive phr.: little bastard, *AmE also* dirty whelp, (young) varmint. - **~dirndl**, *dial.* **~deandl** *n* -s/-n the female counterpart of the former: hay bag, *AmE also* lousy crumb. - **~fraß** *m* -es/pl. rare: -e, **~fressen** *n* -s/pl. rare: - **1.** *livestock breeding* = *Sautrank*. → **2.** low *colloq.* said of a disgusting item of food, or dish, set before the speaker to eat: muck, pukey mess, *AmE also* yuck, yucky stuff. - **⌃geil** *attrib. adj, modern juvenile sl.* excellent: socking good, bully good, strictly solid. - **⌃gemütlich** *adj, colloq.* & *hum.* completely comfortable *(urgemütlich)*: (as) snug as a bug in a rug, as happy as pigs in shit; *da herinnen ist 's* ~, *und was auf den Tisch kommt, ist ein Gedicht* it's as snug as a bug in a rug in here, and the food that comes to the table is sheer poetry. - **~preiß** the *dial.* pronunciation and spelling of **~preuß** *m* -en/-en, rarely **~preuße** *m* -n/-n low *colloq.* **1.** damn Prussian; son-of-a-gun Prussian; *die Bezeichnung ~ bedeutet hierzulande nicht unbedingt eine Beleidigung; es kann mit ihr, bei entsprechendem Tonfall und freilich nur in extremen Fällen, sogar bewundernde Anerkennung für einen cleveren, redegewandten Nordgermanen ausgedrückt werden* in this country, the expression ~ is not necessarily an insult; in fact, intonation can, in extreme cases to be sure, make it an appreciative comment on an astute North Teuton who has the gift of the gab (cp. *Preißensau*). → **2.** a gen. invective for a foreigner: damn foreigner, foreign bastard (as in the punch-line of an anecdote which has an irate Munich street-vendor mutter at a choosey would-be customer from the Far East, '~, *japanischer!*'). - **~trank** *m* -(e)s/...tränke, *dial.* ...trank *livestock breeding* food for pigs, mostly made of unwanted bits of human food: pigswill, swill.

Schạchtel [-ɔ-] *f* -/-n: **alte** ~ [this metaphorical phrase harks back to centuries when minor family trinkets and keepsakes, e.g. a *Fatschenkind*↑, were saved by the female members of the household in chip, or splint, boxes (G *Spanschachteln*), to be taken out and admired at appropriate times; these boxes, often beautifully painted, were inalienable possessions, and grew old with their owners] *hum.*, but mostly *sarc.* an elderly woman, made the butt of a thoughtless or cruel remark simply because of her advanced age: old hag (*or* frump).

Schạchterl [ˈ-ʌ-] *n* -s/-(n) [dim. of *Schachtel f* 'box'] little box; *emot.*, esp. when expressing praise: *das ist (aber) ein süßes ~, das du da hast!* that's a sweet little box you've got there || a *colloq. phr.* describing a disappointing and sometimes even critical state of disarray or bewilderment in one's personal life: *jetzt hab ich den* (or *an) Dreck im ~!* this is a real mess I've landed up in!

Schạchterlteufel *m* -s/pl. rare: - **1.** a children's small toy box holding an amusing figure, often that of a devil, on a spring, which jumps up when the top is opened *(Kastenteufel)*: jack-in-the-box, *AmE also* jack-in-a-box || in *fig. colloq.* used of a person dancing and skipping about like a jointed figure, also known as jumping jack *(Hampelmann)*: *ein Sänger, dem das schweißnasse Hemd am Leibe klebte, sprang vor den Musikern wie ein ~ hin und her* a singer, his sweaty shirt all stuck to his body, was up and down like a jack-in-the-box in front of the orchestra. → **2.** *colloq.*, often *hum.* a person with an explosive temper: spitfire, *AmE also* half brother [sister] to a shot of dynamite; *er [sie] geht auf wie ein ~* he [she] 's an easy (*or* quick) one to blow his [her] top (*or* stack).

Schachterlteufel

Schädelweh

Schädelweh *n* -s/pl. rare: -(s) *dial., med. (Kopfschmerz[en])* headache; *i hab heut früh sakrisch ~ ghabt* I had a God-awful headache this morning.

Schäffler *m* -s/- [an agent noun, < *Schaff n* 'tub'] the name of a trade *(Fassbinder)*: cooper, barrel-maker. - **~tanz** *m* -es/pl. rare: ...tänze *folklore* "Coopers' Dance", a procession and dance of the Munich coopers, alternating with scenes of hoop-swinging, performed every seventh year in January, to commemorate the town's deliverance from the fearful Plague in 1517; towards the middle of the last century, a Munich journeyman-shoemaker carried the tradition to Nonnenhorn, in the Bavarian sector of Lake Constance, and more recently the custom has spread to some twenty other towns as far apart as Geisenfeld, Eichstätt, Landshut, and Garmisch-Partenkirchen.

Schafkopf *m* -(e)s [< *Kopf* 'head' + *schaffen* 'to work'] *cards* "brainwork", one of the oldest and most popular card games, not unlike poker or *Watten*↓; the 4 or occasionally 3 players can choose between *Fragespiel*, where two play against two, and *Solospiel*, where three play against one; the pack contains 32 cards and Queens and Jacks are trumps, as well as one of the four suits; money is bet on each hand.

Schariwari *m* -s/-(s) = *Charivari.*

schẹps, also **schẹbs** *pred. adj* & *adv* [< Yid. *schibes gehn* 'to get lost'] *colloq. (schief)* said of a household (etc.) object that is not exactly in the right position, and thus slightly annoys the eye of the fastidious by lying or hanging **1.** diagonal: cater-cornered, kitty-cornered; **2.** slanting: cockeyed, slantingdicular; and **3.** generally not straight: crooked, askew; *das Bild da ist* (or *hängt*) ~ that picture there is hung crooked, ... is hanging askew *or* skew-whiff.

Scher *m* -(e)s/-e *zo., dial.* a small furry animal living chiefly underground, digging tunnels with its strong forefeet *(Maulwurf)*: mole, *BrE dial.* mowdywarp [*lit.*, 'one that throws up earth'] mowdyrat, mowdy. - **~falln** *f* -/- *dial.*;

scheps

rarely semi-StandG **~falle** *f* -/-n *(Maulwurfsfalle)* mowdy-trap. - **~fanger** *m* -s/- *dial. (Maulwurfsfänger)* mole-catcher, *BrE dial.* mowdy-catcher. - **~haufen** *m* -s/- a small mound of earth made by a mole *(Maulwurfshügel)*: molehill, *BrE dial.* mowdy(warp)-hill.

Schẹrzl *n* -s/-(n) *comest. (Anschnitt oder Reststück e-s Brotlaibs)* end *or* heel (of a loaf of bread), crust (of bread).

schiach, less often **schiech** *adj, dial.* **1.** unattractive and unpleasant to look at *(hässlich)*: ugly, *AmE also* homely; *i hab no selten so a ~e Larvn [= Gesicht* 'face'*] gsehn* I've hardly seen such an ugly mug before; *~ wia die Nacht* ugly as sin, *AmE also* homely (*or, iron.*, pretty) as a mud fence, homely enough to stop a clock (*or* train). - **2.** unpleasant to see, experience, or feel *(unfreundlich, schlecht)*: nasty, beastly; *bei so am ~n Weda jagt ma ned amal an Hund vor die Tür* you wouldn't even send a dog out in a beastly (*or* rotten) weather like this; *des is ganz a ~a Schnupfn, den i da hab* this cold I've got is a real stinker. - **3.** feeling or showing strong emotion about a person who is considered unacceptable, unfair, cruel, or insulting *(wütend)*: angry (*auf* - at *or* with), *esp. AmE* mad (*auf* - *AmE* at, *BrE* with).

Schlạcht... *cul.*: **~fest** *n* -(e)s/-e "butchering party", a village custom by which a farmer, on having slaughtered a pig, gives a dinner of fresh meat, fresh home-made sausages with sauerkraut etc. to neighbours and friends. - **~platte** *f* -/-n "platter of fresh meat and sausages", a slightly more sophisticated

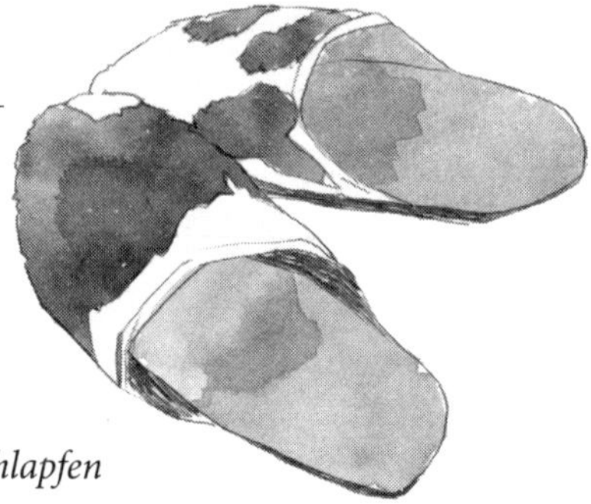

Schlapfen

variant of *Schlachtschüssel*↓, garnished with pickles, tomatoes, small onions, and asparagus shoots. - **~schüssel** *f* -/-n "bowl of fresh meat and sausages", a popular selection of boiled pork, liver sausage and black pudding, served with sauerkraut, dumplings or brown bread.

Schlagerl *n* -s/-(n) [dim. of *Schlag* 'sudden illness caused by a problem in the brain, which can impair a person's motion, feeling, and thinking'] *med., colloq.* slight stroke, *NorBrE also* seizure ['si:ʒə]; *Ihre Tante hat leider ein ~ gestreift* I'm afraid your aunt has had a slight stroke.

Schlạmpen ['ʃlampm] *f* -/- low *colloq., contp.* **1.** a plain unfashionable woman: (old) frump, *BrE also* old trout, *AmE also* hagbag, bag with a sag. - **2.** a woman who is, or seems to be, sexually immoral and whose appearance is rather vulgar and untidy: floozy, *also* floozie.

Schlạpfen *m* -s/- *colloq.* a light shoe with the top made from soft material, usu. worn indoors *(bequemer Hausschuh)*: (carpet) slipper.

Schlawụzi *m* -/- [a blend of *Schlawiner m* 'rogue', 'good-for-nothing' and *Wuzi m* & *n*, a form of endearment for a pleasantly plump little child (cp. *Wuzerl 3*

[1])] *hum.* a child who plays tricks but is regarded with fondness: little rascal (*or* rogue, *or* savage); *wo hat denn mein ~ den Schirm (hin) versteckt?* where has that little mischief of mine (gone and) hidden the umbrella?

Schleimer, *vulg. also* **Schleimscheißer** *m* -s/- *contp.* a sycophant, often a child, trying to curry favour with someone in authority *(schmieriger Liebkindmacher)*: grease rat, crawler, creeper, toady.

Schlụchtenscheißer *m* -s/- *vulg. hum.* a Lower Bavarian's ribald, yet often also good-natured epithet for an Austrian, who is pictured as a hardy cragsman living a vigorous outdoor life at high altitudes and readily answering calls of Nature to depths all "measureless to man" (cp. *Distelscheißer*): "ravine crapper," *AmE also* "Alpine wax dropper" (*or*, "... load dumper").

Schmai, rarely **Schmei** *m* -s/no pl. [a dialect abbreviation of *Schmalzler*↓, with an /l/ mouillé represented by the letter <i>, as in *Waidler* < *Waldler*] *dial.* =

Schmạlzler *m* -s/no pl. [< *Schmalz* 'grease' + the compound suffix *-ler*, signifying occupational relationship with what is expressed in the first element] originally a *trade name*: "butter snuff", North Bavarian type of snuff, chiefly made from Brasilian-grown tobacco: its leaves are ground together with melted butter to keep the tobacco moist; assorted scented ingredients and a fine glass powder are also added, the latter to provide stimulation to the mucous membranes; *der Kenner schüttet ein bisschen ~ in die Mulde am Ansatz des gestreckten Daumens, knapp oberhalb des Handgelenks, und zieht es genussvoll in die Nase ein* the connoisseur taps out a little bit of snuff into the pocket formed at the base of the straightened-up thumb just above the wrist, and then inhales it through the nose with deep satisfaction. - **~dose** *f* -/-n, *dial.* **~dosen, ~dosn** *f* -/- *(Schnupftabak([s])dose)* snuff-box. - **~glasl** *n* -s/-(n) *dial. (Schnupftabaksglas)* snuff-bottle, made of glass or earthenware, shaped like a small *Bocksbeutel*↑ 'Franconian wine bottle' and closed with a wooden stopper; *in den gediegenen Brauereigasthöfen stellt der Wirt aus Kulanz ganz selbstverständlich ein ~ auf den Stammtisch* in the quaint old brewery-inns, the landlord makes a habit of placing a bottle of snuff on the regulars' table as a token of his appreciation. - **~tüachl** *n* -s/-(n) [second el., dim. of *Tuch*, here 'handkerchief'] *dial.* "snuff hankie", a

Schmalzler-tüachl

large and gaily coloured handkerchief used for wiping away remnants of snuff after use.

Schmạnkerl *n* -s/-(n) *colloq.* **1.** *hist. cul. (angebrannte Kruste [am Geschirrrand])* crusty bit (of food, e.g. of porridge), once appreciated by the poor as an extra dainty. → **2.** *cul. (gastronomische Spezialität)* any of the many Bavarian dishes prepared as a culinary delicacy: gourmet offering - for samplings, see *Dampfnudel, Geselchte, Kirchweihgans, Kletzenbrot, Krautwickerl, Züngerl, Obatzte, Presssack, Radi, Ripperl, Schlachtschüssel, Schweinerne, Tellerfleisch, Wammerl,* etc. → **3.** *cul.* a small piece of particularly nice food *(Leckerbissen)*: choice morsel, titbit (*AmE* tidbit). → **4.** *fig.* always *apprec. (Besonderheit)*: (1) specialty, special feature, highlight (of a programme, etc.). - (2) special event. - (3) special treat.

Schmạrrn, less often **Schmạrren** *m* -s/- *dial.* **1.** *cul.* a simple dish originally made in a pan from a mixture of flour, semolina or bread (curds or forest berries, sugar or cinnamon being later additions); today the dough consists of flour, milk, eggs, salt, and sugar, all fried in hot fat and duly chopped up into irregular lumps with a small iron shovel *(fett gebackene Mehlspeise)*: (dessert of) hot, torn-up pancake, scrambled pancake || the variety of gustatorial refinements, and hence of titular dubbings, is great - here is a threesome: (1) *Apfel~* "apple scramble cake", featuring two or three mellow apples, peeled and cubed, in the mix, with everything poured into the pan, scrambled and baked. - (2) *Erdäpfel~* "potato scramble cake", boiled potatoes grated and fried, optionally sprinkled with flour. - (3) *Kaiser~* "woodsmen's scramble cake", a rich creamy pancake broken into small pieces while being baked in butter, with sultanas or raisins added. - **2.** *colloq.*, often *contp. (Geringfügigkeit)* pittance; *sie kriegt, wo sie jetzt ist, einen ~ bezahlt* she gets paid a (mere) pittance in her present job; *ja, hör einmal, Spatzl, musst du denn dei Naserl in jeden ~ neinstecken?* now listen, sweetie(-pie), do you have to be poking your nose into every abbreviated piece of nothing? - **3.** *colloq.*, often *contp. (wertloses Zeug)* something worthless; *das Essen ist ein ~* the food's not worth eating; *die Uhr ist einen (großen) ~ wert* the watch isn't worth a (damn) thing; *ich bin zu alt für so einen neumodischen ~* I'm too old for such newfangled trash. - **4.** *colloq.*, often *contp. ([verbaler] Unsinn)* nonsense: hot air, rubbish, twaddle, *AmE also* hokum; *einen ~ zusammenreden* to be talking through one's hat; *red nicht so einen ~ daher! BrE* don't talk such rot!; *so ein ~!* get away with you, (and) don't be silly!; *das ist doch ein (ganz großer) ~!* oh, this is just (a load of) rubbish!; *Ehrenwort, ohne ~!* on my honour, cross my heart (and hope to die)!, honest Injun! - **5.** *colloq.* a rudely emphatic way of expressing negation: (1) *einen ~ macht er sich draus!* a fat lot he cares! - (2) *einen ~ hat sie ihm verziehen!* like hell she forgave him! - (3) *das geht dich einen ~ an!*

this is none of your bloody (*AmE* goddamn) business! - (4) an energetic, yet at the same time rather mildly worded refusal to do something (, preceded by the rhetorical question, *ich [soll] das machen?): einen ~ werde ich das!* I will - on never-never day, *BrE also* I will - like billy-oh.

schmạtzen *v/i colloq. (plaudern)* to chat: to gab, *BrE also* to natter; *es war nett, mit euch, lieben Leutln, zu ~* it was nice having (had) a chat with you, dear people. - **Schmạtzer** *m* -s/- *colloq.*, often slightly *contp. (einer, der viel daherredet)* a talkative person: chatterbox, *AmE also* gabber; *der Mann ist dir ein ~, da kommst du fei gar nicht zu Wort!* my, what a talker that man is - you can't get a word in edgeways. - **Schmạtzerer** *m* -s *colloq.* an angry curt remark: taunt; *er hat die Tür noch einmal wutentbrannt aufgerissen und einen ~ hineingeworfen* he angrily yanked open the door once again, firing off a vicious parting shot.

Schmu̱ *m* -s, also **Schmu̱geld** *n* -(e)s/pl. rare: -er *colloq.* a reserve of money secretly, and often piecemeal, laid by for private ends: (itsy-bitsy) savings on the side, nest-egg; *(wollen wir) wetten, dass er einen Schmu auf der Seite hat?* (do you) want to bet that he's got some shekels on the side?; *was soll's? das Kleid hat sich die arme Hausfrau kleinweis mit ihrem Schmugeld zusammengespart* what the heck, that poor housewife's been putting away bits and pieces for her nest-egg to get that dress.

Schmu̱ser *m* -s/- *colloq.* a broker who does business in all kinds of rural transactions, e.g. the buying and selling of cattle, agricultural produce, and homesteads: go-between || → *Hochzeits*~, *Hopfen*~.

schnạckeln *v/i* [the base of the word is due to sound imitation] *colloq.* **1.** said of an action accompanied by what may be taken to be a slight explosion: to (go) pop. - **2.** said of what is heard when the latch in a spring-bolt lock falls into place: to snap to, to click (shut). - **3.** said of slight short sounds made by a human being with either of two organs: (1) to click one's tongue. - (2) to snap *or* click one's fingers; *sie hat nach der Musik geschnackelt* she clicked her fingers in time to the music. - **4.** said with reference to a metaphorical snap of sudden recognition or comprehension: to catch the drift, *BrE* to tumble to the racket; *es hat geschnackelt* came the dawn, *BrE also* the penny has dropped, he's twigged, he got the message; *es hat schon seine Zeit gebraucht, bevor es bei ihm geschnackelt hat, was eigentlich gemeint war* it was a long time before he got the hang of (*or*, before he tumbled to) what was really meant. - **5.** an appreciative comment, again using the 'snap' metaphor, on a mutually satisfactory boy-meet-girl situation: *es hat (bei [or, zwischen] denen) geschnackelt* they hit it off; *beim Hans und bei der Anna hat es gleich auf Anhieb geschnackelt* John and Anne clicked (with each other) as soon as they met.

schnạckerlfide̱l *adj* [first el., < *schnackeln* 3; the basic idea conveyed by the compound is that a Bavarian in exuberant high spirits gives vent to his feelings by snapping his fingers and clicking his tongue] *colloq.* cheerfully energetic: bright and breezy, bright-eyed and bushy-tailed.

Schna̲dahüpfl, Schna̲derhüpfe(r)l, Schna̲derhüpfl *n* -s/-(n) [< *schnattern* 'to chatter' + *Hüpfl* 'hop'] *mus.* a characteristic feature of Alpine merrymakings *(neckender Vierzeiler)*: "chatter ditty", a gay and teasing little song of four lines, with innumerable verses, each taken up, or improvised upon the preceding one, by a different person:

Ja, Leutln, seids achtsam,
der Wirt braucht sei' Ruah:
bis zwölfi da habts wohl
fei gsuffa grad gnua!

*Yer landlord's a' tired,
Drink up, folks, an' pay:
By twelve you've been boozin'
Enough for the day!

Schna̲ke *f* -/-n, *dial.* **Schnạckn** *f* -/- *zo.* *(Stechmücke)* mosquito, midge, *BrE also* gnat. - **Schna̲kenstich** *m* -(e)s/-e, *dial.* **Schnạcknstich** *m* -s/- mosquito bite, *BrE also* gnat bite.

Schnake

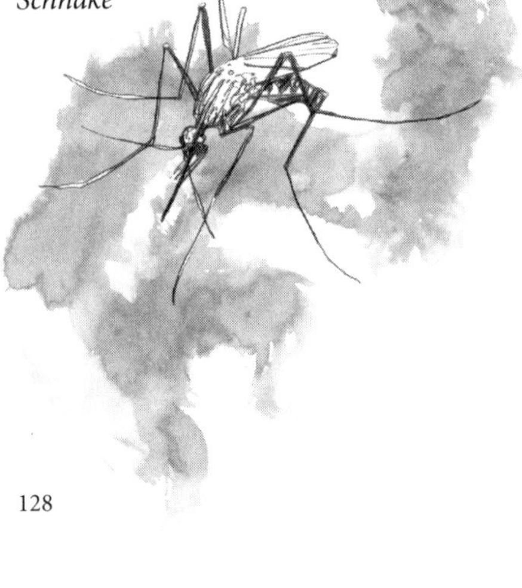

schnạllen *v/t* [< *Schnạlle f* 'buckle', a piece of metal or plastic attached to, and used to fasten, a belt: buckling a belt, therefore, metaphorically speaking, conveys the idea of grasping, getting a firm hold of something] *colloq.* to (begin to) understand what is wanted or meant *(begreifen)*: to catch on, to get the hang (of), *AmE also* to make connections || most often in the p.p. form: *sie hat's geschnallt* she got the message.

Schne̲i̲d *f* -/-(e)n [< StandG *Schneide* (see below, sense 1)] *colloq.* **1.** cutting edge (of a tool); *das nennst du ein scharfes Messer? die ~ ist ja ganz stumpf!* you call this a sharp knife? why, its edge is all blunt (*or*, it wouldn't cut butter)! - **2.** *mount. (Grat, Bergkamm)* narrow ridge, usu. long and straight, maintaining the same height for some distance; *so ein Stucker sechzehn Gams sind gstanden oben auf der ~* there were some sixteen chamois standing up on the ridge. - **3.** *(Mut und Entschlusskraft)* courage and determination: dash, ginger, go, guts *pl.*, pluck, snap, spunk || *phr.*: (1) *j-m die ~ abkaufen* to prove to someone that it is not good to be overly confident: *das wär doch gelacht, wenn ich dem nicht die ~ abkaufen könnt* it would be ridiculous if I couldn't take him down a peg or two (*or, AmE* ... make him come down out of his pink balloon). - (2) *~ haben* to be plucky; *meine Lehrerin hat gemeint, ich würde in der Schule viel besser mitkommen, wenn ich mehr ~ hätte* my teacher said I would get along a lot better in school if I had more spunk. || a young man's challenge to a fist fight, and his adversary's truculent response: A - *geh nur her, wenn du a ~ hast!* put them up, I dare you! B - *geh nur d u her, von dir lass ich mir die ~ noch lang net abkaufen!* y o u come and get it, I'm the last one to crawl before you! - (3) *es braucht schon einige ~, durch den Kamin da zum Gipfel zu kraxeln* it takes some guts to scramble through that chimney to the summit. - (4) an Alpinist's outlook on life, as proudly proclaimed in the quatrain of a chatter ditty:

An da Schneid hats ma nia gfehlt,
aba öfta am Geld;
is ma liaba koa Geld
als koa Schneid auf da Welt!

*Well, I've never lacked ginger,
But I often lacked cash;
What the dickens is cash
Without ginger and dash?

Schneuztüchl, *dial.* **Schneiztüache** *n* -s/- [second el., dim. of *Tuch n* 'piece of cloth'] low *colloq.* a (pocket-)handkerchief: sneeze-rag, nose-rag, nose-wipe, nose-wiper, *NorBrE also* nose-clout (cp. *Rotzhadern*, sub *Hadern*); *die Manschettenknöpfe an militärischen Uniformen sind dazu da (so heißt es), den Soldaten drastisch nahe zu bringen, sich die Nase nicht an den Ärmeln abzuwischen, sondern gefälligst das ~ zu benutzen* cuff-buttons on military uniforms (the story goes) are meant to teach soldiers the hard way not to wipe their noses on their sleeves but to jolly well use their sneeze-rags instead.

scho *adv* [< *schon*] a *dial.* affirmative, with varying vowel length due to varying emphasis: **1.** [ʃo] or [ʃo:] giving simple consent *(ja)*: aye [aɪ]; yes, I do [etc.]; *A: Hast du Hunger? B: Scho.* A: Are you hungry? B: Aye. - **2.** [ʃo:] stressing the speaker's insistence on being right *([aber] doch)*: I do [etc.], though; (of) course I do [etc.]; *A: Du hast ja den Sepp gar net gsehn. B: Scho!* A: Why, you didn't see Joe at all. B: (1) I did, though. - (2) more emphatically: Course I did!

Schrat, **Schratz**, **Schraz** *m* -es/-e and -en/-en, **Schrazel**, **Schrazl** *m* -s/-(n) **1.** *folklore (Heinzelmännchen des Waldes)* woodland gnome. - **2.** *contp. (uneheliches Kind)* child born out of wedlock, *contp.* bastard.

schuhplatteln *v/i.* (pr. t. *ich schuhplattle, du schuhplattelst,* p.p. *geschuhplattelt) folklore* to do an Alpine clog dance. - **Schuhplattler** *m* -s/- *folklore* "foot-slapper", a native Alpine clog dance symbolizing the strutting of the black-cock in front of the demure grey-hen; unless

schuhplatteln

waltzing with their female partners, the men slap soles of shoes and thighs alternately, turn somersaults or cartwheels between the slaps and do other gymnastics in time to the music while the girls waltz slowly round in a circle.

Schụpfen *m* -s/-, sometimes also **Schụpf** *f* -/-en *colloq.* **1.** a lightly built single-floored building, often wooden, used esp. for storing things *(Schuppen)*: shed || the specific use is often indicated by composition, e.g. *Garten~* 'garden shed', *Geräte~* 'tool shed', *Wagen~* 'coach-house', 'carport', though not necessarily so: *trag mir eine Ladung Holz aus dem ~ rein* get me an armful of wood from the shed. - **2.** a small, often roughly made building that rests against the side of a larger one *(Wetterdach)*: lean-to, shelter, carport; *du könntst ja den Wagen auch in den ~ stellen* you might as well put the car under the lean-to (*or,* in the carport).

Schụsser *m* -s/often pl.: - **1.** *colloq.* *(Spielkügelchen, Murmel)* marble (ball). → **2.** *sl.*, pl. only - round, wide-open, and shining eyes, esp. when bulging and rolling *(kugelige Augen)*: *BrE* beady eyes, *AmE* bug(ging) eyes, buggers, banjo eyes || *phr.* describing a person's surprise or excitement: *dem Buben hat's vor lauter Freud die ~ rausghaut* or *raustriebn* the boy's eyes almost popped out of his head with delight. - **~augen** *n* pl. *colloq.* = *Schusser 2; er hat ~ BrE* he's got beady eyes, *AmE* he's bug-eyed *or* banjo-eyed. - **schụssern** *v/i colloq.* **1.** *(mit Murmeln spielen)* to play marbles → **2.** *sarc. phr.: mit j-m ~* to show unwelcome familiarity in relation to s.o.: to chum together with s.o., *AmE also* to hunt in couples with s.o.; *ich kann mich nicht erinnern, dass wir schon einmal miteinander geschussert hätten* I can't remember ever having pulled off the palsy-walsy (*or,* hand-in-glove) act with you, ... having palled around (*or, AmE also,* buddied) together with you.

Schwạmm *m* -(e)s/Schwämme *myc.* & *cul.* *(Pilz)* mushroom; *giftiger ~* toadstool. - **Schwạmmerl** *m* -s/-(n) [dim. of prec. entry] *colloq.* = *Schwamm* || phr.: (1) *wie die Schwammerl aus dem Boden schießen* to grow like mushrooms, to mushroom. - (2) *~ in den Knien haben* → *Knieschwammerl, 2.* - (3) usu. said in anger: *da wachsen ihm vorher die ~ unterm Hut* he'll be covered with moss by the time that [*i.e.*, something made clear by the context] happens, he won't live to see the day, much water will flow under the bridge until then.

Schwe̲i̲nerne *n*, with *adj decl.*: -n *cul.* *(Schweinefleisch)* pork; a typical dish: *~s mit Kraut* pork and sauerkraut (*or,* pickled cabbage) || a proverbial warning that it is impossible to change the real character of a person, especially to make a gentleman or lady of one who is not: *man kann aus einem ~n kein Rindfleisch machen* you can't make a silk purse out of a sow's ear; what can you expect from a pig (*or,* a hog) but a grunt?; *IrE* it's only the Lord can make a racehorse out of a jackass; *AmE also* you can take the boy out of the country, but you can't take the country out of the boy.

Schweins...: **~äugerl(n)** *n pl. colloq.* a person's small eyes: (1) if hereditary - *iron.* or *contp.* piggy eyes. - (2) if due to temporary fatigue - *hum.* in a comment on s.o.'s drowsiness: *du hast ja schon ~!* you've already got dust (*or*, sand) in your eyes. - **~braten** *m* -s/- *cul.* joint of pork; if boiled: roast pork; *Herzstück einer oberbayerischen Gasthaus-Speisekarte ist seit eh und je der ~ - wer Schweinebraten sagt, verrät sich als unangepasster Preiß* roast pork is, and for aye has been, the mainstay of gourmet offerings at Bavarian inns; anyone, though, asking for *Schweinebraten* (instead of *Schweinsbraten*) is bound to give himself away as a Prussian misfit. - **~hachse** (standard spelling, very rare), **~haxe** *f* -/-n, *dial.* **~hax(e)n** *f* -/- *gastr.* pig's foot used as food *(Eisbein)*: pickled knuckle of pork, *BrE also* pickled pork trotter, *AmE also* pork knuckle, ham hock.

schweißeln, *dial.* **schwoaßln** *v/i* [< *Schweiß m* 'perspiration' + iterative suffix *-eln*] *colloq.*, used in respect of a person or persons, or pieces of underwear (usu. a vest or socks) when sweat glands are, or were, overactive - to smell unpleasantly of sweat *(nach Schweiß riechen)*: *BrE* to pong of sweat, *AmE* to (give off a) funk; *in dem Zimmer schweißelt's* there is a muck (*or, BrE also* pong) in this room; *nach vier Stunden Unterricht schweißelt's da wie nicht gscheit* after four hours of class this room smells like merry hell; *deine Socken ~* (with a rude innuendo thrown in: ..., *machst du dir deinen eigenen Fuaßkas?*) your socks are sweaty (..., producing your own limburger [*or* limberger] cheese, eh?).

Schwieger...: **~leute**, *dial.* **~leit** *pl. colloq.* one's relatives by marriage, esp. the father and mother of one's husband [wife]: in-laws; *sind das deine ~?* are these your in-laws?

schwoabn; in its assimilated, truly dialectal form, **schwoam** *v/t dial.* **1.** *(fortschwemmen)* to wash away; *der Platzregn hat den ganzen Dreck von der Straßn gschwoabt* the downpour sluiced

schweißeln

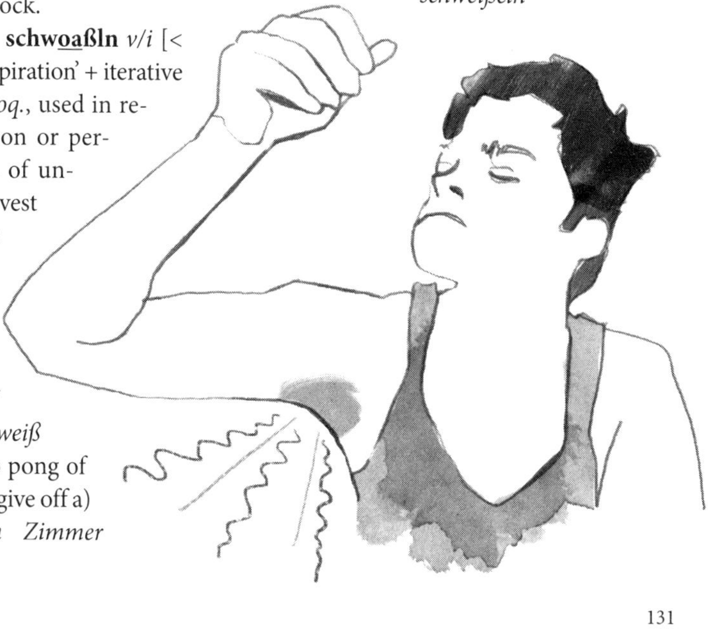

all the muck off the road. - **2.** *(spülen)* to rinse; *nach dem Waschn schwoabt man die Wäsch im reinen Wasser, damit die Seifenreste rausgehn* the laundry is being rinsed in fresh water in order to remove soap after washing.

Sẹmmel *f* -/-n *bak. (Brötchen)* (bread) roll, *AmE also* semmel; *geriebene ~(n) = Semmelbrösel 2* || *fig., colloq.* said of merchandise that is much in demand (the thought here being of bread rolls crisply fresh from the oven, and therefore tasting particularly good [cp. F *se vendre comme des petits pains*]): *die Sachen gehen (weg) wie warme ~n* the things sell (*or* go) like hot cakes.

Sẹmmel...: **~brösel** *n* -s/- **1.** *bak.* roll crumb; *da liegt noch ein ~ auf dem Boden, klaub's bitte auf!* there's another (roll) crumb on the floor, pick it up please. - **2.** *cul.* usu. *pl. (Paniermehl)* stale bread rolls, grated for use in dumplings, for coating meat, fish, celery, slices of vegetable, etc. before frying: breadcrumbs; *~ reiben* to grate (*or* grind) stale (bread) rolls. - **~knödel** *m* -s/- *cul.* a light and soft ball of boiled dough made from dried rolls (soaked in milk), onions and parsley (duly chopped and braised), eggs, and salt, usu. served with a hearty roast: (white-)bread dumpling. - **~schmarrn** *m* -s/- *cul.* a simple yet delicious rural dish made from stale rolls, sliced, soaked in milk and eggs, fried in clarified butter, sugared and served with stewed fruit: scrambled bread rolls. - **~teig** *m* -(e)s/pl. rare: -e *bak.* dough for rolls. - **~wecken** *m* -s/- *bak.* an oval-shaped loaf made from wheat flour: white-bread oval (loaf).

Sẹnn *m* -(e)s/-e = *Senner.* - **~alm** *f* -/-en, **~alpe** *f* -/-n *husb.* mountain dairy, attended by a dairymaid or dairyman (opp. *Galt[vieh]alm, -alpe*); *seit langem schon werden aufgelassene Sennalmen in Galtalmen verwandelt* it has long been a practice to convert disused mountain dairies into stabled pasture-land for young cattle. - **Sẹnne** *f* -/-n rarely: mountain pasture. - **Sẹnne** *m* -n/-n, **Sẹnner** *m* -s/- *husb.* **1.** *(Alpenhirt)* alpine herdsman, alm cowherd [ˈkaʊhəːd]; **2.** *(Bewirtschafter einer Sennhütte)* alpine dairyman. - **Sẹnnerei** *f* -/-en **1.** *(Almwirtschaft)* alpine dairy farming; **2.** = *Sennhütte.* - **Sẹnnerin**, **Sẹnnin** *f* -/-nen alpine dairymaid *or* dairywoman, who tends cattle on the mountain pasture, makes butter and cheese, usu. for home consumption at the valley farm. - **Sẹnnhütte** *f* -/-n mountain dairy hut, alpine dairy, chalet [ˈʃæleɪ].

sẹrvus [ˈzɛrvʊs] [< L *servus* 'slave'] *colloq.* **1.** *interj* [actually, the rest of a hist. phrase expressing abject obeisance, "I am your humble servant"] in broad *dial.* also **sẹrvas**, a jovial greeting - (a) when meeting: hello!; (b) when leaving: so long!, see you! [if in reply, this could be Englished by: yes, see you (*or*, ... be seeing you)!], *BrE also* cheerio! - **2.** $\overset{x}{\sim}$ *m* -(ses)/-se usu. *hum.* one's signature: moni(c)ker; *schreiben* or *setzen Sie da Ihren ~ drunter!* add your monicker here, *AmE also* put your John-Hancock (*or*, John-Henry) here.

Note: When the United States of America declared their independence on July 4, 1776, John Hancock was one of the signatories, and in fact the president of the proceedings; his name became immediately famous for his cockily outsized signature on the Declaration.

Singerl *n* -s/-(n) [a dim. qualifying the stem form of *singen* 'to sing', specifically 'to cheep' or *AmE* 'to peep', i.e. to sound the quickly repetitive weak high noise made by young birds in reply to the mother bird's call] *colloq.* **1.** often *apprec.* small farmyard chicken *(Küchlein)*: chick(abiddy), *AmE also* baby chick, peep; *schau dir nur die süßen ~ an, wie die immer fleißig hinter der Mutter hertrippeln!* just look at those darling chicks anxiously scurrying after their mother! - **2.** [ex a little chicken's early confusion and unpurposiveness] in *iron.* phrases aimed at s.o. giving the speaker a vacant or uncomprehending stare: *schau mich nicht an wie ein ~ (*or, ... *wie ein Kalbl, wenn's blitzt)!* don't look at me as if I was talking double-dutch!

Singerl

soachen *v/i dial* & *vulg.* (< StandG form *seichen*) to piss, *ScotE* to pish. - **Soacher** *m -s/- dial.* & *vulg. (Seicher)* pisser, *ScotE* pisher. - **Soachspieler** *m* -s/- *dial.* & *card-players' sl. (Ersatz für einen wegen Austretens vorübergehend abwesenden Kartenspieler)* "bathroom stand-in," *AmE also* "bathroom pinch hitter," a kibitzer substituting for a cardplayer who goes out to relieve himself of his excess beer. - **soachwarm** *adj dial.* & *vulg.* said of tepid drinks: peewarm.

Soachwasser *n* -s/pl. rare: - low *colloq.* & *contp.* = *Pfeiferlwasser.*

sodala *interj.* [< a contentedly retrospective phrase, *so da* 'so there (then, things stand)' + the echoic suffix *-la* (like *hoppala*↑, *huschala*, etc.) borrowed from cosy nursery talk] a quiet little note of satisfaction when bringing, or having brought, a minor matter to a successful close - **1.** said to oneself: that's it! [ˈðætsɪt] - **2.** meant to encourage an aged or ailing person, when helping him or her to stand up, sit down, or change to a more comfortable position: oops-a-daisy; *bist (du) soweit, Omi? auf geht's ... ~!* are you ready, Granny? come on then - oops-a-daisy (*AmE also* upsy-daisy)!

solala, a shortening of **sosolala** *comp. adv* [a repetitive creation, the balancing act of a wordsmith (and of his untold imitators) performed, one is tempted to believe, on the initials of StandG *so leidlich*; however, such seesaw pattern has its analogues elsewhere, e.g. in It *così così*] *colloq.* **1.** a less than enthusiastic comment on how somebody fared in a competition: (only) so-so; *seine Zensuren in der Prüfung waren grad ~* his results in the exam were only so-so. - **2.** a rather disgruntled response to the query, *wie geht's dir [Ihnen]?* 'how are you?' — moderately well *(nicht gut, nicht schlecht)*: fair-to-middling, just middling.

Spassẹtteln *n pl. colloq.* **1.** playful little jokes *(Witz, Scherz)*: *~ machen* to crack jokes; *immer zu ~ aufgelegt sein* to be always game for jokes. - **2.** annoying jokes *(Albernheit)*: *lass diese albernen* (or, *Schluss mit deinen) ~!* none (*or*, no more) of your silly jokes!; *die ~ gehn mir zu weit* all this is beyond a joke, this joking has been carried too far.

Spạtz *m* -en/-en *colloq.* **1.** *ornith. (Sperling)* sparrow, *BrE also* spadger, spag; a *prov.* advising us to accept something small than to reject it and hope to get more later on: *besser ein ~ in der Hand als eine Taube auf dem Dach* a bird in (the) hand is worth two in the bush, *IrE also* a trout in the pot is better than a salmon in the sea, a wren in the hand is better than a crane to be caught. - **2.** sometimes also *contp.* a person who is small and weak, or poorly developed *(kleiner Kerl)*: little imp, puny feller, *AmE also* wimp; *schau dir (nur) den ~(en) an; der tratzt in einem fort seine große Schwester* (just) look at that little imp, he's continually teasing his big sister. - **3.** *emot.* a pet name for a young person, often one's adolescent son or daughter: darling, dear, honey, *AmE also* (my) love, sweetheart; *wir müssen uns schicken, ~, sonst kommen wir zu spät!* we must hurry up, darling, or we'll be late.

Spạtzen... used in uncomplimentary metaphors levelled at persons in contempt or good-humoured raillery: **~hirn** *n* -s: *ein ~ haben* (1) to be stupid or silly: to be bird-brained. - (2) to forget things easily: to have got a mind (*or* a memory) like a sieve. - **~wadel**, **~wadl** *n* -s/usu. pl. -(n) spindly calf (*pl.* calves): *dem seine ~ sind eine Schau!* those spindle-shanks (*or* sparrow-legs) of his are a sight!

Spạtzl [-ʌ-] *m* & *n* -s/-(n) *colloq.* **1.** *zo.*, sometimes *emot.* ([sweet] little *or* young) sparrow, *ScotE also* spuggy. - **2.** *emot.* a woman's form of endearment when addressing a male, usu. her son or husband: dear, pet, *AmE also* hon [-ʌ-]; *wie war's denn in der Arbeit heute, ~, alles in Ordnung?* did you have a good day at work, dear?; *~, wann du getrunken hast, fahrst (du) net!* you don't get behind the wheel, dearie, when you've been drinking. - **3.** usu. *pl.* [the unumlauted Bavarianized equivalent of the typically Swabian diminutive form in *-le*] *cul.* = *Spätzle.*

Spạ̈tzle *n* -/usu. pl.: - *cul.* a well-known Swabian food substance made at home from flour, eggs, water or milk, and intended for ready consumption: spaetzle(s), spätzle(s), Swabian noodle(s).

spei̱ben [ʃp-] *vt/i dial.* & low *colloq.* to vomit: *colloq.* to be sick; low *colloq.* to puke, to spew; *das Miezerl hat auf'n Teppich gschpiebm* Pussy's bin sick on the carpet || *phr.* the graphic descrip-

speiben

tion of a sickly-looking person: *ausschaun wia a gschpiebms Apfelkoch* to look like a living corpse (*or, more luridly even*, ... like death warmed up).

Spekuliereisen *n* -s/- [first el., < *spekulieren v/i dial.* 'to look pensively'; second el., a reminiscent throwback, verbally, to the times when the frame and arms of eye-glasses were all made of metal] *hum.* (a pair of) spectacles *(Brille)*: specs, blinkers, gig [g-] lamps, *BrE also* barnacles; *ja sag einmal, wo ist denn mein ~?* well, where are my specs, I wonder?

Spezi [short for (*der* or *das*) *Spezielle* '(the) special'] **1.** *m* -/- or, *dial.*, Spezen *colloq.* an intimate friend or companion: chum, pal, *AmE also* buddy; *ein alter ~ von mir* an old pal of mine. - **2.** *n* -/- *colloq.* > *stand., bev.* a mixed drink: half-and-half of Coca-Cola and lemonade; *bitte ein ~!* one lemon-and-coke (mix), please! - **~wirtschaft** *f* -/-en = *Spezlwirtschaft*↓.

Spezl *m* -s/-(n) [a variant of the former, with the diminutive suffix *-l*] *colloq.* **1.** an intimate friend or companion: chum, pal, mate (in cockney rhyming *sl.* > china [plate]), *AmE also* buddy; *die beiden sind schon von ihrer Bubenzeit an echte ~* the two have been as thick as thieves ever since their boyhood days; *er sitzt jeden Abend mit seinen ~n im Wirtshaus* he spends every evening at the pub with the lads. - **2.** *iron.* or *sarc.* (influential) friend: crony; *er hat in allen Ministerien seine ~ sitzen* he has his "boys" in (*or*, his old-boy network spreads into) all the Ministries; *der Bürgermeister schanzt seinen ~n gewiss das eine oder andere zu* the mayor is sure to be doing a favour or two for his cronies. - **~wirtschaft** *f* -/-en *iron.* or *sarc.* favouritism, cronyism, *AmE also* logrolling; *dass der Sohn des Spezls den Posten gekriegt hat, war ein klarer Fall von ~* giving that job to his friend's son was a clear case of cronyism; *diese ~ geht einmal zu weit!* this "old-boy network" has spread too far.

spicken *v/i school sl.* to copy dishonestly from s.o. *([als Schüler] unerlaubt abschreiben oder ablesen)*: to crib; *ich habe die Antworten nicht gewusst und drum bei meinem Nachbarn gespickt* I didn't

spicken

know the answers and so I cribbed them off my neighbour; *man hat ihn beim ~ erwischt* he was caught cribbing. - **Spịcker** *m* -s/- *school sl.* **1.** one who copies in a written examination from his neighbour or neighbours: cribber, copycat. - **2.** an illicit student aid, esp. a tiny manual that offers a literal translation, gives answers to questions, etc.: crib, *AmE also* pony, trot. - **3.** any secretive sheet neatly compiled by a candidate for a written test and carefully tucked away from invigilators' roving eyes; also known as **Spịckzettel** *m* -s/-: crib sheet.

Springịnkerl *m* -s/-(n) [second el., an ablaut variation of *Gankerl*↑ 'little devil'] *colloq.* a person, esp. a child, who moves his body around restlessly, so that he annoys people *(Zappelfritze, -philipp)*: fidget, fidgeter || falling into the cosy vernacular, a Bavarian and a North Briton might equally be tempted to coax: *sitz stad, Bua, sei net so a ~!* sit still, lad, (and) stop fidgetin'.

Sprụchbeutel *m* -s/- *contp.* = **Sprụ̈chmacher** *m* -s/- [first el., dial. form of *Sprüche* pl. 'idle talk'] *contp.* **1.** a person given to meaningless talk: = *Ratsche(n) 2 (1); was soll man denn so einem ~ überhaupt zuhören?* what's the point of listening to such a gurgling gargoyle? - **2.** a person given to rash promises: promise-monger; *der ~ redet dir fei das Blaue vom Himmel herunter!* that big-mouth just about promises you the moon (*or* the earth). - **3.** a person who brags a lot: boaster, *BrE also* romancer; *sie ist ein ~* she blows her own trumpet (*or* horn), *AmE also* she's her own cheerleader.

stad [ʃtaːt], sometimes with the semi-phonetic spelling **staad** *adj* & *adv colloq.* **1.** *adj (still, ruhig)* quiet: (1) *pred.* (a) *(sei) ~!* be quiet!, hush! - merry drinkers favour the following singsong, which is accompanied by rhythmic swayings of their bodies and, for emphasis, their giddily lifting the table around which they are sitting:

Stad, stad, dass 's di' net draht!
Gestern an Rausch, heut an Rausch,
wer woaß, wia 's morgn ausschaut?
Stad, stad, dass 's di' net draht!

*Slow, slow, steady on, whoa!
Boozy last night, same thing tonight;
will we tomorrow be right?
Slow, slow, steady on, whoa!

|| a verbal threat to cow a bawling child: *wennst net glei ~ bist, nacha friss i' di'!* if you don't dry up at once I'll put you on the chopping block! - (b) *um den berühmten Schauspieler ist es ~ geworden* there is hardly any more talk about (*or*, ... any more mention of) the famous actor. - (2) *attrib.* (a) said of a quiet, decent, and reflective sort of person, one whose philosophical bent the

speaker is well aware of, but also said of a secretive, often introvert, individual: *ein ~(e)s Mannsbild [Weibsbild]*, also in the form of an adj noun, *ein ~̽er [eine ~̽e]* a deep one. - (b) said of Advent, or of wintertime in general, when there is comparatively little open-air activity, and many hours are spent by the "fireside clime" with "weans and wife" (in preparation for Christmas, and in expectation of Spring, respectively): *die ~e Zeit* the off-season, the season of lull and leisure. - **2.** *adv* at a regular pace, quietly and unwaveringly, gently not hectically: *phr.* (1) *~ anfangen* to set to work without any hurry. - (2) *sich ~ halten* (a) *(nicht sprechen)* to keep quiet. - (b) *(sich nicht bewegen)* to keep still. - (c) *fig. (geduldig abwarten)* to lie low. - (3) *schön ~ machen!* go easy!, steady on!, don't rush things! - (4) *~ tun* to go easy (on the speed and intensity of work or any other activity, from climbing a rock face to downing quantities of alcohol). - (5) *schön ~ a so weitermachen!* carry on the good work, slow and steady carries the day!

Stadel, **Stadl** *m* -s/- *husb. (Scheune)* barn; *Heu~̽* hay-hut (usu. on high-lying meadows, for temporary storage until called for in winter) || *colloq. phr.: wir haben das Heu nicht im gleichen ~* we do not agree, *colloq.* we don't talk the same language, *AmE* we don't jive, *IrE also* we don't dig with the same foot, *when referring to a third person, also* he (*or* she) is not my cup of tea.

Stạmmtisch *m* -(e)s/-e chiefly in rural inns: **1.** table reserved for regular guests, *colloq.* table for the regulars, habitués' table || as a sign: *~: Dasitzndededaallweidasitzn* Permanently Re-

Stammtisch

served: Theresfortheblokeswotsalwayssitsthere. → **2.** *colloq.* old boon companions, drinking cronies, regular crowd; *er ist zum ~ gegangen* he's gone off for a drink with his gang, *or* ... with the local gang. - **~bruder** *m* -s/...brüder *colloq.* **1.** = *Stammtischler.* - **2.** slightly *contp.* drinking crony, fellow froth-blower; *deine Stammtischbrüder können mir alle gestohlen bleiben!* I don't give a hoot for those boozing friends of yours!

Stạmmtischler *m* -s/- *colloq. (Mitglied einer Stammtischrunde)* one of the habitués, regular, *colloq.* one of the boys, one the lads, one of the gang; *mit echt preußischem Beharrungsvermögen hat er sich beim Kartenspielen vom Kiebitz zum „Soachspieler" hochgedient und ist schließlich etatmäßiger ~ geworden* with truly Prussian persistence, he worked his way up in card-playing from kibitzer to "bathroom stand-in" and was finally accepted as a registered regular.

Stạmperl *n* -s/-(n) *colloq. (kleine Alkoholmenge)* shot, *AmE* jigger (of gin, whisk[e]y, etc.); *wie wär's mit einem ~?* how about a little drop?, what about a little pick-me-up? - **~glas** *n* -es/...gläser *(Schnapsgläschen)* shot-glass, *AmE* jigger.

strawạnzen *v/i* to wander around with no very clear purpose *(herumstrolchen)*: to roam about, to loaf (around). - **Strawạnzer** *m* -s/- mostly *hum.* a juvenile or adult who stays out for unduly long hours: stop-out, gadabout; *ich habe versucht, dich anzurufen, aber du warst den ganzen Abend nicht zu erreichen, du alter ~!* I tried to give you a call, but couldn't get hold of you all evening, you old stop-out.

Stẹckerl *n* -s/-(n) [dim. of *Stock* and *Stecken* 'stick'] *colloq.* little *or* thin stick.

Stẹckerl...: **~beine** *n pl. colloq.* thin legs, *colloq.* matchstick legs. - **~eis** *n* -es/- *colloq.* ice-on-a-stick, *AmE* popsicle; *~ ist beliebt, weil man es unterwegs essen kann* ice-on-a-stick is popular because you can eat it under way. - **~fisch** *m* -(e)s/-e fish-on-a-stick, *i.e.* a small river fish, e.g. bream, roach, redeye, charcoal-grilled on a spit for ready consumption, nowadays also salt-water fish like mackerel and herring; *auf der Wies'n gibt es viele ~bratereien für hungrige Mägen* at the Munich October Fair there are many eat-as-you-go fish grills to feed hungry stomachs; → *Wies'n-hendl.*

Stịftlkopf *m* -(e)s/pl. rare: ...köpfe [first el., dim. of *Stift* 'pin', 'wire brad'] *colloq.* a very closely cut style of hair: crew cut.

Steckerlfisch

Streithansel

Stọck *m* -s/Stöcke **1.** *forestry* stump (of a tree); *holst du einen ~ vom Wald, dann wirst du dreimal warm - beim Ausgraben aus der Erde, beim Zerkleinern zu Haus, beim Verbrennen im Ofen* getting the stump of a forest tree home makes you nice and hot three times - digging it up out there, chopping it up at home, and burning it up in your stove. - **2.** *curl.* short for **Eis~** (wooden) curling stone. - **3.** *contp.* a stupid awkward ungraceful person: lump, clod; *du bist mir so ein ~!* what a bump on a log you are!

stọck... [this is a purely emphatic element, semantically based on the sense of *Stock 1*↑] *colloq.* **~katholisch** *adj* ultra-Catholic: out-and-out Catholic; *sie sind ~* they are rigid Catholics. - **~nạrrisch** *adj* very angry: hopping mad. - **~sauer** *adj* thoroughly disgusted: pissed off.

Stọckzahn *m* -(e)s/...zähne [here again the sense is that such a tooth is as firmly rooted in the gums as is the stump of a tree in its native soil] *med. (Backenzahn)* molar (tooth), back tooth, cheek tooth, grinder; *colloq.: auf den hinteren Stockzähnen lachen* to give a hearty guffaw: to give a belly-laugh (*or* horse-laugh), to laugh oneself to pieces, *ScotE also* to laugh one's socks off.

Stọffel *m* -s/-(n) [< *Christoph(orus)* 'Christopher,' one of the many instances of a Christian name used in a generic and pejorative sense] *colloq.* a taciturn *or* uncommunicative person *(unfreundlicher, mundfauler Mensch)*: clam(-trap), muff, *AmE also* pallbearer.

Streichhölzl *n* -s/-(n) [dim. of *Streichholz,* with the same meaning] *colloq.* match; if a singleton, esp. one that has been used: matchstick || a *hum.* or bantering remark to someone very sleepy, and apparently in need of a mechanical aid to prop open his eyelids: *jetzt brauchst du fei gwiß* (or, *ich borg dir fei gern) ein Paar ~!* now look, use toothpicks to hold open the eyes (*or*, I'll be glad to lend you a couple of matchsticks)!

Streithans(e)l *m* -s/- *colloq.* a quarrelsome person *(Streithahn)*: fire-eater, *(esp. if a woman)* spitfire; *AmE also* splutterfuss.

Strudel *m* -s/- **1.** *geol.* & *hyd. eng.* a place with circular currents of water in a river, which can be very dangerous: whirlpool, eddy (of water). → **2.** [ex the outer resemblance, vague to be true, of water whirls solidified to a golden brown delicacy in the baking pan] *cul.* a pastry of fruit or cheese rolled up in a thin sheet of dough and baked *(Rolle aus dünnem Nudelteig mit Füllung)*: strudel ['stru:dl, *AmE also* 'ʃt-]; hence, e.g., *Apfel~* apple strudel, *Kirsch~* cherry strudel, *Topfen~* curds strudel || ~**teig** *m* -s strudel batter; *für den ~ gibt man das Mehl auf ein großes Nudelbrett, verquirlt dann gut 1/8 l Wasser, Öl, 1 Ei und das Salz, gießt schließlich das Ganze nach und nach zum Mehl* to prepare the strudel batter, whip 1/2 cup of water, oil, 1 egg and the salt, and gradually pour over flour.

Stube *f* -/-n preferably used in rural areas **1.** often *dial.* **Stubm** or even **Stumm** *f* -/- (or -a) a room used, esp. by a family, for varied individual and shared social activities: living room, *BrE also* sitting room || *hist. früher einmal hat es oft zwei Wohnräume im Verbund gegeben, eine ~ mit Ofen, daneben eine Schlafkammer, die lediglich hoch oben in der Trennwand durch zwei winzige Fenster von nebenan etwas Wärme bezogen hat* in earlier times, the rooms often came in pairs, a living room heated by a stove and an adjoining bedroom which obtained but a modicum of heat from next door through two tiny windows high up in the partition wall. - **2.** a small dining room in a country inn or restaurant decorated in the local style, usu. wainscotted *(holzgetäfelt)* and with hunting trophies on its walls: small lounge. - **3.** *colloq. phr.* (1) said of a married couple that is blessed with many children: *eine ~* (often dial., *a Stubm) voller Kinder* a quiverful of children.

Voi Freud han i gheirat't,
do trauri' dann ghaust:
a Stubm voi kloane Kinda
und a Wei', dass 's ma graust.

In glee I got married,
Yet life proved a drag:
A roomful o' li'le kiddies
An' a scarecrowy hag.

- (2) a hearty invitation for one standing at the threshold, usu. a visitor, to enter whatever the speaker considers to be his or her home ground: *(nur) herein in die gute ~!* (ah,) do come right in!, step right in and make yourself at home!, *AmE also* come on in, join the party!, *ScotE also* come into the body of the kirk! - **Stüberl** *n* -s/-(n) [dim. of the above] **1.** *colloq.* a small, cosy room *(Stübchen)*: snuggery. - **2.** = *Stube 2.*

Stubenmusik; often in its dial. form, **Stubm-** or **Stummusi** *f* - *mus.* "parlour music," muted, reflective and slow South and East Bavarian folk music, with the instruments accordingly limited to the dulcimer *(Hackbrett)*, to strings such as the violin, zither, and guitar, and to mellow-voiced brass, such as the flute and French horn; as a

Suffgurgel

folk-musical form, it is of urban origin and has been particularly cultivated since 1945.

Suffgurgel *f* -/-n *contp.* someone who drinks a lot of alcohol *(Trunkenbold)*: boozer, *BrE also* slush bucket, pisshead, *AmE also* guzzle-guts *sg.*

Süffling *m* -s/-e [the stem syllable is an umlaut variant of *Suff* 'booze', with suffixal *-ling* adding, in both E and G, a note of contempt] *colloq.*, sometimes contp. = *Bierdimpfl 1.*

sündteuer *adj, colloq.* very expensive *(überaus teuer)*: frightfully *or* wickedly expensive; *das Gewand war ~* the suit [dress, *etc.*] cost a wicked amount of money.

Suppenbrunzer *m* -s/- *hist. folklore* "soup pisser," a big glass globe with a tapered end below, hung as an economical measure over the dining-room table in farmhouses of SE Bavaria in order to catch, and return as condensation, the vapours rising from the steaming bowl around which all the family are gathered to ladle their broth.

Sur *f* -/-en *cul. (Beize zum Einpökeln von Fleisch)* a liquid - water, plus - used to preserve meat, (1) with vinegar and spices: pickle, souse; (2) with salt: brine.

Sur...: **~fass** *n* -fasses/...fässer *cul. (Behälter zum Pökeln)* salt(ing) tub, pickling tub. - **~fleisch** *n* -(e)s *cul. (Pökelfleisch)* pickled pork. - **~haxe** *f* -/-n, *dial.* **~hax(e)n** *f* -/- *gastr.* a delicacy served roasted, grilled, or boiled, with sauerkraut as a side dish: (1) pickled leg of veal; (2) pickled pork trotter, *AmE* (pickled) ham hock.

T

Tagwerk *n* **1.** -s day's work (of ploughing, or of any other activity); *wir haben heute schon unser ~ getan, lassen wir's gut sein* we've done our share of work for today, let's call it a day. → **2.** -s/- [actually, a field that could be ploughed in one day; cp. the English field-name *Day(s) Work*, examples of which have been found with numerals as high as *Twelve*] *husb.* tagwerk, an area measure of 3.33 square metres, = *100 Dezimal*↑; *drei ~ sind ein Hektar* three tagwerks equal one hectare.

Tandler *m* -s/- *com. (Gebrauchtwarenhändler)* **1.** second-hand (*or* junk) dealer. - **2.** old-clothes man, wardrobe dealer.

Tauben..., *dial.* **Daum...**: **~kobel** *m* -s/- *zo.* = *Taubenschlag.* - **~schlag** *m* -(e)s/...schläge *zo.* pigeon house, dovecot(e) || *fig.* uses in *hum.* banter: (1) describing a place full of noisy movement or activity: *da geht's ja (*or *fei) zu wie in einem ~* it's like a railway station (*specifically also [BrE]* ... like Waterloo Station; *[AmE]* ... like Grand Central Station) here. - (2) a cheerfully indiscreet observation about a male's trouser-fly *(Hosentürl*↑*)*: *dem sein ~ steht offen* (or *auf)!* his shop-door is open!, *NorBrE also* the cage is open, but the beast 's asleep!

Teller *m* -s/- plate || in the *colloq.* phrase humorously, or patronizingly, warning a greedy eater not to scrape the bottom of his plate for the last remnants of soup, etc. (the English equivalent being based on the use of rustic crockery): *iss den ~ nicht mit!, dass du den ~ nicht aufisst!* leave the pattern on the plate! - **~fleisch** *n* -(e)s *gastr.* a popular mid-morning snack, served on a wooden plate: boiled forerибs of beef, boiled and sliced, to be eaten with bread rolls, some horse-radish and chives, one gherkin (or a few slices of beetroot), and washed down with a pint of beer.

Theresienwiese *f* - [< Princess Therese of Saxe-Hildburghausen, the bride in 1810 of the future King Ludwig I] *place-name* "Theresa's Meadow," a large open space on the outskirts of Munich, at the foot of the gigantic statue of Bavaria, where the *Oktoberfest*↑ is held every year; cp. *Wies'n.*

Tod *m* -(e)s death - there are some marked parallels in colloquial lore: (1) *der ~ sucht sich seine Ursach* death doesn't come without a cause. - (2) *für den ~ ist kein Kraut gewachsen* there's neither herb nor cure for death. - (3) *contp.* said of a notoriously slow person: *der ist gut um den ~ schicken* he'd be a good messenger to send for death.

Toten...: **~brett** *n* -(e)s/-er *folklore* in the Bavarian Forest *(Leichen-* or *Gedenkbrett)*: "death board", "memorial board", a bier to rest a recently deceased person on before the body is put into a coffin (cp. *Brett*); after the funeral the board is carved, sometimes painted, and erected with a fitting inscription either somewhere near the farmhouse, by the wayside or in the forest as a simple memorial; the custom is probably of pagan origin, intended to ward off the spirits of the departed, and was later assimilated by Christianity. - **~frau** *f* -/-en, **~weib** *n* -(e)s/-er = *Leichenfrau.* - **~vogel** *m* -s/...vögel *superstition* "death bird", a telltale secondary name for the screech owl *(Käuzchen)* or little owlet *(Steinkauz)*, whose strident notes at night are taken as a bad omen by the anxious, esp. if there is someone ill in the family. - **~wache** *f* -/-n *folklore*, largely *hist.* a ritual observed at the home, or by the side, of a recently deceased person: deathwatch, vigil, *IrE* & *ScotE* wake, i.e. a gathering,

Tauben

on the night before the burial, to grieve over the loss sustained, sometimes accompanied by special food and drink; *die ~ halten* to keep the death-watch (*or* vigil), to watch over the dead. - **~zehrung** *f* -/pl. rare: -en *(Leichenschmaus)* funeral banquet.

traamhappert, **tramhappert** *adj dial.* **1.** not feeling very awake *(schlaftrunken)*: drowsy, dozy. - **2.** slow to react mentally or physically, as if under the influence of a drug *(benommen)*: dopey. - **3.** unintelligent *(einfältig)*: simple(-minded).

Tracht *f* -/-en [< *tragen* 'to wear (clothes)'] *folklore* the concept of tradition and regional identity as materialized in people's distinctive apparel: festive peasant dress, regional costume; *sie hatte die* (or *ihre) ~ angelegt* she had dressed in her traditional costume.

Trachten... *folklore*: **~anzug** *m* -(e)s/...anzüge (a man's) regional suit. - **~fest** *n* -(e)s/-e a festive occasion where traditional costume is worn: costume festival. - **~gruppe** *f* -/-n group (dressed) in traditional costume; *~n aus Bayern* groups in (traditional) Bavarian costume. - **~jacke** *f* -/-n, **~janker** *m* -s/- **1.** jacket worn as part of traditional costume. - **2.** traditionally styled jacket (made of thick woollen material). - **~kostüm** *n* -s/-e (a woman's) suit made of thick woollen material. - **~pflege** *f* - (the custom of) wearing the native costume. - **~verein** *m* -(e)s/-e society for the continued use of traditional costumes. - **~zug** *m* -(e)s/...züge parade (*or* pageant) of traditional costumes, folklore procession.

Trachtler *m* -s/- *folklore* **1.** man wearing the (proper) festive suit of the region. - **2.** member of a regional folklore society.

Tragl *n* -s/-(n) [< *Trage* 'carrier', 'container', 'case' + diminutive suffix *-l*] *colloq.* *([Bier-* etc.*]Kasten)* crate; *Milch~* milk crate (if there are no bottles or if the bottles are empty; otherwise: crate of milk *[~ Milch]*); *ich könnt noch zwei ~ Bier brauchen* I could do with two more crates of beer. - **traglweis** *adv colloq.* *([bier-]* etc. *kastenweise)* by the crate, by the case; *wenn ihm danach ist, schwoabt er das Bier ~ nunter* whenever he's in the mood he downs (*colloq.* he swigs) his beer by the crate.

Trambahn *f* -/-en [first el., < E *tram*, originally a line of wood or iron along which wheeled trucks were drawn in coalmining] *tech.* **1.** a public passenger car, often having one or two trailers, operated on rails along a regular route, usu. through city streets *(Straßenbahn)*: *BrE* tram, *AmE* streetcar, trolley car, surface car; *mit der ~ fahren* to go by tram [streetcar]; *wo ist denn bittschön die nächste ~station?* excuse me, where is the nearest tram stop, please?; *die ~ Nr. 25 geht nach Grünwald* the No. ['nʌmbə] 25 tram goes (*or* runs) to Grünwald. - **2.** *(Straßenbahnnetz) BrE* tramway(s), *AmE* streetcar system.

tratzen *v/t colloq.* to annoy on purpose: to tease; *hör auf und tratz den Hund nicht - der beißt dich noch einmal!* stop teasing the dog, it's going to bite you some day! || → *Magentratzer (1).*

Trottoir [-'wɑ:(r)] *n* -s/-e or -s [< F *trottoir*, a substantivization of F *trotter* 'to trot', 'to trip (along)'; probably of Germanic origin] *colloq.* *(Gehsteig [neben der Fahrbahn]) BrE* pavement, footpath, *AmE* sidewalk; *geh, steig vom ~ runter!* step off the kerb, will you?

Trụmm *n* -s/Trümmer, *dial.* before numerals sometimes - *colloq.* **1.** *(großes,* often also *dickes Stück [von einem Ganzen]* a big portion or piece, e.g. of food: chunk; *jeder hat ein ~ Butterbrot gekriegt* each got *or* had a chunk *or* doorstep of bread-and-butter; *ein ~* [emphatically: *Mords-~* or *Riesen-~*] *Kalbsschnitzel so groß wie ein Abortdeckel* a [great] big veal cutlet the size of a manhole cover. - **2.** *(großer, unhandlicher Gegenstand)* an unwieldy piece, e.g. of furniture: hulking big thing; *ein ~ Holz* a big chunk of wood. - **3.** *(große, ungeschlachte Person)* hulk of a man [woman]; *er ist ein ~ (von einem) Mannsbild* he's a bull of a man, he's a man-mountain. - **4.** a *contp.* reference to a person, at the same time impugning a negative quality of his or hers, e.g., *so ein fades ~!* what a pepless pimple (lumberheels *sg*, wearybones *sg*, *AmE also* sad sack)!

tratzen

U

ü̲berstandig *adj* [an unumlauted dialect variant of StandG *überständig* 'overmature,' actually a technical term in forestry applied to a tree or stand of trees that was allowed to reach an age at which its all-round usability for timber is beginning to decline] *iron.* said of a spinster or bachelor who is on, or possibly even beyond, the brink of marriageable age *(überreif): ein ~es Mädchen* an overripe lass; *mit seinen 36 Jahren ist der Schori schon lang ~* Georgie is 36; why, he's been sitting on the shelf for quite a while.

Ụmständ *m pl.* [< StandG *Umstände* actually, 'things standing around and thus impeding smooth and swift progress'] *dial.* difficulties, trouble || *phr.* (1) said in appreciation of the courtesies shown by the person addressed: *Sie machen sich aber ~ um mich, das wär' ja gar net notwendig!* you do go to such lengths of trouble for my sake, there'd surely be no need for all that. - (2) a warning to s.o. who hesitates, or who puts forward all kinds of flimsy excuses not to do a thing that the speaker thinks needs to be done: *mach koane ~!* don't make a fuss!

Ụmstands...: **~gewand** *n* -(e)s *med. (Umstandskleid)* maternity dress (*or* frock). - **~kramer** *m* -s/- *colloq.*, often slightly *contp.* someone who is too concerned about unimportant details *(Umstandskrämer)*: fusspot, fussbudget.

Umstandsgewand

ụnbandig *adv* [< obs. *Unband m* 'wild-caught hawk'] a *dial.* intensifier meaning 'very (much)', 'a great deal', 'exceedingly': *ich hab mich ~ über das Wiedersehen mit dir gefreut* it was just wonderful meeting you again; *dank dir recht schön für den Brief - er hat mich ~ aufgebaut* thanks a lot for your letter - why, it cheered me up no end; *er ist ~ stark* he's got plenty of brawn, he's as strong as an ox (*or* a horse).

U̲r... 'original': **~bayer** *m* -n/pl. rare: -n, **~bayerin** *f* -/-nen *colloq.*, often *hum.* a person whose parents and grandparents come of Old Bavarian stock: solid (*or, hum.*, primeval) Bavarian; *die beiden sind Urbayern durch und durch, da ist kein Österreicher, aber auch kein Franke angestreift* the two are solidly Bavarian, through and through, with not a touch of the Austrian or indeed the Franconian brush added. - **~viech** *n* -(e)s/-er [for the second el., see *Viech*] *colloq. hum.*, often used in appreciation — a person, usu. male, of much originality and liveliness, at the same time tending to reflect (or indeed clearly reflecting) the cultural likes and dislikes as well as the speech mannerisms, of the region where he was born *(kraftvoll humoriger Mensch)*: one loaded with personality, knockout of a fellow, (real) card *or* character, prize exhibit, *AmE also* one hell of a guy, prize package; *der Hans ist ein ~, bei dem kommst (du) aus dem Lachen gar nicht mehr raus* Jack is quite a scream, he has you all in stitches (*or,* in fits of laughter); *er ist ein bayrisches ~* he's a robustly Bavarian natural.

Urbayer

V

verbạndeln [< *Band(e)l n*, a dim. of *Band n* 'ribbon,' 'piece of string,' 'length of twine'] *v/t colloq.* **1.** *concr.* to tie with a ribbon, cord, etc.: to cord; *verbandel die beiden Schuh' und trag sie über die Schulter!* lace the two shoes together and carry them over your shoulder. - **2.** *fig.* (1) to establish a business or other connection: to get s.o. together; *es wäre doch schön, wenn sich die drei Firmen irgendwie miteinander ~ ließen* it would be a good thing if the three firms could be got together (*or*, could be made to fall into line) somehow or other. - (2) to arrange for a boy and a girl, or a man and a woman, to become acquainted: to get up a blind date for; *man hat mich seinerzeit mit meiner Frau richtig verbandelt; ich war völlig ahnungslos, dass ich ihr begegnen würde* I first met my future wife on a blind date. - (3) in the passive voice only - *verbandelt werden* to get married: to get hitched; *sie werden nächste Woche miteinander verbandelt* they're getting hitched next week. - **verbạndelt** *p.p.* & *adj, colloq.* said of a regular romantic or sexual relationship, but hardly ever (as might be inferred from the prec. instance) of the marital status proper *(in festen Händen): ~ sein* to be going steady; *im Augenblick is s' mit koam ~* she doesn't have a steady at the moment.

Vergẹlt's Gọtt *R.C.* a common phr. expressing appreciation for kindness, alms, or help of any kind: **1.** *interj* God reward you!, God bless you!, thank you kindly! → **2.** *n* -/- heartfelt thanks, God's Blessings || in post-funeral thank-you notices in newspapers: *ein ~ der hochwürdigen Geistlichkeit für die trostreichen Worte am Grabe* heartfelt thanks to, *or* God's Blessing on, the Reverend Clergy for their comforting words at the graveside.

verprịtschen *v/t* [see *pritschen*] *dial.: j-n ~* to tell about the wrongdoings of a friend, etc.: to snitch on s.o.; *Kinder sollten einander nicht ~* kids shouldn't tell tales.

verrẹck [seemingly an imperative of *verrecken* 'to die (a wretched death)' but actually a syntactic shortening of self-addressed *da verreck (ich) doch gleich!*] *interj*, often preceded by *ja* - an expression of sudden strong feeling, either of annoyance or pleasant surprise: well, I'll be (*or*, I'm) damned!, well, I'll be blowed!; *BrE also* well, I'll be jiggered!; *AmE also* I'll be John(ny) Browned!

Verstẹckamandl, **Verstẹckermandl** *n* -s [cp. *Fangamandl*] *colloq.* a children's game in which some hide and others search for them: hide-and-seek; *wie wir noch ganz klein waren, haben wir am liebsten im Stadel ~ gespielt* when we were very young the game we loved to play most was hide-and-seek in the barn.

verwụrstelt, often in the *dial.* form **verwụrschtlt** *p.p., colloq.* said of a dress, carpet etc.: *([in Falten] verschoben, in Unordnung [gebracht]) BrE* rucked up, in a tangle *or* mess, *ScotE also* (all) fankled up, *AmE* (all) tangled up, all wrinkled up, screwed up; *am Tag der Offenen Tür mussten die Schonteppiche schon bald neu gespannt werden, sie waren durch die vielen Füße ganz ~* on the day of Open House, the roll-out carpets soon needed to be straightened out because they were messed up from all the feet tracking over them.

verzụpfen *v/refl colloq.* **1.** *hum.* to go away: to be off; *pfiat di [enk], ich verzupf mich jetzt* toodle-oo, I'm off (*NorBrE* awa' [əwɑː]) now. - **2.** *emot.* to retreat - either (a) stealthily *(sich heimlich verdrücken)*: to sneak off when no one is looking; *~ wir uns beizeiten!* let's slip away while the going 's good; or (b) quickly *(abhauen)*: to clear out; *verzupf dich!* beat it!, *BrE also* hop it!, *AmE also* scram!, get lost!

Vẹsper [ˈfɛspə]; *dial.* [ˈfɛʃpə] *f* -/-n [< L *vesper* 'evening (star)'] less often, and more specifically, used than *Brotzeit*↑: snack (between meals), *esp.* mid-afternoon. - **vẹspern** [ˈfɛspən]; *dial.* [ˈfɛʃpən] *v/i* to eat *or* have a (mid-afternoon) snack.

Vi̲ech [fiːχ] *n* -(e)s/-er *dial. (Vieh)* (*sg.* head of) cattle pl. || *dial. hum.* said of an entertaining and amusing person, usu. male: *~ mit zwoa Haxn = Urviech.*

Vo̲gel...: **~scheuche** *f* -/-n, often *dial.* **~scheichn** *f* -/- **1.** *agr.* an object (usu. old clothes hung on sticks) in the shape of a person, which is put in a field where crops are growing in order to frighten birds away: scarecrow, *ScotE* potato-bogle, *AmE also* bird scarer. → **2.** *contp.* often *alte ~* a thin and very untidy-looking person, often a destitute old woman: scarecrow, *AmE also* old rag doll, hay bag.

Vogelscheuche

W

Waagscheitl, **Wagscheitl** *n* -s/- [literally, 'a piece of wood (meant to be held) in balance', + dim. *-l*] **1.** *agr., colloq.* a crossbar, pivoted at the middle, to which the traces of a draught animal are fastened for pulling a cart or farm implement: *BrE* swingle-tree, swivel-tree, whipple-tree, *SouBrE* spreader; *AmE also* singletree, whiffletree. → **2.** *contp.* a drunkard staggering under the load of alcohol consumed: punch-drunk (*or* top-heavy) boozer; esp. in the dial. outcry: *so a bsuffas [< besoffenes] ~!* what a booze hound loaded to the barrel!, look at that booze hound and his staggers!

Wadl *n* -s/-(n) *anat. colloq. (Wade)* calf || said of an aggressive dog: *j-n ins ~ (*or, *in die ~[n]) beißen* to snap at s.o.'s leg (*or*, legs).

Wadl... *colloq.*: **~beißer** *m* -s/- **1.** a popular name, in farming communities, for (1) the stable fly *(Stomoxys calcitrans)*: "cattle stinger", and (2) any breed of dog trained to snap at the ankles of cattle and other domestic animals in order to make them go faster or move in a certain direction: "cattle nipper". - **2.** *fig., hum.* or *contp.* a disciplinarian who makes people work very hard: pusher, slave driver, whip cracker; *er ist ein ~* he puts the screws (*or*, the squeeze) on. - **~strumpf** *m* -(e)s/usu. pl.: ...strümpfe *folklore* tight-fitting calf coverings worn by men as part of their regional costume *(Wadenstrümpfe)*: half hose.

Wạld *m* -(e)/no pl. *geog. proper name* an endearingly possessive abbreviation of *Bayerische(r) ~*, therefore often in its dialect form **Woid** (with an /l/ mouillé represented by the letter <i> [cp. *Schmai*]), *colloq.*: "Forest"; *ich komm vom ~*, dial. *i bi(n) vom Woid dahoam* I come from (*or*, I'm a native of) The Forest, I'm Forest-born.

Wạldler (in its dialect spelling **Waidler**) *m* -s/-, **Wạldlerin** *f* -/-nen [reference here is always to the Bavarian forest] *place-name derivative* an inhabitant of, usu. one born and raised in the Bavarian Forest: Forest man [Forest woman].

Wạllfahrt *f* -/-en *R.C.* **1.** pilgrimage; *eine ~ machen* or *unternehmen* = *wallfahrten.* - **2.** = *Wallfahrtsort; die ~ auf dem Bogenberg bei Straubing* the pilgrimage church on Bogenberg Hill near Straubing. - **3.** (sacred place for the) cult of a saint; *ein besonderer Schmuck der bayerischen Landschaft*

Wadlbeißer

sind die zahlreichen alleinstehenden Kapellen und Kirchen, von denen viele ihre Entstehung einer alten, meist längst erloschenen ~ verdanken the great number of solitary chapels and churches dotting the Bavarian countryside have an attraction all their own, and many of them owe their origin to an ancient cult of a saint often now long extinct.

wallfahrten *v/i*, ~ **gehen** to go on a pilgrimage; *nach (*dial. *auf) Altötting* ~ to seek the shrine of Altötting.

Wammerl *n* -s/-(n) *cul. (Schweinebauch)* pork belly, the fat meat from the pig's abdomen; lean bacon, occasionally smoked *(geräuchertes ~)*, served steamed or roasted in chunky slices.

wampert *adj, dial. (dickbäuchig)* fat, big-bellied; *prov.: ~ macht schlampert* fat and sloppy go together. - **Wamperte** *m, f* -n/-n fat man *or* woman, *sl.* tub of lard (in direct address: tubby, *AmE* fatso).

Wampn, Wamp'n *f* -/- *dial.*, often *contp. (Wanst)* paunch, pot(-belly); *er kriegt eine richtige* (or *saubere, schöne*) ~ he is getting quite a (little) paunch; he's going to waist || in a German spoonerism: *i' gang so gern auf d' Kampenwand, / wann i' mit meiner ~ kannt* I'd like to climb a steepy crag :/ Too bad there's Paunchy's creepy sag.

Watsche *f* -/-n StandG, rare, for *dial.* **Watschen, Watschn** *f* -/- [prob. an echoic word] low *colloq.* or *vulg.* **1.** *(Ohrfeige)* box on the ear, clip over the ears, slap in the face, *ScotE also* scud on the lug || *phr.* (1) *du fangst gleich eine (~)!* I'll land you one in a minute, you'll get a thick ear in no time, *Western AmE* I'll wat you one if you don't watch out. - (2) *j-m eine (saftige) ~ herunterhauen* to give one a (good) sock on the ear-hole, *IrE* to hit one a (great) clout in the lug, *Western AmE* to give one a (good) wat in the face. - **2.** *fig.* said at the sight of ill-matched architectural styles, colour patterns, etc.: *das gibt einem eine ~* it's a smack in the eye. - **3.** *prov.: Gusto und Watschen sind verschieden* there's no accounting for tastes; tastes differ (*or*, every man to his own taste), said the farmer as he kissed his cow; *AmE also* one man's meat ball is another man's hamburger.

Watschen...: **~baum** *m* -(e)s [jocularly, on the analogy of *Maibaum*↑, *Kirtabaum*, etc., and the ceremony of felling

Watschenbaum

the tree in the end; on the "tree", which nominally deputizes for the blow-in-the-face-happy arm, hang choice fruits like "figs" (Ohr*feigen*) and "dates" *(Dachteln)*, with the hand to take quick action as their potential dispenser] *fig., colloq.* "ear-clout tree", an imaginary tree hung with "clips" and "clouts" that tend to come down rather suddenly on an incessant taunter, or other frivolous offender, once the victim's patience is exhausted: (1) *der ~ fällt um* "the ear-clout tree" falls, i.e. you *etc.* get a box on the ear (at last). - (2) a jocular warning to the unsuspecting, usu. a wanton child:

Rüttle nicht am Watschenbaum:
Die Frucht, sie reift, du merkst es kaum!

*Do not shake the ear-clout tree:
The blow will fall, quite suddenly. -

(3) a whimsical notice found in the public gardens of a Bavarian health resort:

Gemeinsinn hat dies Werk vollbracht
Und freudig-stolz das Herz uns lacht:
Zerstörern geben wir bekannt:
Der Watschenbaum wächst hierzuland.

*Through common efforts ne'er denied
The park here stands, our civic pride.
To roughs let this a warning be:
Our native growth's the "ear-slap tree". -

~gesicht *n* -(e)/-er usu. *contp.* **1.** bloated *or* pudgy face. - **2.** face arousing antagonism; *der hat ein richtiges ~* that ugly face of his is just asking for a punch, he's got the sort of face you'd like to put your fist into. - **~schuhplattler** *m* -s/- *folklore* & *mus.* "box-your-ears" clog dance, a type of *Schuhplattler*↑ in which faked face-slapping symbolizes the mock rivalry between two male dancers for a beautiful girl.

wạtten *v/i* to play (the game of) "watten"; **Wạtten** *n* -s *cards.* "watten", a card-game between 2, 3 or 4 players with a tarot pack (hearts, bells, leaves and acorns) of 32 cards, from which each player is dealt five cards; elder hand names the denomination *(Schlag)* which for the time being is to outrank any other, and the opposing party does so for the suit *(Farbe)*; besides, the king of hearts *(Max)*, the seven of bells *(Belle)*, and the seven of acorns *(Biese)* are permanent trump cards *(Kritische)*; a game is over if a player wins three tricks.

Wẹcken *m* -s/- *bak. (Brot in länglicher Form)* oval loaf (of bread). - **Wẹckerl** *n* -s/-(n) [dim. of prec. entry] *bak. (kleines, längliches Gebäck)* oval-shaped roll, *BrE also* finger roll; cp. *Eiweckerl.*

Weiber..., *dial.* **Weiba...** or **Weiwa...** *contp.*, often out of the mouths of macho men; but sometimes *hum.* or (as in the first comp. pair) devoid of any connotations, purely in the sense of 'typical of, or reserved for, woman': **~fasching** *m* -s;

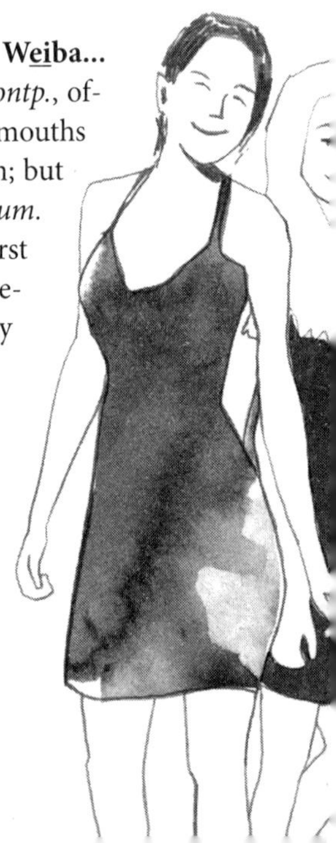

outside Old Bavaria, **~fastnacht** *f - folklore* the Thursday preceding Shrove Sunday *(Faschingssonntag)*, the Sunday before Ash Wednesday, close to the end of the carnival merry-makings, on which the "feminine gender" assumes hilarious control of the revels for that one day: "Women First" Carnival. - **~leit** *n* -s/- [< *Leute* pl. 'folk(s)'] *dial.* a woman or girl *(weibliches Wesen)*: female, *hum. also* wench; *ich möcht mit dem ~ nix zu tun habm* I can't be bothered with that female; *für den Kurs haben sich nur ~ eingetragen* it's all womenfolk have signed up for this class.

Weiberer, *dial.* **Weiwara** *m* -s/- *contp.* a libertine *(Weiberheld)*: womanizer, *AmE also* woman-chaser; *der Mann von der Nachbarin lauft auch hinter jedem Rockzipfel her, der alte ~!* our [my] woman-neighbour's man is quite keen on dangling after petticoats, that old lecher!

Weiberer

Weibsbild *n* -(e)s/-er *colloq.*, often *emot.* a female person: woman; *sie ist der Traum von einem ~* she's the answer to a man's prayer; *so ein ausgeschamtes ~!* what a brazen *or* shameless female!

Weihbrunn, *dial.* **Weichbrunn** *m* -(e)s/-en *R.C. (Weihwasserbecken)* holy-water font, stoup; *(Weihwasserkessel)* holy-water bowl; *einen ~ nehmen* to bless (*or* cross) oneself with holy water; *sie wollten alle die tote Großmutter noch einmal sehen und ihr ~ geben* they all wanted to see their dead grandma one more time and to sprinkle her with holy water.

Weißbier, also **Weizenbier** *n* -(e)s/-e *bev.* a typically Bavarian light ale, sparkling but fairly dry (since including a mixture of barley and corn), brewed from wheat grain, malt and top-fermentation yeast: weissbier; *~ ist die köstlichste Erfrischung für durstige Gemüter und belebt schlappe Zeitgenossen; drum gehört es einfach zur bayerischen Vormittagsbrotzeit wie zum Katerfrühstück nach einer durch-„drahten" Nacht* weissbier is the most refreshing drink imaginable for thirsty souls, and it reactivates Tired Tims; it is part and parcel, therefore, of a Bavarian mid-morning snack and comes in handy as a pick-me-up for those with a hangover after "a night on the tiles."

weiß-blau, **weißblau** *adj* & *adv* blue-and-white **1.** denoting dynastic or regional colours, of or within Bavaria: *durch seine Vermählung mit Ludmilla von Bogen übernahm 1204 ein Wittelsbacher, Ludwig der Kelheimer, die ~en Rauten der in der Straubinger Gegend beheimateten Grafen von Bogen in sein Wappen; es ist seither neben dem pfälzischen Löwen das vornehmste Wahrzeichen aller Linien des verzweigten Fürstenhauses und des heutigen bayerischen Staates geworden und findet sich schließlich als wesentlicher Bestandteil vieler niederbayerischer Gemeinde- und Landkreiswappen* the blue-and-white diamond field of the Counts of Bogen, from the vicinity of Straubing, was taken over by a member of the Wittelsbach dynasty, Ludwig of Kelheim, when he married Ludmilla von Bogen in 1204; together with the Palatine Lion, it has since become the noblest emblem of all the lines of this royal family with its many branches and of the modern State of Bavaria, as well as a prominent element in the coats of arms of a great number of Lower Bavarian communities and districts; *Bayern sind die Franken und Schwaben nur den gemeinsamen ~en Landesfarben nach; in ihrer Sprache sind sie es nicht und ihrem Charakter auch nicht* Franconians and Swabians may share the same blue-and-white flag with Bavarians, but their languages differ, and so do their characters; → **2.** *journ.* & *colloq.* denoting things Bavarian, esp. Bavarian realia, institutions, and characteristics: *innerhalb (außerhalb) der ~en Grenzpfähle* inside (outside) the pale of Bavaria; *fast 80.000 Tonnen Käse überschreiten jährlich die ~e Grenze* nearly 80,000 tons of cheese roll out of Bavaria every year; *Freunde und Liebhaber unseres ~en Landes* friends and fans of this country of ours (with its blue-and-white); *das ~e Nationalgetränk* the national drink of the South, i.e. beer; *wenn sie hier in einem Biergarten sitzen, die frische Mass vor sich, daneben einen tränenden Radi und eine resche Brezn, dann sind sie alle - die Einheimischen, die Zugereisten und die Weitgereisten - sich darüber einig, dass der Himmel ~ und die Welt schön ist* when they sit in a beer garden, with a fresh mug of beer in front of them and alongside it a well-salted giant radish and a crunchy pretzel, then everyone - born here, moved here, or visiting from abroad - is united in the assurance that God's in his heaven and all's right below in Bavaria.

Weißkraut *n* -(e)s *bot.* *(Weißkohl)* white cabbage.

Weißwurst *f* -/...würste, *dial.* ...würscht *gastr.* a snack-time speciality "discovered" by a Munich apprentice butcher on February 22, 1857: white sausage, *ScotE* white pudding, a fat white delicacy filled to bursting point with calves' brains, spleen and veal; if eaten in style, the gourmet's fingers and teeth do the squeezing || *phr.* since its consistency does not last for many hours, it is well to follow the warning: *die ~ darf das Zwölfuhrläuten nicht mehr hören* (or *erleben)* a white sausage must have gone the way of all flesh before the clock strikes the hour of twelve.

Weißwurst... in *comps.*, mostly *hum.* or *contp.* in the sense of '(typically) Bavarian': **~äquator** *m* -s, **~grenze** *f* - *hum. (Mainlinie)* the River Main, considered by a staunch Bavarian to be the northern frontier of his beloved homeland, a visible divide to shield what is near and dear to him in his cultural "hemisphere": *Bavarian defence line.

Weißwurstgrenze

Weiz *m* -es *folklore* disembodied spirit, esp. a "poor soul" which, because of some misdeed committed while a human being or because of leaving this life as a result of torture or suicide, has to roam the earth and cannot find peace until somebody performs a particular deed, or uses a particular formula, to relieve the spectre of its wanderings. - **weizen** *v/i* said of a felonious person or one who has met a violent death *(geistern, umgehen, gespenstern)*: to haunt a place; *es weizt* there is a ghost haunting the place, the place is haunted, the place has a ghost; *im Schloss weizt der Geist eines ermordeten Ahnherrn* the ghost of a murdered ancestor walks in (*or* haunts) the castle; *für im Leben begangene Untaten musste man nach dem Tode ~: Hölle und Fegfeuer der Kirche waren dem einfachen Volk als Strafen zu ungewiss* one who had committed a crime in his lifetime was condemned to wander about as a ghost after death - the Church's hell and purgatory were too uncertain modes of punishment for the unsophisticated to accept.

Weizen *n* -s/- *bev., colloq.* short for *Weizenbier (= Weißbier↑)* - the habitué's, and insider's, word form when shouting his order, e.g. „*Oa ~!*"

wer ko, der ko! [*ko < kann*] *colloq. phr.* (used both in dialect texts and as a dialect implant in standard language) a self-confident answer cheerfully flung in the face of one who has just dared make a miserably envious remark about, or who has cast some doubts on, the speaker's manual skill or mental potential: those who can, do!; he who can, does!; *das positive Bild, das die Münchner zu Recht von ihrer Stadt haben, entspricht ganz ihrem Selbstverständnis, das da lautet: „~ ~, ~ ~" - und München „ko" eben* the positive view natives of Munich have of their city is entirely in tune with their view of themselves, which is that "Those who can, do!" - and Munich can and does, period; *du hast wohl geglaubt, dass ich den Schlüssel gar nimmer rauskrieg - da schaust aber jetzt, gell? ... ja, ~ ~, ~ ~* you thought I wouldn't be able to get the key out, didn't you? why, now, eat your words ... he who can does, see?

Wies'n *f* - *colloq. place-name* in Munich: "Meadow," a popular abbreviation for *Theresienwiese*↑, the scene of the October Fair, the biggest folk festival in Europe; *auf der ~* at the Fair; *auf geht's zur ~* off (we go, *etc.*) to the Fair. - **~bier** *n* -(e)s *bev.* "Meadow beer," a special tangy beer almost twice as strong as ordinary beer, brewed for the event and served in numerous beer tents to the accompaniment of music played by colourfully costumed farmers. - **~braut** *f* -/...bräute *hum.* "Meadow bride," temporary sweetheart (good for one day's fun at the fairground), sweetheart of the day. - **~fest** *n* -(e)s/-e = *Oktoberfest.* - **~gast** *m* -(e)s/...gäste visitors to (*pl. also* those attending) the October Fair (*or, more colloq.*, the October do). - **~hendl** *n* -s/-(n) *cul.* "Meadow chicken" **1.** fried *or* grilled chicken, a staple item of consumption at the October Fair; *der Steckerlfisch des Münchner Oktoberfestes schmeckt gut und kostet wenig, er gilt als das ~ des kleinen Mannes* at the Munich October Fair, grilled fish-on-a-stick is an inexpensive treat, and passes for the poor man's fairground chicken. → **2.** *hum.* any chicken dish eaten vicariously at home or elsewhere during that period. - **~rennen** *n* -s/- October Fair Race, staged annually, excepting war years, since 1810. - **~wirt** *m* -(e)s/-e October Fair (brewery) landlord. - **~zeit** *f* -/pl. rare: -en *colloq.* the span of days the (Munich) October Fair (*or, more colloq.*, the October do) is on; *während der ~* while (*or*, as long as, *or*, throughout the days) the October Fair is on; *zur ~* when the October Fair is [was; will be] on, at the time of the October Fair; *das offizielle Faschingsprinzenpaar wählt sich die Narrhalla schon um die ~ aus* the choice of the official carnival prince and princess is made by the Narrhalla Society as soon as the October Fair comes round.

Wimmerl *n* -s/-(n) *med. colloq. (Eiterbläschen, Pickel, Pustel)* pustule, pimple, *colloq.* hickey, hickie, doohickey, do-hinky; *er hat sich alle ~(n) im*

Gesicht ausgedruckt he squished out all the hickeys in his face.

Wọlpertinger *m* -s/pl. rare: - [< *Wolperting*, an imaginary Bavarian place-name (containing the elements *Waldbrecht* 'famous in the forest' + *-er* 'inhabitant (of)'] *folklore hum.* a mysterious forest animal, with a highly prized fur, that allows itself to be caught only by candlelight in a bag patiently held open by the midnight stalker; the story is a hoax directed at gullible non-Bavarians, preferably 'Prussians', whom natives boast to have kept waiting in lure for hours while themselves enjoying the successful prank over rounds of beer at the local inn *(→ derblecken)*: dodgie, fadger, bodger-fax, wadger-beasel, *ScotE* haggis, *AmE* catawampus, snark, hoofen-poofer, whiffen-poof, woofin-whiffle, *PaG* elpentrecher, elbedritch || a spurious invitation to the unsuspecting: *j-n zum ~fangen schicken* to send s.o. on a wild-goose chase; *gemma* [< dial. *gehen wir*] *~fangen!* let's go dodgie (*etc.*)-hunting!

wụrst or **wụrscht**, invariably pronounced [-ʃt] *adv* [the metaphor probably rose from the sense impression, ever-recurring to millions of knife-wielding people every day, that it makes no difference whether they start cutting their sausage at one end or another] in the *colloq.* phrase cluster *das ist mir ~*

Wolpertinger

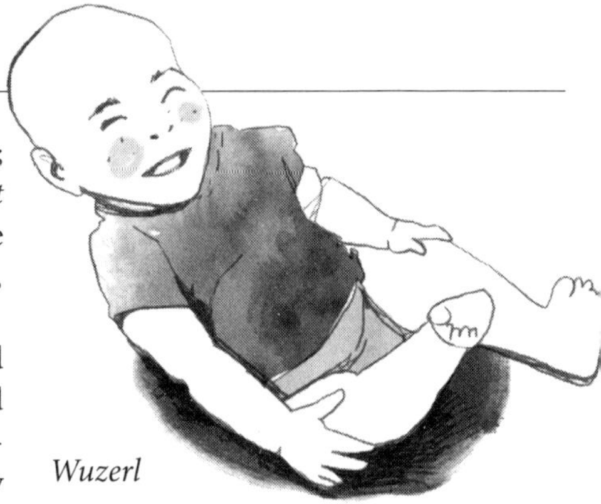

Wuzerl

[gewesen] I'm not [I wasn't] bothered; *das soll mir doch ~ sein, ob er kommt oder nicht!* as if I cared whether he comes or not!; *das ist mir völlig ~ (*or, *~egal)* I couldn't care less.

Wụrzelsepp *m* -s *colloq.*, often *hum.* and in appreciation - a robust and bearded type of person who is rooted in his native, usu. sylvan, surroundings: burly backwoodsman; *er ist der* (or, *ein*) ~, *wie er im Buch steht* he is the perfect example of a Woodland Joe || cp. *Urviech.*

wuzeln *vt/refl* [< a word stem that tries to imitate the motion and the sound made in the characteristic action] *colloq.* **1.** *v/t* (1) always with reference to something very small, soft, or little resistant to the touch, that invites a human being, often unwittingly, to roll it into a pellet *(drehen)* — to roll up and down between the fingers: to roll around; *ja weißt denn du nichts Bessres als deinen Rotz zu ~?* haven't you got anything better to do than roll around your snot? - (2) with reference to a cigarette or a cigar *(wickeln)*: to roll, to make (by rolling); *ich wuzel mir jetzt eine* I'm going to wrap (myself) one up. - **2.** *v/refl* to twist one's way with some effort: *sich durch die Menge ~* to worm (*or* wriggle) one's way through the crowd.

Wuzerl *n* -s/-(n) [either an imitative parallel of *wuzeln*↑, or a dialect variant of *Butz(en)*↑, quite possibly a combination of the two, + *-erl*] *colloq.* **1.** any small light loose waste from wool, or human skin peeled off (e.g., after excessive exposure to the sun), which one sometimes tends to pick up and roll into a tiny ball before throwing it away: twiddlybit (of wool, peeled skin, etc.). - **2.** *(Fussel)* a feather-light adhesion, occasionally resembling an uncannily insubstantial roundness, of soft thin hair and dust particles that hover on or gently waft along the floor of an untidy room: *BrE* fluff, *AmE* fuzz, lint. - **3.** *hum. (Dickerchen)* a fat and round person; (1) if a child: humpty-dumpty; *die Kleine ist ein süßes ~, gell?* the little one's a sweet roly-poly, isn't she? - (2) if an adult: chubby chops; *das ~ könnte auch einmal ans Abspecken denken!* ('t) wouldn't be a bad idea if chubby chops were to go and shed a few pounds. - **4.** *physiol. (Nasenkrümel)* a piece of hardened mucus: bogey, *NorBrE* crow, *vulg.* blob (*or* piece) of snot.

wuzerl... *colloq.*: **~dick**, **~fett** *adj* with reference to babies and little pigs, usu. connoting cheerful appreciation — nicely rounded: pleasantly plump; *seine ~en Handerln* his podgy (*or* pudgy) little hands. - **≗viech** *n* -(e)s/-er [for the second el., see *Viech*] *dial.* an unidentified small creeping animal, vaguely associated with the beetle-cum-spider population: creepy-crawly.

Z

Zahnspangler, by reviving an old umlaut variant also **Zahnspängler**, *m* -s/- *colloq.*, usu. *hum.* = *Fotzenspangler*↑.

Zamperl *m* -s/-(n) *colloq.* **1.** *hum.* or slightly *iron.* - a small dog: little yapper. - **2.** *sarc.* a small nondescript dog, often saddled with the onus of doubtful parentage: pooch, *AmE* mutt.

Zander *m* -s/- *ichth.* a predatory freshwater fish in the East and South of Germany, also known as **Schill** *m* -(e)s/-e *(Lucioperca sandra)*: pike-perch, zander [ˈzændə]; a new delicacy now in East Anglia, where the fish is bred by the Great Ouse [u:z] River Authority.

zaundürr *adj colloq.* of a person who is very slim *(spindeldürr)*: (as) thin *or* lean as a rake, (as) thin as a lath, skinny, spindly || → *Hopfenstange 2.*

zeckerlfett *adj* [first el., dim. of *Zeck(e)* 'tick', i.e. a very small insect-like animal that can gorge itself to several times its original size] *colloq.* of a person, often *hum.* obese, esp. replete with food (and/or drink): full as a tick.

zefix; if given more weight, **zäfix** *interj.* [an abbreviated, and therefore de-emphasized, form of *Kruzifix* which, besides its factual meaning, 'crucifix', is a full-bodied curse, '(God) damn it (by the holy cross on which His Son had to die)!'; the English equivalents here offered are euphemisms for *Jesus* and *God*, respectively] a rather mild cry of annoyance: jeepers!, by golly!; *jedesmal wenn ich rausgeh - ~! -, fängt es zu schütten an* it starts pouring (*NorBrE also* teeming with rain) every blessed time I go out.

Zeitlang *f* - *dial.* **1.** *(Sehnsucht)* longing, yearning; ~ *haben nach* (dat.) to long *or* yearn for, to miss (a person, a place, etc.). - **2.** *(Heimweh)* homesickness; *ich hab'* ~ I'm homesick. - **3.** *(Langeweile)* boredom; *schrecklich ~ haben* to be bored stiff, to be bored to tears.

zaundürr

Zinken *m* -s/pl. rare: - *colloq.*, often *hum.* or *contp.* a person's sharp, angular nose: beak, *BrE also* hooter, pecker, *IrE* Concorde nose; *dem seinen ~ könnt' man fei als Pflug hernehmen* his beak might as well serve as a plough.

Zipferl *n* -s/-(n) [dim. of *Zipfel m* 'end', 'tip'] **1.** *colloq.* the small, tapering (or tied-up) endpiece of an article of food, esp. that of a length of sausage: end bit. - **2.** low or domestic *colloq.* a child's penis: tassel, *BrE also* winkle, *AmE also* wag; cp. *Pfeiferl 2.*

Zoigl *m* & *n* -(s) [see etym. note under 2] *folklore* in the northern Upper Palatinate: **1.** *bev.* a type of homemade beer, light and sweet, for whose production, on a small-scale private basis, a couple of peasants have made a point of joining forces: local home brew; *unser ~ enthält Fluor und ist die reinste Medizin* our home brew contains fluorine, and is a cure-all good and proper. - **2.** [< the verb stem of *zoign*, the dial. variant of StandG *zeigen* 'to show,' 'to draw attention to' + the dim. suffix *-l*] *com.* a sign displayed in front of the house where the home brew is offered for neighbours and passersby to sample: welcome sign (for lovers of the local home brew).

Zornbinkel *m* -/-(n) *colloq.*: hot-tempered person: hothead; *hast du je schon so einen ~ gesehen?* have you ever seen someone fly off the handle like that (*or*, someone lose their temper like that)?

Zuagroaste *m* & *f* -n/-n [the popular South German variant of *Zugereiste* 'newcomer', actually the past participle noun of a defunct verb, *zureisen* 'to travel there'] *dial.* any person who, either recently or years ago, has moved into the community; one looked upon, sometimes indeed looked *down* upon, as a non-native *(Zuwanderer[in])* - **1.** if from another town, or part, of Germany or from a German-speaking country *(Zuzügler[in]*, colloq. *Neue)*: newcomer, *colloq.* young-timer, Johnny [*if female*: Jeanie]-come-lately. - **2.** if from further abroad, esp. from the East *(Ausländer[in])*: immigrant, foreigner, *slightly contp.* one of those aliens; *jeder fünfte Münchner ist ein Ausländer; mit seinen „~n" aus aller Welt ist München unter den Spitzenreitern in der Republik* every fifth citizen of Munich comes from abroad; in this country, the town

Zuagroaster

is among the front-runners as regards population influx from all over the world.

Zubrot, *dial.* **Zuabrot** *n* -(e)s [actually, 'additional bread'] *colloq.* extra income *(zusätzlicher Verdienst)*: something earned to boost (*or*, up) one's salary a bit; *a wengerl a ~ verdienen* to make a bit on the side.

zündeln *v/i colloq.* **1.** nearly always referring to a child, or children, impishly engaged in incendiarism: to play with fire (*or* with matches) || a common folk belief, and a scary warning to potential culprits: *wer zündelt, bieselt in der Nacht ins Bett* he who plays with fire will wet the bed (*or*, will pee in bed). - **2.** said of one gripped by an uncontrollable, or criminal, desire to start fires: to be a firebug. - **Zündler** *m* -s/- *colloq.* **1.** (1) child (*or, less often*, youngster) playing with fire. - (2) child having caused fire damage through the act of playing with live matchsticks: child incendiary. - **2.** arsonist: firebug, *AmE also* torch (man), torcher.

Zunftbaum *m* -(e)s/...bäume *folklore* erected in the centre of some villages as a permanent landmark of communal identity and pride: "guild pole", the trunk of a huge forest tree or a steel mast (in either case some thirty feet high), bearing at regular intervals, both left and right, some distinctive "guild emblems" *(Zunfttafeln)*, the sometimes almost life-sized silhouettes of people or their occupational instruments (a man scything, a woman gathering sheaves of grain, a breweryman and his dray, etc.) which are typical of that village in its day-to-day activities.

zünftig *adj colloq.* **1.** *(prächtig)* fine, grand; to express satisfaction at being in a convivial group: *~ ist's!* it's just grand!, it's really groovy!; *ein ~er Kerl* a jolly good fellow. - **2.** *(herzhaft)* genuine, proper; hearty; *zu einer ~en Brotzeit gehören Bauernbrot, Brezen, Salzstangerln oder Kümmelweckerln* a hearty snack includes black bread, pretzels, salt sticks, or crisp caraway-seed rolls.

zusammen...: **~rucken** *v/i colloq.* **1.** usu. said of a convivial group of people seated on a bench or around a table, and trying to accommodate one or more comers: to move up closer, to huddle together; *der Bayer liebt volle*

Wirtshäuser, Bierzelte und Biergärten; am liebsten zwängt er sich, entschuldigend um Gunst buhlend, mit einem „Ruck ma a bisserl zamma, bittschön!" an einen bereits voll besetzten Tisch a Bavarian is fond of jam-packed inns, of brewery tents and beer gardens; and he just loves to edge in on a fully-seated bench with a coaxingly apologetic, "Let's move over (*or*, squeeze together) a wee bit, shall we?" - **2.** to start quarrelling: to have a set-to; *mir werden fei bald ~, mia zwoa, wann des so weitergeht!* we'll soon have it out, me and you, if things go on like that! - **~saufen** *v/refl* low *colloq.*, among intimate friends *(austrinken)*: to finish one's drink; *sauft's euch* (dial. also *enk*) *z'samm, wir müssen gehen!* drink up, it's time (for us) to go! - **~trinken** *v/refl colloq. = zusammensaufen.*

zuzeln, less often **suzeln** *vt/i dial.* [< *Zuzel m* 'nipple', related to E *teat* and *tit* 'nipple of breast or udder'] **1.** *vt/i (saugen)* to suck. - **2.** *v/i (mit spitzen Lippen undeutlich sprechen)* to speak unclearly, using [θ, ð] for [s, z] (e.g. saying *er tthutthlt* ['tθu:tθlt] for *er zuzelt*): to (have, *or* speak with, a) lisp.

zuzeln

Zwẹtschge *f* -/-n *bot.* plum || if dried (and gently boiled before eating), prune.

Zwẹtschgen...: ≃**blau** *adj* (as) blue as a plum; *durch jahrelangen Alkoholgenuss war seine Nase ~ geworden* steady years of drinking had turned his nose a mottled red-and-blue. - ~**datschi** *m* -(s)/-(s) *bak.* flat plum cake (made on a baking tray). - ~**knödel** *m* -s/- *cul.* plum dumpling. - ~**mandl** *n* -s/-(n) "fig-and-prune man" **1.** *folklore* & *com.* a distinctive feature of, and a popular take-home present from, any Bavarian Christmas Market since about the early nineteenth century: a quaintly decorative wire figure in peasant costume, its lean body made up of figs, and its arms and legs of dried plums; indeed, this "laddie" may appear in various guises, e.g. as a chimney-sweep or a dwarf, and he may have a "lassie" by his side to make a pretty bridal pair. → **2.** low *colloq.* a lean or even emaciated male person: skinny-malink, bag of (skin and) bones; if justified by appearances, a favourite invective, e.g. by an irate offender for a policeman: joker. - ~**mus** *n* -es/-e *cul.* plum jam. - ~**schnaps** *m* -es/...schnäpse, ~**wasser** *n* -s/...wässer *bev.* plum brandy.

Zwịckerbusserl *n* -s/-(n) [first el., 'anybody or anything that pinches or nips' (here, the action of pinching is meant); for the second el., see *Busserl*↑] *colloq.*, always used in a cheerful mood — a playful pinch given by an elderly person to a youngster's cheek or cheeks, either with the thumb and forefinger or the forefinger and the middle finger, in a spirit of bonhomie: friendly little

Zwickerbusserl

tweak; *der Direktor hat dem Buben ein ~ gegeben* the headmaster gave the boy a friendly little tweak.

Zwiderwurzn *f* -/- *dial. colloq.* a person with no sense of humor, who always complains and is never satisfied *(Griesgram)*: grumbler, grouch, sourpuss [-pʊs], *AmE also* crosspatch, (old) crabbie, glumpot, vinegarpuss, Adam Sourguy [Calamity Jane].

Zwiefache *m* -n/-n *mus.* "double trouble", gay Bavarian dance music involving alternation between 2/4 and 3/4 time; surprise changeovers for those unfamiliar with the particular tune often cause them to lose step, thus providing extra merriment for all concerned.

Zwịrl *m* -s/- [related to E *twirl* 'sudden quick spinning movement'] *dial.* **1.** *concr.* (1) a twisted mass of something, such as hair or thread *(Knäuel)*: ball, tangle. - (2) knot (in a thread). - **2.** *fig.* a confused situation: snarl-up; *da muaß jemand wo an ~ neibracht habm, gemma's oiso wieda von vorn an!* someone must have made a mess-up (*AmE also*, ... must have goofed) somewhere, so it's back for us to square one.

Schnadahüpfl ... Chatter Ditties

Gúat schauts es aus,
grüaß enk Gott,
setzts enk her, wiast und hott!
Leutl, seids alle do?
Na fang ma o!

Geht's ums Schnádahüpfl-Sínga,
ja, da reiß i was z'samm;
wer mi aussinga will,
muaß 's grad büachlweis habm.

I bin a jungs Bürscherl
und hab a jungs Bluat,
i ka tanzn und plattln,
dass 's funkazn tuat.

Und mi gfreit grad a Gsangl,
recht frisch, net vadraht,
und a Tanzl, dass 'n Staub
vo da Stub'm aufwaht.

A Herz wiar a Vögerl,
a Bluat wiar a Fisch,
koa Mensch kunnt ma 's glaabm,
wia wohl dass mar is.

Was nutzt oan des Grantln,
was nutzt oan des Sorgn?
's Le'm geht ja eh grad
von heut bis auf morgn.

God bless you all,
what a fine sight!
Sit you down, left and right.
Ain't no one missing, though?
Here, then, we go!

Singing chatter ditties dainty,
I am sure I can score;
Why, the one that outsings me
Must know oodles more.

A lively young laddie,
I'm all out for larks -
I can dance and can foot-slap
And throw off bright sparks.

Don't I like a fresh song
From the heart, without guise,
And a dance full o' stomping
The dust's bound to rise!

My heart's like a birdie's,
Blood's cold as a fish:
No man might believe
There's nowt else I could wish.

Now why do folks worry,
Why grumble and groan?
Life that's today
Will tomorrow be flown.

Nimm i d' Hanni? Oda d' Nanni?
Is fei gsprunga als wia ghupft:
die óa, die is stützi,
die ander is gschupft.

Eyeing Jeannie? Trying Annie?
What'll I tweedle-dum-dee-do?
The one acts all snooty,
The other's coo-coo.

Wannst gar so viel busslst,
derfst dirs net vahehln:
Gehn d' Bussln dir aus,
tuans im Ehstand dir fehln!

A hamper of kisses
In youth idly spent
Will set you, once married,
In search where each went.

Dass Bussln oan scheckat macht,
dees is erdicht't:
Grad oft waarn dann d' Deandln
schiach scheckat im Gsicht.

Pure myth it is
Kissing brings out facial blight:
Why, lasses would then
Be a weird spotty sight.

Deandl, spreiz di net so,
aus 'n Troad wird a Stroh,
aus de Bleamln a Heu,
grad vier Wochn is Mai!

Don't you hum, lass, don't haw:
Summer's grain turns to straw,
Flowers fair wilt to hay,
There's but four weeks in May.

Mei Deandl hoaßt Juli,
die riacht nach Patschuli,
die Woch grad oamal ...
und asonst nachm Stall.

My sweetheart's called Jody,
Her Sunday scent's eau de.
All week, though - tough luck! -
Her choice scent's stable muck.

Habm mei Deandl und i
grad amói uns verkracht,
nacha trotzn ma bei Tag,
aba net bei da Nacht.

Should my lassie and I
Have a tiff or a fight,
We'll just sulk while it 's day,
But have done comes the night.

As Bettstattl is kloan,
muaß drin schlafn alloan;
aba bsuacht mi mei Schatz,
hab ma alle zwoa Platz.

Right narrow is the bed
For to rest there my head;
With my love, though, with me
Room for two there will be.

Jétzt waar's zum Hoamgeh Zeit,
's Hoamgeh is nia mei Freid.
Hoam geh i scho -
aba jétzat net nó!

Time has come I should leave,
Leaving's my constant peeve.
Home I will go -
Yet still bide for a mo.

Und jetz háb i mei Häusl
mit Lebzeltn deckt,
und drum bring i die Deandln
vom Dach nimma weg.

Got my gingerbread house
A new roof nice and sweet,
So the lasses are aye
On the tiles for a treat.

Bald acker' i am Bifang,
bald acker' i am Roa;
bald hab i a schöns Deandl,
bald bin i alloa.

Now ploughing in mid-field,
Now ploughing far out;
Now charmed by a lassie,
Now left a poor lout.

Im Winta san Kletzn,
im Summa san Birn -
das allaschönst Lebm
is das Privatisiern.

Pears 's plenty in summer,
In winter there's prunes.
"Hurray for the bach'lor!"
's the best of all tunes.

Auf da Wélt is aus mi'm Stréitn
und es geht alls in Ruah,
wann der oan halt' 'n Mund
und die andern hörn zua.

Life has done away with quarrels
And no trouble appears
If one party shuts up,
And the rest is all ears.

Und es bleibt scho beim Altn,
es bleibt scho beim Brauch:
wann der Schoaß draußn is,
ja da gfreit si der Bauch.

Here 's a time-honoured custom
We'll keep without doubt:
'Tis the belly's delight
When the fart thunders out.

Wann's an Leberkaas regnt
und Bratwürschtl schneibt,
nacha bitt' ma an Herrgott,
dass 'as Wetta so bleibt.

If there's sausagey snowfalls
And meatloafy rains,
May the Lord go on pouring
Such heavenly gains.

Heut gibt's Knödl und Krapfn
und Nudln auf d' Nacht:
das Herzerl im Magn wird
ganz hupfert und lacht.

O for dumplings and donuts
And sweet cubes tonight!
The heart in my tummy
Just bounds with delight.

Du himmlischa Vata,
auf da Welt wär's bessa z' blei'm,
wann's nur oamal a halbe Stund
Zwanzger tät schnei'm.

This life here on earth, Lord,
Would, I reckon, be more worth
If it snowed for a hálf hour
Pound notes to earth.

Bin i gsund, is' s ma recht,
Bin i krank, geht's ma schlecht;
han i a Geld, bin i froh,
han i koans, geht's aa so.

If I'm well, fair enough,
If I'm ill, why, that's tough;
If I've got cash, I am high;
If I've none, I'll get by.

I kénn scho dein' Brauch
und a wó ma di' findt:
im Wirtshaus ganz vorn,
in da Kirchn ganz hint.

I know all your likes
And what places you mind -
In the pub, right up front;
In the church, way behind!

Fúrt in da Fruah, hoam af d' Nacht,
só hat's mei Vata gmacht.
Furt af d' Nacht, hoam in da Frua,
so macht's sei Bua.

Óff at the dawn, home when it's night:
Thát's what my Dad thought was right.
Off, when it's night, home with the sun:
That's Laddie 's fun.

Kimmst hoam mit an Rausch,
nix redn brauch i
als „Grüaß di Gott, Weiberl!" -
das andre redt sie.

Once home, reelin' drunk,
I gingerly purr,
"God bless you, dear wifie" -
The rest's said by her.

Schrei fei eini in d' Felswand -
horch, wia 's Echo kimmt raus!
I brauch koane Berg net,
wann mei Weib is im Haus.

If you shout up a rock wall
Hear the echo reply!
I dón't need no rock wall
If my wife stands close by.

D' Schwiegamuatta und da Bandwurm
san a Plag spat und fruah,
so lang no da Kopf dran is,
gebms koa Ruah.

Mothers-in-laws are like tapeworms,
They're a pest night and day:
As long as their head is on
There's the devil to pay!

Alle Gstanzln san gsunga,
de Klampfn hat a Ruah;
seids es alsdann am End,
machts des Büachl staad zua!

All the ditties are sung,
And to rest's come my guitar;
Gently make the book to
When you've done this last bar.

Jetzt pfüat enk Gott, Leut,
packts z'samm und gehts ham.
So schön und so jung
kemma net wieda z'samm!

Good-bye, folks, farewell,
Our songs are now sung!
We won't meet again
Quite as fair and as young.

Da Auswärts

Ganz staad und stoiz
schwingt si a Hobicht ume übers Hoiz.
Und durch de Baam,
do geht a hoamlichs Rauschn
ois wia a Wiagnliad.

Im Roa dro hoit si d' Sunn
und warmt de erschtn Bleamen o.
A Käfa, der hod aa scho aussagschaut,
doch 's Fliagn probiern hod er si no ned traut,
weil's letzte Nacht nomoi an Reif hod gmacht.

Und über d' Fejda her,
do trogt da Wind a Glockngläut:
„A scheene Zeit, a scheene Zeit!"
Ganz wurlat bin i und eiwendi volla Freid,
denn ejtz, do woaß i 's gwiß,
dass des da Auswärts is.

Gerd Maier (*1945)

Springtime

All stealth and pride,
A hawk wings over to the forest side.
And there the treetops
Gently sway along
Like a murmured cradle song.

Uphill the sun 's well set
To cheer the first pert flowers on.
A beetle, too, peeped out and on around.
To try his wings, though, seemed as yet unsound
'cause frost last night
Brought back a hoary sight.

And o'er the fields the wind
Now wafts some church bell's chime,
"A happy time, a happy time!"
So in a dither, yet aglow with joy sublime,
My heart leaps up to sing,
"Aye, surely this is Spring!"

Beim Michael

Beim Michel geht's aufs letzte End,
As Wei steht da und woant und flennt
Und jammert halt, was 's jammern kann.
Denn schaug, er war a guater Mann.
„Gel, Weibei,", schnackelt er so hin,
„Gel,", sagt er, „bal i gstorben bin,
An Mann, den brauchst ja dengerscht - und -
Na heiratst - halt an - Sepp von Gmund."

„O mei,", flennt sie, dass sie 's ganz z'sprengt,
„An den da han i aa scho denkt!"

At Michael's

With Michael, life drains soft away,
His missus bawling through the day;
And bawl and moan is all she can
For, mind, he was a right good man.
"Look, wifey, please," his voice, near fled,
Comes halting, slow, "Please, when I'm dead
A man you'll be in need of, though ...
You could - och - marry Lake-End Joe."

"Oh my," and fast her tears forth well,
"That's one I've thought of, too, mysel."

Karl Stieler (1842 – 1885)

’s Gebet

A gar kloans Diendl mit der Muatta
hat in der Kirch’ in Sunnta’ ’bet’t
und is halt g’west so voller Andacht,
als wann ’s es glei’ recht nöti’ hätt’;
dees hat der Muatta gar guat g’fall’n
und nach der Kircha sagt s’ dazua:
„Du bist amol a recht a Frummi,
du hast scho bet’t, in aller Fruah’;
was hast jetz’ ’bet’t, dees muaßt ma sagn,
du Schatzerl du, so brav und nett?“
Und ’s Maderl sagt auf ihra Frag’n:
„Dass d’ Kirch bald aus werd, hon i ’bet’t.“

The Prayer

At Sunday mass a tiny lassie
Was kneeling by her mother’s side;
Hands folded, eyes cast down and humble,
As though in need when help ’s denied.
Mum liked the sight. And duly taken,
On leaving church, she bent her head:
“God loves a child that is so pious,
’twas sweet the morning grace you said.
And now, what did you pray? Come tell, pet?
What pretty thoughts could God hear there?”
The lassie’s answer proved right candid:
“That church ’s soon over, was my prayer.”

Franz von Kobell (1803 – 1882)

Bhoit 's Glück a weng bei dia

Manchmoi hod ma 's dumpfe Gfui,
as Lebn macht grod, wos' sejba wui,
denn oiss laaft schiaf und nix haut hi,
„Is des gerecht?", so frogt ma si.

Wia a Baaz klebt 's Pech an dia
und zwingt di imma mehr in d' Knia.
Verzweifeln kaanst, koa Kraft host mehr,
ja, as Lebn is oft scho schwer.

Doch lass di niamois unterkriagn,
schwarze Woikn, sie verfliagn,
und an dem Doog, wos 's Unglück weicht,
do wird oiss Schwere federleicht.

Dann bhoit 's Glück a weng bei dia
und lass's auf koan Foi wieder z' früah
irgendwo ins Nichts entschwebn,
acht's ois größtes Gschenk im Lebn!

Andreas Dick (*1964)

Hold on to good luck for a while

Life has freaks, you dimly feel,
and plays them off just as it will:
all plans will topple, grim 's the heap -
you're bound to ask, "Does justice sleep?"

Bad luck 's yours, a slimy gown
to drag you ever further down.
Despair around, no strength to spare -
this life, aye, 's often hard to bear.

Never, though, yield to dismay,
please mind dark clouds will fly away;
and on the day when ends the plight
all heaviness feels feather-light.

Hold on to good luck a wee while,
and see that it won't use a guile
to fade away for evermore -
your choicest gift Life 's had in store.

's Fluachn

Der Vata is ganz ausanand:
„Wia mei *Bua fluacht, dös is a Schand!*
Mei Wei fluacht nit, und i fluach nit.
Und grad der Bua, der gibt koan Fried!
Der Himmiherrgottsakra, der -
Wo hat jetzt der dös Fluachn her?"

Swearin'

Dad puckers up his worried face:
"My lad's foul tongue's sure a disgrace!
The wife don't swear, an' swear don't I;
It's just that lad won't give a try!
God damn it, bloody hell - now where
Did that young devil larn to swear?"

Karl Stieler (1842 - 1885)

Heut san d' Liadln gsunga

An Upper Bavarian farewell ditty, a favourite with community singers

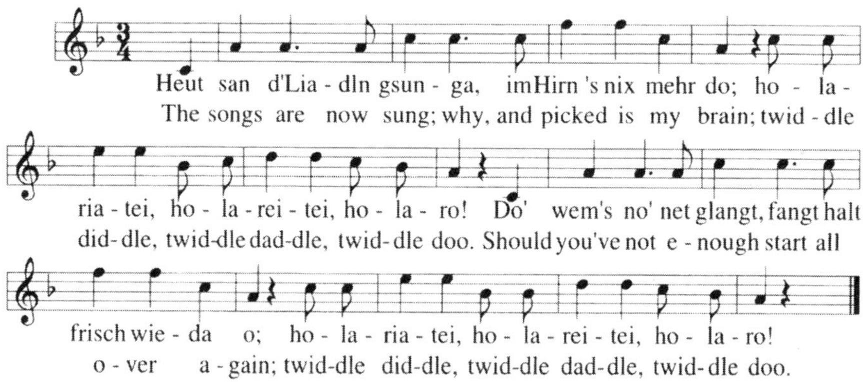

Und lachts und seids lusti,
nia fad und valegn:
A Liadl auf d' Lippm
bringt vielfachn Segn.

And laugh, and be merry,
Show dullness the door:
A song on your lips
Will bring blessings galore.

Drum is ebm a Singweil
a grüawige Freud.
„Bis 's wieda mal is,
pfiat enk Gott, liabe Leut!"

And that's why a singsong's
A jolly good treat.
"May God save you kindly
Till again we can meet!"

♪ ♪ ♫ ♪
Be good to your-selves ...

Abbreviations Used

abbr.	abbreviation
adj	adjective
admin.	administration
adv	adverb
agr.	agriculture
AmE	American English
anat.	anatomy
anthrop.	anthropology
apprec.	appreciative(ly)
approx.	approximate(ly)
archit.	architecture; architectural
arith.	arithmetic
attrib.	attributive(ly)
AusG	Austrian German
AustralE	Australian English
bak.	baking
BavG	Bavarian German
bev.	beverage
bot.	botany; botanical
BrE	British English
brew.	brewery
ca.	circa (L, about)
chem.	chemistry
Chr. n.	Christian name
civ. eng.	civil engineering
colloc.	collocation(s)
colloq.	colloquial(ly, -ness)
com.	commerce; commercial
comest.	comestible
comp(s).	compound(s)
concr.	concrete(ly)
contp.	contemptuous
cp.	compare
cul.	culinary art
Cumb.	Cumberland
curl.	curling
cyn.	cynology
d.	died
decl.	declension
dial.	dialect; dialectal
diet.	dietetics
dim.	diminutive
Du	Dutch
E	English
eccles.	ecclesiastical
ecol.	ecology
econ.	economics, economy; economic
educ.	education
e.g.	exempli gratia (L, for instance)
el.	(compound) element
e-m	einem
emot.	emotional; emotive
e-n	einen
ent.	entomology
e-s	eines
esp.	especially
etym.	etymology, etymological
euphem.	euphemistic(ally)
f	feminine
F	French
fig.	figurative(ly)
for.	forestry
G	German
garm.	garment
gastr.	gastronomy
gen.	general(ly); genitive
geog.	geography
geol.	geology

Germ.	Germanic
Goth	Gothic
Gr	Greek
her.	heraldry
hist.	history; historical
hort.	horticulture
hum.	humour; humorous(ly)
hunt.	hunting
husb.	husbandry
hyd. eng.	hydraulic engineering
ibid.	ibidem (L, in the same place [i.e., in the book just quoted])
ichth.	ichthyology
i.e.	id est (L, that is)
IE	Indo-European
illus.	illustration(s)
imit.	imitative
indus.	industry
interj	interjection
IrE	Irish English
iron.	irony; ironic
It	Italian
j-m	jemandem
j-n	jemanden
joc.	jocular
journ.	journalism
jur.	jurisdiction
L	Latin
ling.	linguistics
lit.	literature; literally
m	masculine
math.	mathematics
ME	Middle English
med.	medicine; medical
MedL	Medieval Latin
meteor.	meteorology
MHG	Middle High German
mil.	military
ModE	Modern English
ModHG	Modern High German
mot.	motoring
mount.	mountaineering
Mt.	Mount
mus.	music; musical
myc.	mycology
myth.	mythology
n	neuter
NorBavG	Northern Bavarian
NorBrE	Northern English
NorG	Northern German
Northumb.	Northumberland
OBav	Old Bavarian
obs.	obsolete
OE	Old English
OF	Old French
OHG	Old High German
ON	Old Norse
opp.	opposite
orig.	originally
ornith.	ornithology
orogr.	orography
PaG	Pennsylvania German
phr.	phrase(s)
phys.	physics
physiol.	physiology
pl.	plural
poet.	poetical
polit.	political
p.p.	past participle
prec.	preceding
pred.	predicative(ly)

prep.	preposition
pr. n.	proper name
prob.	probable; probably
pron.	pronounced; pronunciation
prov.	proverb(s); proverbial
pr. t.	present tense
R.C.	Roman Catholic
relig.	religion
sarc.	sarcastic
scient.	scientific(ally known as)
scil.	scilicet (L, [to be] understood or supplied)
ScotE	Scottish English
sg.	singular
sl.	slang
s.o.	someone
sobr.	sobriquet
SouBrE	Southern English
SouG	Southern German
sp.	spelling
stand.	standard
StandE	Standard English
StandG	Standard German
s.th.	something
tech.	technology
theat.	theatre
UK	The United Kingdom (of Great Britain and Northern Ireland)
UpG	Upper German
usu.	usually
vet.	veterinary
v/i	intransitive verb
vinic.	viniculture
viz.	videlicet (L, namely)
v/refl	reflexive verb
v/t	transitive verb
vt/i	verb used both transitively and intransitively
vt/refl	verb used both transitively and reflexively
vulg.	vulgar
Yid.	Yiddish
zo.	zoology

<	is derived from
>	develops, morphologically or semantically, into
→	(1) see; (2) the sense develops to
[ ]	square brackets (1) contain etymological information; (2) vary, and thus stand within, round brackets; and (3) indicate free variations in model sentences, e.g. boys [girls]
<>	angle brackets enclose individual letters (or graphemes)
~	the swung dash stands for the headword; when its initial letter changes from a capital to a small letter, or vice-versa, a superscript ^{x} is added: $\overset{x}{\sim}$
*	the asterisk (1) marks a deduced, and therefore undocumented, word form; and (2) serves as a warning, before whole sentences, that in the absence of a close equivalent in English the wording offered is an idiomatic, but only more or less literal translation
:	the colon, after due definitory preliminaries, is the curtain raiser for the exact and concise equivalent of the headword; if non-standard, the headword here finds its match on the proper non-standard level (colloquial, slang, vulgar, etc.)